Deuteronomy and the Pentateuch

THE ANCHOR YALE BIBLE REFERENCE LIBRARY is a project of international and interfaith scope in which Protestant, Catholic, and Jewish scholars from many countries contribute individual volumes. The project is not sponsored by any ecclesiastical organization and is not intended to reflect any particular theological doctrine.

The series is committed to producing volumes in the tradition established half a century ago by the founders of the Anchor Bible, William Foxwell Albright and David Noel Freedman. It aims to present the best contemporary scholarship in a way that is accessible not only to scholars but also to the educated nonspecialist. It is committed to work of sound philological and historical scholarship, supplemented by insight from modern methods, such as sociological and literary criticism.

John J. Collins
General Editor

THE ANCHOR YALE BIBLE REFERENCE LIBRARY

Deuteronomy and the Pentateuch

JEFFREY STACKERT

To Jeanne—
with all best
wishes—from one
author to another!

Jeffrey
Stackert

YALE · AYBRL

Yale
UNIVERSITY
PRESS

NEW HAVEN
AND
LONDON

Published with assistance from the foundation established in memory
of James Wesley Cooper of the Class of 1865, Yale College.

Yale University Press books may be purchased in quantity for educational,
business, or promotional use. For information, please email sales.press@yale.edu
(U.S. office) or sales@yaleup.co.uk (U.K. office).

Set in Adobe Caslon and Bauer Bodoni types by Newgen North America.
Printed in the United States of America.

Library of Congress Control Number: 2021948947
ISBN 978-0-300-16751-1 (hardcover : alk. paper)

A catalogue record for this book is available from the British Library.

This paper meets the requirements of ANSI/NISO Z39.48-1992 (Permanence
of Paper).

10 9 8 7 6 5 4 3 2 1

Contents

Acknowledgments

I am very grateful to the many friends, colleagues, and students who have generously discussed aspects of this book with me over the past few years. Primary among them have been Simi Chavel, Joel Baden, Baruch Schwartz, Sam Boyd, Bernie Levinson, and Stephen Young. Each of these colleagues read parts of the manuscript and provided valuable critique and encouragement in response. My students Aslan Cohen Mizrahi, Justin Moses, and David Ridge likewise read draft materials and made helpful suggestions for their improvement, and David compiled the book's bibliography. I was also fortunate to have instructive conversations with, and to receive essential bibliographical suggestions from, Jacob Lauinger, James Osborne, Jessie DeGrado, Tzvi Abusch, Avi Faust, Liane Feldman, David Lambert, and Chloe Blackshear.

Ideas developed in this book and parts of its chapters were presented orally in a number of venues, including meetings of the Society of Biblical Literature, the Middle West Branch of the American Oriental Society, and the Chicago-Yale Pentateuch Colloquium. I offer my thanks to the participants at each of those meetings for their insightful questions and comments. A portion of Chapter 2 appeared in a different form as "The Wilderness without Generation Change: The Deuteronomic Portrait of Israel's Forty-Year Journey," *VT* 70 (2020): 696–721. I am grateful for the opportunity to include that material here. I also express my gratitude to my dean, David Nirenberg, for approving the research leave that allowed me to complete this book. The editorial staff at Yale University Press, including Jennifer Banks, Heather Gold, and Abbie Storch, were most patient and helpful as I worked on this project. John Collins, the editor of the Anchor Yale Bible, was equally supportive. I thank them each warmly. I am likewise grateful to the press's anonymous referees for their judicious feedback and to Saul Olyan, Anchor Yale Bible Reference Library editorial board member, for his careful reading of the manuscript. Jessie Dolch copyedited the manuscript carefully, and it is a pleasure to be able to thank her. Finally, Eve Levavi Feinstein prepared the indexes for the book, and both she and my student Noah Avigan checked the proofs. They did expert work, and I am grateful.

As I worked on this project, I benefited immeasurably from the love and support of my wife, Richelle, and our two children, George and Kate. Our "four family," as we call it, has been a constant source of joy and encouragement, not least through the pandemic shutdown that accompanied my completion of this volume. As a sign of my affection and appreciation, I dedicate this book to Richelle, George, and Kate.

Abbreviations

AB	Anchor Bible
ABRL	Anchor Bible Reference Library
ABS	Archaeology and Biblical Studies
AIL	Ancient Israel and Its Literature
AJSR	*Association for Jewish Studies Review*
AnBib	Analecta Biblica
ANEM	Ancient Near Eastern Monographs
ANESSup	Ancient Near Eastern Studies, Supplements
AOAT	Alter Orient und Altes Testament
ATANT	Abhandlungen zur Theologie des Alten und Neuen Testaments
ATD	Alte Testament Deutsch
AUSS	*Andrews University Seminary Studies*
AYB	Anchor Yale Bible
AYBRL	Anchor Yale Bible Reference Library
BA	*Biblical Archaeologist*
BaAr	Babylonische Archive
BaghM	*Baghdader Mitteilungen*
BASOR	*Bulletin of the American Schools of Oriental Research*
BBaghM	Baghdader Mitteilungen, Beihefte
BBB	Bonner Biblische Beiträge
BDB	Brown, Francis, S. R. Driver, and Charles A. Briggs. *A Hebrew and English Lexicon of the Old Testament*
BEATAJ	Beiträge zur Erforschung des Alten Testaments und des Antiken Judentums

BETL	Bibliotheca Ephemeridum Theologicarum Lovaniensium
BibInt	*Biblical Interpretation*
BibInt	Biblical Interpretation Series
BibOr	Biblica et Orientalia
BibSem	Biblical Seminar
BJS	Brown Judaic Studies
BN	*Biblische Notizen*
BO	*Bibliotheca orientalis*
BWANT	Beiträge zur Wissenschaft vom Alten und Neuen Testament
BZABR	Beihefte zur Zeitschrift für altorientalische und biblische Rechtsgeschichte
BZAW	Beihefte zur Zeitschrift für die alttestamentliche Wissenschaft
CAD	*The Assyrian Dictionary of the Oriental Institute of the University of Chicago.* Edited by A. Leo Oppenheim, Erica Reiner, and Martha T. Roth. 24 vols. Chicago: Oriental Institute, 1956–2010.
CBET	Contributions to Biblical Exegesis and Theology
CBQ	*Catholic Biblical Quarterly*
CHANE	Culture and History of the Ancient Near East
CTH	*Catalogue des textes hittites.* Emmanuel Laroche. Paris: Klincksieck, 1971
CUSAS	Cornell University Studies in Assyriology and Sumerology
DCLS	Deuterocanonical and Cognate Literature Studies
DJD	*Discoveries in the Judaean Desert*
DSD	*Dead Sea Discoveries*
EdF	Erträge der Forschung
FAT	Forschungen zum Alten Testament
FAT/II	Forschungen zum Alten Testament 2. Reihe
FRLANT	Forschungen zur Religion und Literatur des Alten und Neuen Testaments
HALOT	*The Hebrew and Aramaic Lexicon of the Old Testament.*

	Ludwig Koehler, Walter Baumgartner, and Johann J. Stamm. Translated and edited under the supervision of Mervyn E. J. Richardson. Study Edition. 2 vols. Leiden: Brill, 2001.
HAR	*Hebrew Annual Review*
HAT	Handbuch zum Alten Testament
HBS	Herders biblische Studien
HCOT	Historical Commentary on the Old Testament
HeBAI	*Hebrew Bible and Ancient Israel*
HKAT	Handkommentar zum Alten Testament
HSM	Harvard Semitic Monographs
HThKAT	Herders Theologischer Kommentar zum Alten Testament
HTR	*Harvard Theological Review*
HUCA	*Hebrew Union College Annual*
ICC	International Critical Commentary
ISBL	Indiana Studies in Biblical Literature
JAJ	*Journal of Ancient Judaism*
JANEH	*Journal of Ancient Near Eastern History*
JANES	*Journal of the Ancient Near Eastern Society*
JAOS	*Journal of the American Oriental Society*
JBL	*Journal of Biblical Literature*
JCS	*Journal of Cuneiform Studies*
JCSMS	*Journal of the Canadian Society for Mesopotamian Studies*
JESHO	*Journal of the Economic and Social History of the Orient*
JHS	*Journal of Hebrew Scriptures*
JJS	*Journal of Jewish Studies*
JNES	*Journal of Near Eastern Studies*
JSP	*Journal for the Study of the Pseudepigrapha*
JQR	*Jewish Quarterly Review*
JSJSup	Supplements to the Journal for the Study of Judaism
JSOT	*Journal for the Study of the Old Testament*
JSOTSup	Journal for the Study of the Old Testament: Supplement Series

JTS	*Journal of Theological Studies*
KHAT	Kurzgefasstes exegetisches Handbuch zum Alten Testament
LHBOTS	Library of Hebrew Bible/Old Testament Studies
LNTS	Library of New Testament Studies
LSAWS	Linguistic Studies in Ancient West Semitic
LXX	Septuagint
MT	Masoretic Text
NCB	New Century Bible
NICOT	New International Commentary on the Old Testament
OBO	Orbis Biblicus et Orientalis
ÖBS	*Österreichische* biblische Studien
ORA	Oriental Religions in Antiquity: Egypt, Israel, Ancient Near East
OTL	Old Testament Library
OTS	Old Testament Studies
OtSt	*Oudtestamentische Studiën*
PEQ	*Palestine Exploration Quarterly*
RA	*Revue d'assyriologie et d'archéologie orientale*
RB	*Revue biblique*
REJ	*Revue des études juives*
RevQ	*Revue de Qumran*
RINAP	Royal Inscriptions of the Neo-Assyrian Period
SAA	State Archives of Assyria
SAAS	State Archives of Assyria Studies
SAAB	*State Archives of Assyria Bulletin*
SANER	*Studies in Ancient Near Eastern Records*
SAPERE	Scripta Antiquitatis Posterioris ad Ethicam Religionemque pertinentia
SBLAIL	Society of Biblical Literature Ancient Israel and Its Literature
SBLDS	Society of Biblical Literature Dissertation Series
SBLEJL	Society of Biblical Literature Early Judaism and Its Literature

SBT	Studies in Biblical Theology
SBTS	Sources for Biblical and Theological Study
SCS	Septuagint and Cognate Studies
SEÅ	*Svensk Exegetisk Årsbok*
SFEG	Schriften der Finnischen Exegetischen Gesellschaft
StBibLit	Studies in Biblical Literature (Lang)
STDJ	Studies on the Texts of the Desert of Judah
TA	*Tel Aviv*
TDOT	*Theological Dictionary of the Old Testament.* Edited by G. Johannes Botterweck, Helmer Ringgren, and Heinz-Josef Fabry. 15 vols. Grand Rapids: Eerdmans, 1974–2006.
TP	*Theologie und Philosophie*
TSAJ	Texts and Studies in Ancient Judaism
UF	*Ugarit-Forschungen*
VT	*Vetus Testamentum*
VTSup	Supplements to Vetus Testamentum
WD	*Wort und Dienst*
WdO	*Welt des Orients*
WMANT	Wissenschaftliche Monographien zum Alten und Neuen Testament
ZA	*Zeitschrift für Assyriologie*
ZABR	*Zeitschrift für altorientalische und biblische Rechtsgeschichte*
ZAW	*Zeitschrift für die alttestamentliche Wissenschaft*
ZBK	Zürcher Bibelkommentare
ZTK	*Zeitschrift für Theologie und Kirche*

Deuteronomy and the Pentateuch

Introduction: The Importance of Deuteronomy and the Challenge of Its Interpretation

The past several decades have witnessed considerable advances in our understanding of Deuteronomy. Scholars have offered new explanations for the composition, redaction, and reception of its texts, which have resulted in new insights into the meanings of its parts, both large and small. They have done so both by considering new evidence (especially textual and comparative) and by evaluating and refining the conclusions of prior research, adding to an already ample history of scholarship on Deuteronomy—a text that has occupied a central role in the history of modern biblical criticism, a history that extends now more than two centuries.

Deuteronomy has enjoyed this prominence in the field of biblical studies for several reasons. Perhaps most importantly, Deuteronomic thought and language are observable across much of the biblical canon—not least in the Former Prophets (Joshua, Judges, Samuel, and Kings), which together with Deuteronomy have been termed the "Deuteronomistic History."[1] Deuteronomy has thus been a regular resource—and in some instances even a starting point—for investigations of many texts and religious ideas beyond it.[2]

Another reason for Deuteronomy's importance in scholarship, and one related in part to the foregoing, is the foundational role it has played in various historical arguments concerning other biblical texts and the contexts of their emergence. For example, Deuteronomy has often served as a fulcrum for dating texts both within the Pentateuch and outside of it. By correlating the central legal corpus in the book with the account of the Josianic book find (2 Kgs 22–23, 2 Chr 34), scholars have established a date for (parts of) Deuteronomy and an "Archimedean point" for situating other texts in relation to it. This Josianic correlation—the so-called de Wette hypothesis—has also served as a linchpin for scholarly reconstructions of ancient Israelite religion, most famously in Julius Wellhausen's influential (if problematic) *Prolegomena to the History of Ancient Israel*. For Wellhausen, the major shift from an early, lively, prophetic religion in ancient Israel to a late, lifeless legalism that culminated in rabbinic Judaism could be traced to Deuteronomy's legislation.[3]

Deuteronomy also introduces and develops some of the ideas, events, and individual texts most prized in the thought and practices of Judaism and Christianity.[4] Its import in academic scholarship thus mirrors in part its significance for the communities that view its text as Scripture. There has also often been a significant overlap among these parties, with scholars who are themselves religious producing scholarship in service of their religious communities (and other religious communities).

Precisely because Deuteronomy and the ideas epitomized in it are richly attested, extensively treated, and widely esteemed, the scholarship engaging them is varied, complex, and at times overwhelming. Scholars have advanced—and continue to endorse—fundamentally differing perspectives on issues that are indispensable for understanding Deuteronomy, including the text's dating, compositional history, and interactions with other biblical and nonbiblical ancient Near Eastern texts. Disentangling the discussion can be a daunting task, to say nothing of evaluating it.

Deuteronomy and the Pentateuch responds to this situation. Its chapters explore the major issues in the biblical book of Deuteronomy or, as argued in the following pages, first the pentateuchal Deuteronomic (D) source and then the scroll of Deuteronomy. At the same time, this book gives sustained attention to the broader discussion of Deuteronomy in modern scholarship and the various and sometimes mutually exclusive claims that scholars make regarding it. The book's concern is thus twofold: it advances its own theses in relation to the primary text and relevant ancient evidence, even as it seeks to understand and make its claims in relation to the various trajectories of modern, critical scholarship on Deuteronomy. While meant as a monograph, then, the volume also bears some features of a handbook.

Perhaps most importantly, and in service of each of these ends, *Deuteronomy and the Pentateuch* attempts to demonstrate the productivity of its arguments through the exegetical treatments of texts from Deuteronomy that are sprinkled across its pages. These interpretive engagements, some brief and others more extensive, show how and why the various questions raised about what Deuteronomy is, when and how it was composed, and how it has been shaped into its present form make a difference in reading its texts. In some cases, the texts treated will reappear from one chapter to the next, demonstrating the ways in which the various issues discussed across the volume are related to each other and bear cumulatively on the overall interpretation of Deuteronomy.

The Distinctives of This Book

Because the texts explored in this book are ancient, the evidence for reconstructing their composition and historical setting is often frustratingly incomplete. The arguments here are offered in full recognition of such evidentiary challenges, and the book's sequence of chapters is both an acknowledgment of these difficulties and an attempt to ameliorate them, if only in part. Especially across the first four chapters, the discussion moves generally from issues for which there is more evidence to those for which there is less, even as the conclusions drawn in the earlier chapters inform the analyses of the later ones (and, as the perceptive reader will note, some later conclusions are anticipated in earlier analyses). Chapter 1 treats the genre and compositional history of Deuteronomy, with a special focus on the implications of the text's literariness. Chapter 2 considers Deuteronomic compositional method, which is highly revisionary and thus informed by source material. Some of the source material employed in Deuteronomic composition is extant—most notably, the Covenant Code and what I identify as the larger Elohistic source of which it is a part. Chapter 3 then turns to the specific influence of cuneiform materials (especially legal and treaty traditions) upon both D and its Israelite forebears. Chapter 4 considers the impact of D's situation within the compiled Pentateuch in the early history of its interpretation and the transformation it underwent through its inclusion in the Pentateuch. And finally, relying upon the literary evidence adduced in the foregoing chapters and buttressed by additional, archaeological data and historical considerations, Chapter 5 seeks to situate D's composition historically.

The Neodocumentary Hypothesis

The major compositional theory that guides the analysis of Deuteronomy in this book is the Documentary Hypothesis. Specifically, this study employs a modified version of the Documentary Hypothesis that has been termed *Neodocumentarian*.[5] According to this view, the Pentateuch is a compilation of four originally independent literary works—in the order of their initial appearance in the compiled Pentateuch, P (Priestly), J (Yahwistic), E (Elohistic), and D (Deuteronomic). These works may be distinguished from each other on the basis of duplications, literary discontinuities, and content contradictions in the received text. In some instances—as seen especially in Deuteronomic texts—the differentiation of the sources can be corroborated by observing the reuse of one pentateuchal source in isolation from another source with which it is interwoven in the compiled Pentateuch.[6]

In its starting point, namely, the compiled Pentateuch (or, more precisely, the different witnesses to this text), and in its method of isolating putatively earlier material based on duplication, discontinuity, and contradiction in these texts, Neodocumentary scholarship does not differ markedly from other source-critical approaches, including previous articulations of the Documentary Hypothesis. Its distinctive claims concern especially the nature of the compilation of the four largely complete and long-running narrative works that it identifies in the Pentateuch. Such claims, of course, are not the *aim* of the analysis but its *result*. The Documentary Hypothesis presented here is thus properly a solution proposed in response to a specific set of literary problems—the aforementioned duplications, discontinuities, and contradictions in the Pentateuch. It is source-critical in its approach, but it is not itself a method of analysis.

According to the Neodocumentarian theory, the compilation of the pentateuchal sources was accomplished according to three principles: (1) maximal preservation, (2) minimal intervention, and (3) the arrangement of the source materials into a single, chronologically ordered plotline based on the plots of the works combined. These principles are inferred from the combined text itself and are readily demonstrable with examples.

To begin with *maximal preservation*, when the duplications, discontinuities, and contradictions of the Pentateuch are separated from each other, it is possible in most instances to reconstruct independent works that are complete and fully cohesive. For example, when the plague of blood in Exod 7:14–25 is divided (between J and P), each blood episode is complete and internally consistent, even as the two accounts differ from each other markedly.[7] The questions that are prompted by the combined text—Did Moses wield the rod or did Aaron? Did he strike the water with the rod or simply hold his hand over the water? Was only the Nile affected or was it all of the water in Egypt? Was there duration to the wonder or not?—are all answered in satisfactory fashion by the two accounts that can be reconstructed, and nothing is missing from either one.[8]

Minimal intervention is observable in several aspects of the compilation. For example, in combining the works before him, the compiler apparently sought to toggle between these works as infrequently as possible. The result is a combined work with minimal splicing. In fact, notwithstanding the prominence of interwoven episodes (such as the Flood or the Plagues in Egypt) in the history of pentateuchal composition, whenever possible the compiler maintained complete episodes from his source material and did not seek to create a single episode from episodes in different sources. It is only in those instances when the compiler concluded that the episodes in the different works he was combining were accounts of the same historical event that he interwove them into a single account. Even then, if they could be kept separate from each other, this was preferable, as the two creation accounts in Gen 1–2 demonstrate.

The compiler's minimal intervention can also be observed in the balance of material that cannot be attributed to one of the underlying sources. It is almost always the case that all of the received text can be assigned to one of the pentateuchal sources. Moreover, of that material which seems to be secondary, it is likely that most of it postdates the compiler's work. It thus may be concluded that the compiler added very little in the process of creating the Pentateuch.

Minimal intervention is also observable in the compiler's sequencing of materials. When the received text is divided according to its duplications, discontinuities, and contradictions, the sequence in which the parts of a single source appear in the compiled text is usually identical to the order in which these parts cohere as an independent work—a sequence demonstrable on the basis of the literary content of the reconstructed source. Thus, while the combination of these originally independent works is a significant intervention in its own right, one can easily countenance considerable rearrangement of source material that the compiler apparently did not pursue.

Instructive examples of the compiler's minimal intervention are found in Gen 37, the story of Joseph's descent into Egypt. In this case, the compiler encountered two accounts of what he judged to be a single event and thus interwove them.[9] Yet in so doing, he maintained the original sequences of the two different episodes. Thus, when they are separated, each narrative emerges perfectly in order. Moreover, in the midst of this episode, the compiler introduced at most a single word.[10]

Another remarkable feature of the compiler's principle of minimal intervention, also attested in Gen 37, is the occasional introduction of a new plot element—one unattested in the underlying accounts combined—in order to avoid making changes to the wording of the works being combined. An example is found in the coordination of subjects and verbs in Gen 37:28. According to this verse, the <u>Midianites</u> sold Joseph to the <u>Ishmaelites</u>, who then carried him off to Egypt:

> <u>Midianite traders</u> passed by, and they pulled Joseph up from the pit, and they [<u>the Midianites</u>] <u>sold</u> (*wayyimkĕrû*, without stated subject) Joseph to the <u>Ishmaelites</u> for twenty silver pieces, and they [<u>the Ishmaelites</u>] <u>brought</u> Joseph to Egypt.[11]

Read on its own, this verse is unproblematic. Yet situating it within the larger narrative reveals that it is actually a combination of J and E material. It should be divided as follows (with E underlined):

> <u>Midianite traders passed by, and they pulled Joseph up from the pit</u>, and they sold Joseph to the Ishmaelites for twenty silver pieces, and they brought Joseph to Egypt.

In the J narrative, to which the sale-to-the-Ishmaelites plot element belongs, it is *Joseph's brothers* who sell him, not the Midianites. This is clear from the immediately preceding J text (vv. 26–27), where the brothers hatch their plan:

> [26]Judah said to his brothers, "What profit is there if we kill our brother and cover up his blood? [27]Come, let us sell him to the Ishmaelites, but let not our hand be against him, for he is our brother—our flesh." And his brothers heeded him.

The original J section in vv. 26–28 thus would have read,

> [26]Judah said to his brothers, "What profit is there if we kill our brother and cover up his blood? [27]Come, let us sell him to the Ishmaelites, but let not our hand be against him, for he is our brother—our flesh." And his brothers heeded him, [28b]and they sold Joseph to the Ishmaelites for twenty silver pieces, and they brought Joseph to Egypt.

In this reconstruction, the selling action in v. 28b aligns perfectly with the planning in vv. 26–27, and the identification of Joseph's brothers as the unstated subject of the verb "they sold" (*wayyimkĕrû*) in v. 28b is flawless grammatically.[12]

This example illustrates that the minimal intervention prized by the compiler is a *material* one. Indeed, the introduction of a plot point not attested in either of the works being combined—the sale of Joseph from the Midianites to the Ishmaelites—might easily be considered a significant (and hardly nonminimal) intervention. Yet the compiler's concern is to maintain the actual wording of the works he combined. In Gen 37:28, then, reassigning the act of selling Joseph to the Ishmaelites from his brothers to the Midianites allowed the compiler to interweave his sources without adding any material to the text at all.[13]

The principle of minimal intervention relates closely to the compiler's final combinatory principle: *the creation of a single, chronologically ordered plotline* based on the plotlines of the underlying sources combined. It may be observed that, though admitting of a significant lack of internal cohesion (due to its duplications, discontinuities, and contradictions), the narrated timeline of the pentateuchal plot is almost entirely ordered in chronological sequence and is constructed with general deference to the chronologically ordered plotlines of the underlying works combined within it. Genesis 37, just cited as an example of minimal intervention, also exemplifies the compiler's prioritization of a single, chronologically ordered plot. Even though neither J nor E included the sale of Joseph by the Midianites to the Ishmaelites, the compiler introduced this plot element because it allowed him to achieve a single plotline in his combination of the two accounts. How could Joseph be taken both by the Ishmaelites and the Midianites? The compiler's answer was simple: he must have been passed from one group's possession to the other in a sequence of misfortunes. As I discuss in detail in the next chapter, the same principle is on display on a large scale in the compiler's integration of D into the Pentateuch as a mostly uninterrupted block.

The consistency of the combinatory method observed across the Pentateuch makes it likely that a single compiler was responsible for this amalgamation and that it was completed in a single compilational event. Thus, though the individual source documents admit of combinations of earlier, disparate material that they now comprise, and the whole in some instances shows evidence of supplementation after its compilation, it is probably the work of a single compiler that accounts for the particular shape of the Pentateuch as it has been received. Evidence supporting the Documentary Hypothesis is readily available in Deuteronomy, and I point to it often, especially in my discussions of this text's compositional history (Chapter 1) and its revisionary method of composition (Chapter 2).

Literature versus Scripture

As emphasized already, the interpretive approach of this book is literary and historical, and one of its distinctive aspects is that it attempts to engage both the literary and the historical in theoretically informed ways. Yet beyond these two categories, history and literature, a third category, Scripture, has exerted considerable influence upon interpreters of Deuteronomy. Indeed, the history of Deuteronomy's reception is overwhelmingly the history of its interpretation *as Scripture*.[14] Though its origins were otherwise, Deuteronomy has been received as part of the biblical canons (Jewish and Christian) and, crucially, as part of the compiled Pentateuch.

The reception of Deuteronomy as Scripture is important because this identification has functioned as a sort of genre designation, carrying with it a set of reading practices and assumptions to guide its interpretation.[15] In Chapter 1, I discuss at length what it means to identify Deuteronomic texts as historically situated literature, including the implications for this identification. In Chapter 3 I return to the issue of genre in the comparison of Deuteronomic literature with ancient Near Eastern diplomatic and legal works. Yet it is useful here to consider briefly what it has meant to identify ancient Israelite and Judean texts as Scripture and how scriptural reading practices have sometimes been at odds with historical and literary approaches. As I show, at times scriptural interpretive frameworks have exerted significant (if also unacknowledged) influence in the scholarly analysis of Deuteronomy.

What, then, does it mean to read texts as Scripture, and how does this practice differ from reading texts as ancient literature? I do not offer here a full analysis of the category of Scripture; such is a topic for a whole book.[16] Instead, I focus on a number of interpretive assumptions established already in antiquity, first by Jews and then also by Christians, that were applied to a limited set of texts—mostly those that would become biblical.[17] As James L. Kugel has discussed and exemplified at length, these assumptions were that these texts were fundamentally cryptic, relevant, perfect and perfectly harmonious, and divine.[18] Applying such assumptions to biblical (and other) texts facilitated their reception as theologically significant.

Though embedded within specific religious milieux—and thus sometimes exhibiting features based on this situatedness—these interpretive assumptions also responded to and were guided by the contents of the texts themselves. Thus, it was in part their confrontation with content discrepancies such as the duplications, discontinuities, and contradictions of pentateuchal texts that pressed scriptural interpreters to develop reading strategies that could accommodate them. This was especially the case in view of other textual features, such as the chronological arrangement of the pentateuchal plotline and its thematic parallels, that suggested the text was unified.[19] The claim that biblical texts were (and are) at once cryptic and harmonious can be understood as a response to such issues. By means of these assumptions, challenging features of biblical texts were deemed meaningful opportunities for deeper interpretive insight rather than faults that would hamper interpretation (and certainly not deficiencies that resulted from the processes of composition and transmission or that might otherwise undermine the text's prestige and authority).

The development of the assumption that biblical texts were divine was likewise a response to their content, albeit in a different way. Many speeches in biblical texts are presented within their literary frameworks as revelation. In other words, as explicit attributions to the deity, these speeches are, in their voicing, "divine." Part of the claim to the divine origin of Scripture was a generalization of this feature, namely, an application of the divine voicing of some units to the many biblical texts not voiced by the divine character. Through such efforts, interpreters shifted the divinity of biblical material from narrower examples of individual, divinely voiced speeches to the text's overall origin or authorship, a process that resulted in a prophetic conceptualization for much of the biblical text.[20] In some instances, early characterizations of Scripture explicitly invoked notions of spokenness in their reorientation of nonprophetic texts (e.g., 2 Tim 3:16).

Reading biblical texts as revelatory also allowed scriptural readers to draw upon precedents for understanding revelation, including biblical precedents, in line with their experience of the texts' contents. Some biblical texts explicitly characterize mediated divine messages as incompletely transmitted or enigmatic (e.g., Num 12:6). In this way, the literary problems of biblical texts not only suggested that they were cryptic; when combined with these texts' specific, lucid characterizations of revelation, such problems could also serve as confirmation of their divine nature.

In some instances, as the Qumran Habakkuk commentary (1QpHab) demonstrates, early interpreters even believed that biblical prophets may not have comprehended their own messages.[21] It was only through subsequent, inspired interpretation (in the case of the Habakkuk commentary, by the figure labeled "the Teacher of Righteousness") that such divine communications could be deciphered (1QpHab 2:5–10, 7:1–5).[22] This remarkable claim of the Habakkuk commentary is partially explained by the assumption of the biblical text's relevance. The commentary asserts that the biblical Habakkuk's message is for the late Second Temple Jewish community led by the Teacher of Righteousness, not for the community of the prophet Habakkuk centuries before. This example of scriptural reading is in one sense an extreme one, for it not only posits a specific referentiality for the Habakkuk text but an (at least partially) exclusive one that is far removed from Habakkuk's composition. Yet it demonstrates one way that emerging notions of the relevance of biblical texts were influential. It also shows how the assumption of relevance could work in tandem with an assumption of the biblical text as fundamentally cryptic: the message long hidden in the Habakkuk text was to be unlocked by the latter-day Teacher of Righteousness, to whom the text itself refers.

As this brief discussion suggests, the development of scriptural hermeneutics constituted a definition (or redefinition) of the text and its character. One of its major effects was to short-circuit conventional expectations for how language functions and, in particular, expectations for its function in literature. As I discuss in Chapter 1, the interpretation of literature requires a different set of reading practices than those that feature in the interpretation of Scripture. Without preempting the discussion there, it is useful to consider here one important contrast between reading biblical texts as Scripture and reading them as literature.

In her theorization of literature, Barbara Herrnstein Smith has proposed a helpful distinction between *real discourse* and *fictive discourse* in the use of language. Real (or natural) discourse comprises, for Smith, the actual utterances of real beings in real historical situations. As such, they are *events*. Fictive discourse, by contrast, is what appears in literature—what she terms "poetry in the broad sense." Though it can (and regularly does) mimic real discourse, this discourse is fundamentally *representational*. It has no historical occurrence in the real world but is instead only and ever mimetic. Smith observes:

> When we speak of *mimesis* or representation in an artwork, we recognize
> that it does not constitute the imitation or reproduction of existing objects
> or events, but rather the fabrication of fictive objects and events of which

there are existing or possible instances or types—whether they be rural landscapes, star-crossed lovers, or laments for dead friends. In other words, to say that an artist has represented a certain object or event is to say that he has constructed a fictive member of an identifiable class of natural ("real") objects or events.[23]

With language as both the medium of mimesis and that which is represented, Smith concludes that literary works are "fictive utterances":

> What is central to the concept of the poem as a fictive utterance is not that the "character" or "persona" is distinct from the poet, or that the audience purportedly addressed, the emotions expressed, and the events alluded to are fictional, but that *the speaking, addressing, expressing, and alluding are themselves fictive verbal acts.*[24]

In their primary reference, then, literary works are not actual utterances of real beings in real historical situations with specific audiences; nor do they contain such utterances. Accordingly, they cannot be measured in direct relation to the real world. As I discuss in Chapter 1, they instead create for themselves what the literary theorist Benjamin Harshav (Hrushovski) has termed an *internal field of reference,* namely, a fictive framework.[25] It is within and to their fictive framework that literary works are accountable, and it is by recourse to that frame that their cohesion is measured.[26]

Smith's distinction between real discourse and fictive discourse is directly applicable to the distinction between Scripture and literature. For those who endorse the category, Scripture functions as *real discourse:* it is language conveyed by a (putatively) real being (in this case, a deity) and directed to a real audience in the real world—even if not to a single audience in a single moment. As noted above, not only is Scripture understood to be divine; it is attended by the assumption of its relevance, which is iterative. Its address is (repeatedly) to real people in the real world in their continually occurring presents.[27]

This characterization of Scripture as real discourse may seem strained in view of the problems of discontinuity, duplication, and contradiction within the texts so categorized. After all, such features are hardly ideal (or typical) characteristics of conventional language use. Yet such problems do not by themselves undermine real discourse; moreover, as noted already, the assumptions that guide scriptural interpretation mitigate and even lionize the readerly disorientations induced by these texts. Those assumptions do not adhere, however, in the case of literature. In this sense, the fictive discourse of literature and the reading practices associated with it are less supple than those of real discourse—or at least potentially so, as the case of Scripture's real discourse demonstrates.

At least in the case of the Pentateuch and the history of its interpretation, there is also some basis for understanding the prominence of a scriptural hermeneutic as a response to the nonliterariness of the text. I argue that even as the pentateuchal sources individually carry the hallmarks of literature, the compiled Pentateuch does not. There is even a tacit recognition of the latter in the assumption that Scripture is divine and should be read accordingly. The difference between Scripture and other texts was expressed and reinforced by association with the well-established opposition between the human and the divine: if Scripture is understood as divine—and thus fundamentally different from all other texts—its interpretation could (even should) be governed by different rules.

Potentially confusing is that what was once literature—the fictive discourse of the individual pentateuchal sources—has been recontextualized and redeployed in the compiled Pentateuch as real discourse. Smith takes up precisely this scenario, observing various ways that fictive discourse has been transformed into real discourse.[28] A straightforward example that she offers is the poetry found in a greeting card, which is intentionally created not as real discourse but as discourse *to be made real* in the act of giving the card to its recipient.[29] That this sophisticated transformation could become a commonplace—and in such a mundane context—highlights how easily readers can become habituated to this shift.

Unlike in the case of the greeting card poem, however, in the case of the Pentateuch it is often difficult to identify any cognizance of the text's redeployment as real discourse. Scriptural reading is instead regularly attended by what ritual theorist Catherine Bell has termed "strategic misrecognition" in ritual performers. Of ritual performers and their performance, Bell notes: "Ritualization sees its end, the rectification of a problematic. It does not see what it does in the process of realizing this end, its transformation of the problematic itself. . . . ritualization interprets its own schemes as impressed upon the actors from a more authoritative source, usually from well beyond the immediate human community itself."[30] In a basic sense, scriptural reading can be viewed as a kind of ritual practice, the goal of which is the transformation of fictive discourse into real discourse. The result is the possibility, for the reader/listener (= ritual participant), of "being addressed." Moreover, as James W. Watts has observed, the ritual practice of scriptural interpretation is normally attended by other ritual practices—especially oral performance and iconic veneration. These practices are mutually reinforcing within communal religious life.[31]

Smith also observes that some discourse stands "on the margins" between the real and the fictive. This can occur for a number of reasons, including the fact that certain kinds of real and fictive discourse are so similar to each other that their function is difficult to discern, especially without additional, contextual information. In such instances, it is obviously possible to mistake one for the other.[32] In the case of the Pentateuch, the distinctive, hybrid nature of the compiled text, with the mixed signals that it presents to its readers, certainly contributes to the difficulty of its interpretation. Yet any narrative that presents the past—narratives like those of the Pentateuch—may be particularly liable to such misrecognition, even apart from problems of compositional history that they may exhibit.

In his theorization of narrative, Hayden White highlights the constitutive role of the cause-and-effect structure upon which narrative works are built and by which they assert reality. In the case of narratives that present a past, the presentation of ostensibly real events in this form, an activity that entails the imposition of plot structure on these events, creates the possibility of relative significances for realities and, even more so, basic relations among them.[33] This means, then, that for White, narrativizing is essentially a process of meaning making, and narrativizing the past is quite literally to organize *and evaluate* an inherently disorganized temporality. White observes, "Narrative strains to produce the effect of having filled in all the gaps, to put an image of continuity, coherency, and meaning in place of the fantasies of emptiness, need, and frustrated desire."[34] It is on these terms that White observes the attractiveness of historical narrative:

> We can comprehend the appeal of historical discourse by recognizing the extent to which it makes the real desirable, makes the real into an object of desire, and does so by its imposition, upon events that are represented as real, of the formal coherency that stories possess . . . the reality that is represented in the historical narrative, in "speaking itself," speaks to us, summons us from afar (this "afar" is the land of forms), and displays to us a formal coherency that we ourselves lack.[35]

With such substantial appeal, it is clear that narrative also has the capacity to lead astray, for its form—as much as its content—makes it compelling.

In the case of the Pentateuch, the natural appeal of narrative is only buttressed by the assumptions of Scripture.

Together with this book's Neodocumentarian orientation, the differentiation between literature and Scripture and their attendant reading practices provides a starting point for the ensuing chapters' discussion of the Deuteronomic source as a historically situated, literary work and of how that work, as a piece of literature, should be interpreted. The literature/Scripture distinction also introduces the framework that began to operate in the early history of Deuteronomy's interpretation, which I treat in Chapter 4. This book thus progresses diachronically from the literary to the scriptural, and one of its goals is to demonstrate both the substantial changes that Deuteronomic texts underwent along this trajectory and the ways that these changes influenced the interpretation of these texts. Almost all of these developments began in antiquity, and their impact continued to reverberate long afterward, including to the present.

1 What Is Deuteronomy?

An accurate description of Deuteronomy is no mean task, especially if what is attempted is a coherent characterization of all of its parts, their relations to each other, and their historical situation. Scholars who have addressed this issue have toggled between evaluations of the text's form and content, offering labels including "covenant/treaty," "law code," "valedictory address," "constitution/polity," "catechesis," "narrative," and (simply) "Torah"—or some combination of these (or other) genre designations.[1] Moreover, as is clear already in a cursory appraisal of these characterizations, the delimitation of the text itself plays a central role in describing its genre. For these reasons and more, this book's basic question—"What is Deuteronomy?"—proves deceptively complex.

Yet even as some issues must wait for detailed consideration in subsequent chapters (including the claim that Deuteronomy bears the form of a covenant akin to Hittite, Assyrian, and other ancient Near Eastern treaties and loyalty oaths), it is possible to take up this broad, definitional question here. To do so, I consider the specific issues of the text's literary shape and extent, the combination of literary forms attested within it, and its particular contents and aims. The answers that emerge—and especially the procedure necessary to uncover them—are hinted at in this book's title: to understand Deuteronomy requires considering it in relation to the larger Pentateuch of which it is a part. This is first because of the peculiar circumstances that led to the composition and delineation of Deuteronomic texts. Moreover, as the discussion here emphasizes—and as the extended example at the end of the chapter demonstrates—the various literary issues in Deuteronomy are mutually informing. The fruit of this discussion will not be a full compositional or literary analysis of Deuteronomy but a general orientation to its genre and contents that can be applied even to those details not treated in depth here.

Delimiting the Text: Books, Scrolls, and Works

While Deuteronomy is largely free of major text-critical issues,[2] determining literary boundaries is a far-reaching and consequential task in its analysis. Such textual delimitation and, with it, consideration of broader issues of compositional history require situating Deuteronomy in the context of the Pentateuch. This is because Deuteronomy is properly *and only* the final fifth of "the five fifths of the Torah." This observation, while very basic, sets the stage for several important terminological distinctions. Though the texts of Deuteronomy are the contents of a single *scroll,* they are not properly a *literary work* or *composition,* terms that I use in this book interchangeably. The term *book,* so often applied to Deuteronomy in the designation "the book of Deuteronomy," is thus a misnomer if taken in the sense of "literary work." For this reason, I avoid using it.[3] The designation "book" for Deuteronomy originates from the Greek *pentateuch* (πεντάτευχος), a term regularly rendered "five books." Yet this term is better translated "five scrolls," for it referred originally to the text's materiality, including its division into parts and the storage of those parts.[4] This original sense of the label Pentateuch thus supports the claim that I argue for across this chapter: the Deuteronomy scroll is a delineation that results from ancient technological factors, namely, limitations of scroll size, not the literary autonomy of its contents.

As Menahem Haran observed, the compiled Torah was likely divided into five parts because it was too large to fit on a single (conventional) scroll. Yet Haran was also quick to note that none of the individual scrolls that together make up the Pentateuch—Genesis, Exodus, Leviticus, Numbers, and Deuteronomy—strains the limits of ancient Judean scroll length. Rather than exhausting the constraints of the scroll medium, the specific division of the Torah into its five parts was accomplished by following internal, content cues—both narrative arc and themes.[5] Across the history of the Pentateuch's reception, this attention that was paid to the Pentateuch's content in the process of its division into scrolls has sometimes contributed to misunderstandings of these individual scrolls as standalone works.

The scroll of Deuteronomy is to be distinguished from the Deuteronomic, or D, source of the Torah, which is (or was) a *literary work* or *com-*

position. This difference is significant, even as scholars sometimes overlook it or speak of it imprecisely:[6] the Deuteronomy scroll is a *part* of a single, composite text—the Torah/Pentateuch—and is fully integrated into the chronologically arranged plot of the Pentateuch. This scroll's contents are *not* a unit that is literarily or compositionally distinct. By contrast, to delimit and consider D, which in my view encompasses almost all of Deut 1:1–32:47 (itself admitting of compositeness), is to consider a *composition*—a work shaped to stand alone and characterized by a high level of internal cohesion (though not, in the case of D, from a single hand).[7]

The identification of the D source as an independent composition and the specific delimitation of its text are achieved in the same way that all of the pentateuchal compositions can be identified and disentangled from each other. That is, it is on the basis of D's distinctive content—its historical, legal, and theological perspectives—that it may be judged a separate composition from the rest of the Pentateuch.

At this point it is sufficient to offer just a few, brief examples; additional content discrepancies are treated in Chapter 2's discussion of D's revisionary compositional method. According to Exod 18:21–24, in an encounter prior to Yahweh's revelation of law at Horeb, Moses's father-in-law, Jethro, recommended that Moses appoint judges to help him manage Israel's disputes, and Moses did so. According to Deut 1:9–18, Moses appointed judges, but not at the recommendation of Jethro; moreover, D states that this judicial appointment occurred after Yahweh's revelation at Horeb, not before. Similarly, according to Exod 20:24, Yahweh told Moses at Horeb that the Israelites may build as many altars as they would like in order to sacrifice to their god; by contrast, Deut 12 insists that Israel may build and sacrifice at only one altar. It also pejoratively characterizes the alternative as "each man doing what is right in his own eyes" (Deut 12:8). Finally, according to Exod 24:10, the elders saw the god of Israel at the mountain. Deuteronomy 4:12, however, insists that Israel saw no divine form on this occasion but instead only heard Yahweh's voice.

Such content discrepancies, which can be multiplied several times over, suggest that the members of each set of discordant pairs come from different hands—or, more precisely, *different works.* They include mutually exclusive historiographical and theological details that are not attended by any attempt to coordinate the differences between them. In many cases, their theological claims amount to historiographical claims: for example, central issues for D in relation to the other pentateuchal compositions are what Yahweh revealed to Israel and to Moses in the desert, and how these revelations took place. In the Deuteronomic instances just cited, moreover, the texts are not only historiographically and theologically distinct from their counterparts in Exodus (or, in other cases, Numbers); they also correlate with each other and, together with additional material, compose an internally consistent narrative work with an identifiable beginning, middle, and end. Importantly, there is good precedent from the ancient Near East, including from ancient Israel and Judah, of narrative compositions that are internally consistent, suggesting that internal inconsistency is not simply a characteristic of ancient Israelite/Judean literary composition.[8]

The beginning of the D composition corresponds with the beginning of the Deuteronomy scroll, a concurrence that is not merely coincidental. Structured as an introduction, Deut 1:1 served as a fitting beginning for a new scroll, just as it did for the D composition: "These are the words (namely, the words that follow) that Moses spoke to all Israel on the other side of the Jordan" (Deut 1:1a). The Mosaic speeches to which 1:1 refers, situated at the end of the wilderness period before Israel's entry into the land of Canaan, dominate the scroll of Deuteronomy, which then also helps to explain the scroll's ending. Focused on the speeches of this single character, Deuteronomy concludes when Moses dies; it even includes a reflective panegyric that affirms Moses's singularity (Deut 34:10–12).

Yet if such a logic for the beginning and end of Deuteronomy may be observed,[9] content discrepancies and other internal clues in the scroll suggest that it is not all of one piece. The closing chapters of Deuteronomy are a good place to begin identifying material that is not part of the D composition. As just noted, the claim to the end of prophecy in the Mosaic guise in Deut 34:10a stands at odds with the divine instructions in Deut 18:15–22 for the appointment of prophets like Moses after him (i.e., after Moses's death). According to 18:18, Yahweh stated that he himself would elevate prophets subsequent to Moses and that they would be like Moses.[10]

It is likewise notable that Deut 32:45–47, coming as they do before the end of the scroll, contain what appears to be concluding content:

> [45]When Moses finished speaking all these words to all Israel, [46]he said to them, "Be careful concerning all these words with which I have warned you this day, which you should command your children to be careful to do—all the words of this teaching. [47]For it is no small thing for you: it is your life! By this word you will lengthen your days upon the land that you are crossing the Jordan to inherit."

Voiced by the text's omniscient third-person narrator, 32:45 corresponds closely with the story details in 1:5, signaling beginning and end: "On the other side of the Jordan, in the land of Moab, Moses began expounding this teaching, saying . . ." Moses's characterization of his speeches as "this teaching" in v. 46 and the reference to the River Jordan in v. 47 likewise create a bookend, matching the similar details in 1:5. Finally, the material in Deut 32:48–34:12 correlates with the other pentateuchal sources (J, E, P) and is readily assigned to them.[11] Each part of this material, divided into its separate sources, follows directly upon what immediately precedes it in the work to which it belongs. Taken together, these details suggest that the D composition concludes in 32:45–47.

These observations on the beginnings and ends of both D and the Deuteronomy scroll underscore that the compositional analysis of these texts requires a careful consideration of their details not only in relation to each other but also in relation to the Pentateuch as a whole. Indeed, many texts in Deuteronomy—and especially their specific features—are *only* explicable in relation to a larger theory of pentateuchal composition. This claim should not be surprising: as noted already, the scroll of Deuteronomy is properly a section or volume of the Pentateuch.

The Neodocumentarian account of the pentateuchal compiler's work, described in the Introduction, offers a compelling explanation for the situation of the pentateuchal sources in the Deuteronomy scroll. Most notably, the compiler's method explains (1) why D appears in the combined Pentateuch as an almost entirely uninterrupted block, (2) why this block is located as it is in the compiled Pentateuch, and (3) why its accounts of events that are also narrated in the Exodus and Numbers scrolls were not combined with those Exodus and Numbers accounts.

In arranging an overarching, chronologically ordered plotline, the pentateuchal compiler was guided by the internal (and sometimes conflicting) frameworks of the materials combined, not least of which were the respective timelines of these works' plots.[12] The D material, as an account of Moses's valedictory speeches to the Israelites at the end of their wilderness journey and before their entry into the land of Canaan, had to be located precisely where it is in the compiled Pentateuch, namely, after its accounts of Israel's wilderness journey. Moreover, it could be comfortably located in this position because of specific correspondences in its story and those of the other pentateuchal sources. For example, with regard to location, D's situation of Moses's speeches in the plains of Moab at the end of Israel's wilderness journey accords precisely with the geography of the Israelites' travel described in the other pentateuchal sources (cf. Num 33:50; 35:1, 10; 36:13). D's timeline is similarly shared, a point exemplified by the single P verse, Deut 1:3, that was interwoven into a block of D material.[13] Deuteronomy 1:3 situates Moses's speeches at the end of Israel's forty years in the wilderness. In D, too, Moses repeatedly refers to the end of the forty-year sojourn (2:7; 8:2, 4; 29:4).

The combination of source materials at the end of Deuteronomy can be explained similarly. The scroll ends with an account of Moses's death and a summary reflection upon his life (34:1–12), yet none of this material belongs to D. It is instead a combination of J, E, and P texts.[14] Yet the temporal details of the J, E, and P materials here correspond closely with D's chronological claims. For example, in Deut 4:21–22, Moses reflects on his impending death, which will occur before Israel's entry into the land of Canaan. Similar perspectives appear in the narrative in Deut 31:1–8, where Moses acknowledges his aged state, his inability to enter the land of Canaan himself, and Joshua's role as the new leader of Israel. If the combined text's plotline was to be arranged chronologically, the accounts of Moses's death had to appear after his valedictory address, but this juxtaposition also proved eminently logical, for it was the timeline already described in D. Thus, the correspondences among the temporal and geographical frameworks of the different pentateuchal sources, beyond their general content similarities, greatly facilitated the compiler's combination of them.

The setting of Moses's speeches in D likewise explains the compiler's choice not to interweave D's accounts of events that occurred earlier in the wilderness period with accounts of the same events from other sources. The accounts of Israel's wilderness experiences in D, including Moses's appointment of judges, Yahweh's manna provisions, the war with Amalek, the Horeb revelation, and the golden calf rebellion, are all part of Mosaically voiced retrospectives, not anonymous, third-person narrations, as they are in the other sources. Guided by the temporal setting of D's Mosaic speeches, the compiler made no attempt to integrate them with the earlier pentateuchal accounts of the same events; indeed, he could not. In view of these details, the compiler's incorporation of D into the Pentateuch as an almost entirely uninterrupted block is also fully explicable. The story that D relates, which is primarily an account of Moses's speeches to Israel, requires very little narrative time; there was thus little reason to disrupt or rearrange it when incorporating it into the pentateuchal plotline.[15]

Identifying Compositeness within the Deuteronomic Source

Yet even as D should be understood as a single work, there is ample evidence within it that it includes originally disparate material. It is thus necessary to consider this evidence and how it suggests that D attests the combination of material from multiple hands. A starting point is a recognition that the process of identifying compositeness within a discrete composition (such as D) is both similar to and different from the identification of originally independent literary works in a composite text (like the Pentateuch). Specifically, these processes are similar—even identical—in their beginning, but they diverge thereafter.

Whatever the result of the analysis, the identification of compositeness commences on the basis of observed duplications, contradictions, and discontinuities. Yet important differences also obtain between material that should be identified as a stratum/compositionally distinct section of a work and material that should be assigned to an entirely different work. In cases of identifiable strata, it is not possible to reconstruct larger, continuous works by connecting isolated pieces of text with each other—though it is sometimes possible to correlate different, discrete sections with each other as part of a single stratum. As the language of strata suggests (and as scholars have often noted), what is hypothesized resembles an archaeological tel: new material accretes to an earlier layer or layers, with some of these accretions coordinating with each other (usually on the basis of their distinctive content) as parts of a single, larger layer. In many instances, the "excavative" work of redactional analysis suggests that little of what was ever included was subsequently excised; texts instead tended to grow progressively, at least for significant parts of their histories.[16]

It is also the case that stylistic and thematic features—or, more precisely, inconsistencies in style and theme—may point to compositeness within a single work. Yet reliance upon style and theme as primary evidence for multiple authorship can be quite tenuous, for these features often introduce no duplications, contradictions, or discontinuities to a text. Stylistic differences may instead be instances of authorial choice (e.g., for the sake of emphasis or as an expression of aesthetic preference), not evidence of different hands.

One special category of style that has featured prominently in scholarly reconstructions of biblical compositional history is the appearance of multiple genres within a single work. Yet as in the case of stylistic and

thematic variation, formal complexity does not *necessarily* produce duplication, contradiction, or discontinuity and thus need not do any damage
to a text's internal cohesion. The inclusion of multiple genres in a single
work only requires the possibility of such a work, namely, one that includes
multiple genres/subgenres within it. It is on this account that the inclusion
of multiple genres/subgenres may be considered a stylistic choice, and, of
course, it proves to be quite common in biblical compositions, as it does
in other literary works as well.[17] Yet with these cautions in place, there are
also instances, as I discuss below, in which stylistic and thematic inconsistencies are difficult to explain without recourse to compositional theories,
especially when they appear alongside other evidence that suggests compositeness. In such instances, the coordination of multiple lines of evidence
is especially important for diagnosing disunity.

These observations point to another important distinction that should
be made in compositional analysis, namely, the differentiation between material incorporated into a work but not originally composed for inclusion
there and material composed for the purpose of supplementing the work.
While the identification of each of these materials contributes to understanding a text's origins and development, they carry different implications.
It is possible, for example, that the original D work (or works) was not all
its authors' original composition but incorporated some existing materials
as part of the work. If that is the case, some measure of compositeness could
be understood to have existed in D from its inception and did not originate
only from the work's agglutinative growth over time. In identifying such
preexisting material, it should be acknowledged that what is isolated is not
necessarily an earlier stage in the development of D but instead (part of) a
prior, distinct work. Because of the paucity of evidence for reconstructing
such prior works, their identification usually remains especially tentative.

I turn now to specific features that recommend the identification of
compositeness in D. My goal, as noted at the outset, is not to offer a comprehensive compositional analysis. It is instead to identify and exemplify
features that serve repeatedly in D as markers of compositional disunity
or, as in the case of the final feature I discuss, allegedly serve to mark such
disunity.

Structural Duplication

A first such feature is *structural duplication*, which may be observed
already at the very beginning of D. It has long been recognized that D

includes two opening sections, each of which offers an introduction to the laws that follow. One introductory section comprises Deut 1:1–4:40; the other includes Deut 4:44/45–11:31. Though their content differs, these sections are *structurally* equivalent, each presenting a historical retrospective of Israel's wilderness experiences as an introduction to Moses's lawgiving—variously termed *mišpāṭîm, ḥuqqîm, tôrâ*, and equivalents—and framed accordingly. As such, they represent duplication that is unexplained by D and thus redundancy in the work.

Scholars have proposed several explanations for this duplication. Observing the close correspondence between Deut 4:45–49 and 1:1–2, 4, a number have suggested that 1:1–4:40 (or a majority thereof) were added as a second introduction to the already existing first introduction in chapters 5–11,[18] a process akin to what has recently been identified as a broader phenomenon in biblical and other ancient Near Eastern literature and termed "revision through introduction."[19]

Martin Noth famously offered a different suggestion, though also along the lines of "revision through introduction": he argued that Deut 1–3 were not an introduction to D but to a work encompassing the entirety of Deuteronomy–Kings—his Deuteronomistic History. A major factor in Noth's analysis was his claim that Deut 1–3 lack concern for law and thus do not properly introduce the D composition, with its major emphasis upon legislation.[20]

Alternatively, while differing in the details of their analyses, scholars such as Julius Wellhausen and Menahem Haran have argued that D's two introductory sections originally headed different D compositions, each with a subsequent legal section.[21] Among the virtues of this explanation for Haran is its ability to account for the establishment of asylum cities in 4:41–43, which is uncoordinated with the asylum laws in 19:1–13 and seemingly out of place in the current form of D, a subject to which I return below.

Joel Baden recently made an argument that shares certain features with each of the foregoing suggestions. While accepting much of Haran's reconstruction of D, Baden suggested that the nonoverlap between the two sections of historical recollection in 1:1–4:40 and 4:45–11:31 points to the addition of 1:1–4:40 *as a second introduction* to D that exhibits knowledge of Deut 4:45–11:31 and was added to it.[22] On this theory, 1:1–2, 4 can be understood as modeled on 4:45–49, making the latter appear as a repetitive resumption (*Wiederaufnahme*) in the combined work.[23] This reconstruction, if accepted, has potential implications for the ending of D as well.

Deuteronomy 32:45–47 seem to correlate with 1:5, referencing the beginning and completion of Moses's speeches in the plains of Moab. If 32:45–47 is an original ending to D, 1:5 was likely fashioned with knowledge of it. If this ending is not original, it is possible that it comes from the same hand as 1:5.

Content Duplication

A second, well-attested feature of D that suggests compositeness is *specific content duplication*. In these cases, it is not necessarily the structural elements of the work, such as its introduction, that are reproduced; it is instead overlapping details, which in D's case usually means divine instruction. Such duplicated material is normally either uncoordinated or insufficiently coordinated; it also often includes *content contradiction*, which may be treated as a feature of compositeness in its own right.

An example of content duplication is found in D's treatment of cult centralization in Deut 12, which exhibits evidence of the combination of multiple, corresponding cult centralization laws. Many scholars have noted both redundancies and disparities among the different sections in this chapter, and several have suggested that these sections, or parts of them, come from different hands. Particularly compelling is Simeon Chavel's recent analysis, in which he argues that 12:2–7 and 12:8–12 duplicate each other without acknowledgment while 12:20–28 is an interwoven combination of originally distinct and substantially equivalent compositions (vv. 20 + 22–25 and vv. 21 + 26–28; see Table 1). According to Chavel, 12:13–19 is the latest section in the chapter and draws upon and responds to the earlier sections, already in their combined form.[24]

If this analysis is correct, it points to a complex, multiform process of growth in this chapter and, in view of the formative role that centralization plays in other laws, in the D work more broadly. This process included juxtaposing substantially equivalent legal sections side-by-side, interweaving equivalent legal sections, and revising and updating those sections through supplementary interpolation. What Deut 12 does not do is provide clear evidence for a theory like Wellhausen's or Haran's of a combination in D of blocks from multiple, originally independent compositions (though some have argued along these lines).[25] Though tantalizing for the more comprehensive explanations they offer, such theories move substantially beyond the available evidence and, as such, are untestable.

Table 1. Two interwoven originals in Deuteronomy 12

A: Verses 20 + 22–25	B: Verses 21 + 26–28
Border expansion context	
²⁰When Yahweh your god expands your borders, just as he promised you,	²¹If the place that Yahweh your god will choose to designate for himself is too far from you,
Nonsacral meat consumption	
and you say, "I would like to eat meat!" (for your throat longs to eat meat), you shall eat meat at any time your throat desires it.	you may slaughter from your herd and your flock that Yahweh has given you, just as I have commanded you, and you may eat in your gates whenever your throat desires it.
Emphasis that this practice is nonsacrificial	
²²Only just as one eats the deer and the gazelle, thus shall you eat it, the pure and the impure together may eat it. ²³Yet take care not to eat the blood, for the blood is the life, and you may not eat the life with the meat. ²⁴You shall not consume it; you shall pour it on the ground like water. ²⁵Do not eat it,	²⁶You shall still carry your holy offerings and your votive offerings to the place that Yahweh will choose, ²⁷and you shall make your whole burnt offerings, the flesh and the blood, upon the altar of Yahweh your god. You shall pour out the blood upon the altar of Yahweh your god, and the flesh you shall eat.
Motivation to obey	
in order that it may go well with you and your children after you, for you must do what is right in the eyes of Yahweh.	²⁸Listen carefully to all of these words that I am commanding you in order that it may go well for you and for your children after you forever, for you must do what is good and right in the eyes of Yahweh your god.

Content Contradiction (Plot, Law)

Turning to the category of *content contradiction*, D includes instances of significant plot contradiction and legal contradiction, the two of which are often intertwined. A classic example of plot contradiction in D appears in the conflicting references to the writtenness of Moses's speeches. According to the third-person narrative in Deut 31:9, Moses wrote down the laws that he received at Horeb *after* his speeches in the plains of Moab recounting those: "Moses wrote this teaching and gave it to the Levitical priests, those who carry the ark of Yahweh's covenant, and to all of Israel's elders." Yet the act of writing described in this verse stands at odds with the references to the writtenness of the contents of Moses's speeches in texts such as Deut 28:58, 61; 29:19, 20, 26; and 30:10, each of which cites an existing, written scroll containing "this teaching," "the statutes and commandments," or "the curses."

Scholars have offered various explanations for this plot contradiction, including that it does not constitute a contradiction at all or that its contradiction does not rise to a level requiring a compositional explanation. For example, acknowledging the discrepancy with 31:9, S. R. Driver suggested that the references to an already written scroll in D before 31:9 are departures from the fictive claim of the story world and reflect the fact that D originated as a written text.[26] They are thus the views of the author, not the character who speaks them. Yet in view of other evidence for compositeness—the precise evidence of the kind reviewed here—it is all the more likely that distinct strata exist in this case, too.

Uncoordinated Content

Another feature in D that points to its compositional complexity is its combination of *uncoordinated content.* I mean to contrast uncoordinated content with both duplicated and contradictory content, even as the latter are also very much uncoordinated. Uncoordinated content, as identified here, is not *necessarily* contradictory or duplicative; as such, it does not constitute by itself evidence for compositeness to the degree that these other categories of evidence do. Yet it too suggests at least the possibility of multiple hands.

An example of uncoordinated content, as mentioned already, is found in D's treatments of asylum and Israel's establishment of cities of refuge. According to Deut 4:41–43, Moses established three cities in the Transjordan before Israel's entry into Canaan. In Deut 19:1–13, Moses recounts Yahweh's command to Moses to establish three (and then another three) refuge cities in Canaan. There is no direct duplication or contradiction between these texts, either in their specific content or at the level of a shared story world. Moses received Yahweh's instructions before his establishment of the Transjordanian cities in 4:41–43, and the cities described in Deut 19:1–13 for Canaan are definitely different from the Transjordanian cities.

Yet there is an important difference in the way that these two texts treat the establishment of refuge cities. In 4:41–43, this initiative is Moses's alone; in 19:1–13, it is done at Yahweh's command. Moreover, there is no cross-referencing between these texts: the cities in 4:41–43 are established before Moses's recitation of the law in 19:1–13, but Moses makes no reference to his designation of the Transjordanian cities when he gives the command for establishing Cisjordanian asylum cities. Moreover, he offers specific descriptions of what the Cisjordanian cities are to be and how they should function, details presumably already known by the Israelites, given that similar descriptions (in abbreviated but nearly identical language) already appear in 4:42.

By way of contrast with this example of uncoordinated content, it is helpful to observe the coordination between D's rules for asylum in the case of unintentional homicide (Deut 19:1–13) and its Decalogue text. Though D's asylum legislation includes no basic homicide law, the Decalogue does include such a law ("Do not murder," Deut 5:17). The possibility that Deut 19:1–13 relies upon and assumes the Decalogue homicide law is unproblematic, for D presents its Decalogue as legislation for the Israelites.[27] By contrast, the asylum law in E, found in Exod 21:12–14 and from which D draws in Deut 19:1–13, does include a basic homicide law:

> [12]One who strikes a person, who then dies, shall surely be put to death. [13]But he who did not lie in wait, but rather God moved his hand—I will set up a place for you to which he may flee. [14]But if a man plots against his neighbor to kill him craftily, you shall take him from my altar to die.

Lest this law be considered redundant in E in light of its own version of the Decalogue, which also includes the "do not murder" line (Exod 20:13), it should be recalled that the Ten Words appear in E's story world as a demonstration of prophecy, not as legislation for the Israelites.[28] There is thus no redundancy between E's Decalogue and its basic homicide law (Exod 21:12). Yet what is especially relevant for this discussion is the way that, in view of its omission of such a basic rule outlawing homicide, the legislation of Deut 19:1–13 is consciously coordinated with earlier D material (i.e., its Decalogue homicide law) but apparently not coordinated at all with Moses's designation of asylum cities in the Transjordan in 4:41–43.

Stylistic/Thematic Differences (Discontinuity)

A final type of evidence for compositeness is *stylistic and thematic difference*. Such differences might be considered a form of discontinuity, yet like uncoordinated content, they are not as pronounced as duplications, contradictions, or other forms of discontinuity. Even so, they remain worthy of consideration, not least because scholars often cite them as evidence for compositeness.

One example of inconsistent thematic content in D can be observed in its characterization of all Israelites as "brothers." Though this characterization appears frequently across the D corpus, it is notably absent from a number of individual laws—including some laws, such as D's rules for asylum protection just discussed, where it might be expected. Scholars have noted that D's fraternal claim appears most forcefully in laws oriented toward interpersonal relations and protection of the vulnerable.[29] For example, Deut 22:1–3 employ brotherhood as the primary framework for understanding the Israelite obligation to return lost property:

> [1]You shall not see and ignore <u>your brother's</u> stray ox or sheep. You shall instead return them to <u>your brother</u>. [2]If <u>your brother</u> is not close by or if you cannot identify him, you shall take it into your home, and it shall remain with you until <u>your brother</u> seeks it out. Then you shall return it to him. [3]Thus shall you do for his donkey and his cloak. You shall do the same for any lost item belonging to <u>your brother</u> that, having gone missing from him, you find. You shall not ignore it.

Given the comparatively greater vulnerability present in a case of manslaughter, the emphasis upon a kinship framework in D's treatment of lost property makes its absence from D's homicide and asylum laws all the more conspicuous.

When assessing this inconsistent appeal to Israelite brotherhood, it is striking that among D's laws that are revisions of Elohistic laws, the brotherhood emphasis is substantially muted. This observation is relevant to the present discussion because it points to an alternative explanation for D's inconsistent thematic. The notion of brotherhood is entirely absent from E's laws, and D's close reliance upon E material for some parts of its legal content but not for others suggests that where the brotherhood framework is absent, D's laws may be adhering closely to the discourse of its legal patrimony.[30] Thematic discrepancies in D thus may not be indicators of strata but instead reflect other aspects of this text's composition—in this case, D's use of diverse source materials and/or its sporadic employment of such sources.

The "block model" advanced by Norbert Lohfink and Georg Braulik is an example of a larger theory of Deuteronomic composition that relies especially on identifications of thematic discontinuity. Lohfink has argued that a legal core in Deut 12:2–16:17, focused on the cult's regulation, was supplemented during the exilic period with the "laws concerning offices" in 16:18–18:22. The distinction that Lohfink draws is largely thematic: "A new theme is introduced abruptly at Deut 16:18."[31] These sections are further supplemented by blocks of laws in Deut 19–25, within which bridging material is also identified. For Lohfink and Braulik, thematically discontinuous—and thus originally independent—materials are held together through associative links and arrangements of (parts of) the laws of Deut 12–26 according to the sequence of the Decalogue.[32]

Like thematic variations, stylistic differences may point to the existence of multiple hands in D, though their value for such identifications also requires careful scrutiny. In many cases, observations concerning style are combined with other observations in service of compositional reconstructions. One stylistic anomaly in D that scholars have used in compositional analysis is its number variation (*Numeruswechsel*), that is, the commonly observable alternation in D between Moses's second-person singular and second-person plural address of his fictive Israelite audience. In some instances, the patterns of D's number variation do correspond with the division of strata reached on other grounds. Yet in other cases, they do not.[33]

The example of Deut 12 discussed above exhibits some such patterning: the address in vv. 8–12 consistently uses the second-person plural (with the exception of the formulaic ending of v. 9), while the address in vv. 13–19 is formulated entirely in the second-person singular. At the same time, the section in which Chavel identifies two interwoven originals, vv. 20–28 (A: vv. 20 + 22–25; B: vv. 21 + 26–28; see Table 1), contains only second-person singular address. Consistent formulation of Moses's address in D is thus hardly a sufficient marker of the text's unity. In addition, scholars have recognized that it is not always possible to reconstruct one or more cohesive precursors by separating D's texts formulated in the second-person singular from those formulated in the second-person plural. Not surprisingly, the ancient witnesses exhibit some discrepancy in the second-person formulation preserved in individual instances, complicating the matter further. Finally, comparable examples of number variation are attested in other ancient Near Eastern texts, suggesting that a different rationale may exist for this phenomenon in ancient composition.

The Deuteronomic Source as Literature

As highlighted already, D is almost entirely a series of first-person, retrospective speeches to the Israelites that are voiced by Moses. The speeches in chapters 1–11 are primarily exhortatory and make their argument through a selective recollection of Israel's wilderness experience. The speeches in chapters 12–26 are primarily legal. They are Moses's communication of the laws that the deity revealed to him alone after Yahweh's direct revelation of the Decalogue to all of the Israelites (Deut 5:28). D's central legal discourse is immediately followed by a speech outlining a series of blessings and curses, and the work concludes with additional exhortatory Mosaic speeches.

These speeches are set within a sparse, third-person omniscient narrative framework that begins in 1:5 and describes the actions of its characters (usually Moses's initiation or conclusion of speech). The narrative also includes other brief details of setting and plot, including Moses's writing of his teaching and provisions for its future recitation (e.g., 4:41–43; 5:1; 28:69; 29:1; 31*; 31:30; 32:45).[34] The existence and import of this narrative framework has occasionally been recognized, and Michael V. Fox has even observed several ancient Near Eastern parallels to it, including in the book of Qohelet in the Hebrew Bible.[35] D's narrative framework proves significant for understanding its genre, its story world, and, as I show in Chapter 3, how to adjudicate proposed ancient Near Eastern comparisons.

As the foregoing comments imply, identification of D as a narrative requires a clarification at the beginning of the work. That is, it is important to differentiate between the beginning of D's narrative and its paratextual heading or, according to the categorization of Gérard Genette, *preface* (Deut 1:1–2, 4; as noted above, v. 3 belongs to P).[36] This distinction clarifies particular content and literary characteristics in D and contributes to the compositional analysis discussed already. It also corrects common misconceptions concerning D's genre, misconceptions that are prompted in part by D's preface.

D's preface describes the work's contents as "the words that Moses spoke" (v. 1a). This characterization is mostly accurate, for D does mostly comprise speeches voiced by Moses. Yet the expression "the words of Moses" does not describe accurately all of D's contents. Omitted from it are D's third-person omniscient narrations, which are not "the words that Moses spoke" but instead the words of a separate voice—that of the narrator. This incompleteness in the preface's description is not ultimately problematic, however—and thus presents no cause for identifying multiple hands—for the preface's purpose is to direct the reading of the work.[37] That is, its goal is not necessarily a comprehensive characterization of D's contents. It instead means to focus the reader's attention on D's Mosaic speech content, which is, of course, that part of the work that contains its message.

The incompleteness of D's prefatory description also helps to distinguish vv. 1–2, 4 from 1:5, for it highlights the shift in addressee between them. In v. 5, the narrator begins to recount the story, and its deixis, which falls within the storytelling discourse, accurately points to the following speeches ("this teaching"). In this case, the narrator addresses the narratee. With the deictic reference in v. 1—"These are the words that Moses spoke"—the speaker is not storytelling but characterizing the work's contents. In so doing, this (anonymous) speaker properly addresses the text's real reader.[38] Though it is easy to overlook, the difference between preface (paratext) and narrative in D is actually marked as it so often is in literary works: Deut 1:1–2, 4 stand *outside of* D's narrated story, whose beginning and end, as discussed already, can be identified in the correspondence between 1:5 and 32:45–47.[39]

Beyond any presupposition that readers may bring to the text, this brief description, with its focus on plot, narration, and characterization, suggests that D is *literature*. Yet as theorists have observed, plot, narration, and characterization (as well as other so-called literary features) are actually not the exclusive domain of literature. Thus, to solidify D's categorization as literature and to weigh its implications, it is necessary to treat in some detail what "literariness" means and what its applicability is to a work such as D. Put simply, what makes D's narrative literary?

This consideration is especially pressing on three, related counts. First, it has sometimes been suggested that modern literary theory, including the category of literature itself, is an ill fit for ancient compositions.[40] The arguments below serve as a rebuttal to such a claim. Second, sometimes the literariness of biblical texts has been taken for granted, that is, asserted without being defined.[41] Yet failing to define this basic category—or defining it in only the most rudimentary of ways—can result in all sorts of inaccuracies (some of which I reference below). Finally, in the history of biblical studies, literary analysis has often been pitted against historical analysis, with these two inquiries characterized too simplistically as alternatives to each other.[42] My arguments here call this dichotomy into question by showing how historical/compositional and literary analyses are mutually informative. In this discussion, then, I seek to recover certain virtues of nineteenth-century pentateuchal scholarship while also introducing more recent theoretical advances, especially from beyond the field of biblical studies.

The Internal Field of Reference

Particularly instructive for understanding D as a literary work—or, indeed, any of the pentateuchal sources as literary works—is Benjamin Harshav's theorization of literature. Harshav has argued that literature is characterized by three interrelated elements: an internal field of reference; the autonomy and closure of the individual text; and the use of norms and conventions of literature that themselves are subject to revision and change over time.[43] Of these characteristics, the definitive (and thus definitional) feature is the internal field of reference that a literary text creates for itself and that governs its interpretation, from the individual word or sentence to the paragraph, the chapter, and the work as a whole. Harshav observes, "The experience and interpretation of literary texts is not a matter of language alone: language in literature can only be understood *as embedded in fictional or projected constructs*—situations, characters, ideas—no matter how partial or unstable these may be."[44] These different elements, which Harshav terms "frames of reference," together combine in a work of literature to create its *internal field of reference* or *fictive world*. Dilating on the way that readers encounter this internal field of reference, Harshav appeals to a familiar image: "A literary text builds the boat under its own feet while rowing in the sea. . . . In other words, a work of literature projects its own 'reality' while simultaneously describing it."[45]

This means, among other things, that as the literary work constructs its fictive world, it offers cues for how it should be read and, in so doing, prioritizes its construction in instances of discrepancy that might arise between internal and external evaluations of any particular detail.[46] Put differently, though a literary work may sometimes draw, even extensively, from the world beyond it—and thus also evinces what Harshav terms an *external field of reference*, knowledge of which is indispensable to readers—it is free to depart from that external world at will.[47] The internal field of reference, the work's *fictiveness*, thus requires readers to submit themselves to it to understand the work (even if they might object to the values described within it, its characterizations, or other perspectives contained within it). And important for the present discussion, a literary work may be deemed successful as such insofar as it creates and maintains its internal field of reference. Accordingly, Harshav characterizes the internal field of reference variously as a work's "internal structure and coherence" or its "unity."[48] He also concludes that the internal field of reference, in line with its definitional role, is the arbiter among all interpretations: "Hypotheses of interpretation involve hypotheses on ... [a text's] interdependencies and may be refuted when one of the terms is exposed as wrong."[49]

A brief example can illustrate these points. In a historical novel, characters recognizable from the "real" world may, in the story world, act in ways that are contrary to what is known of them from beyond the story. Likewise, a realistic event that did not actually happen in the real world may occur in the novel. A novel may thus include an account of Adolf Hitler's invasion and conquest of the United States during World War II, or of the total defeat of the Germans at the hand of the Jews in the Warsaw Ghetto Uprising. That such claims do not accord with occurrences in the real world, even as they draw on a recognizable external field of reference, is irrelevant to their function within the literary work. What does matter is whether those claims are consistent with the novel's other details—that is, if they accord with the work's internal field of reference. In our example, it is important that Hitler be portrayed as the aggressive German Führer and not as, say, a mild-mannered milkman; in the same way, to describe a Jewish victory in Warsaw credibly, the novel must claim that the Germans invaded Poland. As long as a story's details are interdependent and internally consistent, they are literarily acceptable, whatever correlates or divergences they may exhibit with the world beyond the story. Harshav thus asserts that one who marshals externally derived counterevidence against a literary depiction misunderstands the literary work.[50]

This prioritization of the internal field of reference, it should be observed, applies equally to a comparison of details between literary works. As noted above, Harshav identifies autonomy as a characteristic of literary works. Thus, just as a story world may sometimes correspond with the real world and sometimes depart from it, so too may the story world of one literary work accord with or diverge from that of another work. Harshav observes that literary departures from what is known from the real world can be particularly revelatory of a perspective important within the internal field of reference.[51] The same may be said for disparities between literary works and their respective internal fields of reference.

Literary Theory and Compositional History

Harshav has not served as a regular conversation partner for pentateuchal critics or even biblical scholars more generally.[52] Yet applying his insights to pentateuchal texts permits a redescription of their compositional analysis that, though stated anew, hearkens back to this endeavor's early characterization as "literary criticism" (*Literarkritik*). In fact, the history of pentateuchal studies reveals that something close to Harshav's theorization of literature, at turns inchoate or partial and almost always uninvoked, has guided many scholars' disentanglements of the pentateuchal sources and their identification of them as originally independent literary works. It has also guided the identification of strata within them. What Harshav perceived for literary works generally biblical scholars have observed for the works combined in the Pentateuch: the distinctive contents (settings, plotlines, religious ideas, portrayals of characters, etc.) of the pentateuchal sources and their strata constitute their mutually exclusive internal fields of reference, and the cohesive assemblages of these distinctive contents point to each work's autonomy.

It is because of the governing role that each of these features plays in the interpretive process that the reader of the compiled Pentateuch is thwarted: the texts' contradictions, duplications, and discontinuities, particularly in their narration and characterization, are problems of competing autonomies and internal fields of reference. Harshav identifies precisely the problem that readers of the Pentateuch encounter: "An author rarely tells us anything directly, he does it through various speakers and narrators, who are committed to the same truth within the Internal Field of Reference or are exposed as being ironical, ignorant, lying, or unreliable."[53] In the case of the Pentateuch, it is necessary to add an additional explanation: speakers and narrators presumed to be singular may be unaligned because they are the products of different hands. The narrator's (or, better, narrators') descriptions prove inconsistent, yet no explanations for such inconsistencies are forthcoming in the text. Neither do they serve any discernable narrative purpose. For example, there is no indication that a pentateuchal author intentionally deploys an unreliable narrator.[54] The story's characters similarly exhibit discrepant identities, knowledge, speech, and actions. In D, the characterization of Moses is especially at issue: in the absence of any accounting for the incongruities in his speeches, for example, the Mosaic character proves confused and perplexing. In Harshav's terms, though Moses is assumed to be "committed to the same truth within the Internal Field of Reference," he deviates from this commitment without explanation.

This application of literary theory to the Pentateuch—both to the compiled whole and to the sources of which it is composed—prompts another question: Does the compositeness of these texts call into question their categorization as literature? To what extent do these texts' duplications, discontinuities, and contradictions diminish their literariness or even suggest for them a different classification? The answers to these questions, I would suggest, are different for the pentateuchal sources than for the compiled Pentateuch, and the basis for these different answers relates to what remains when their respective duplications, discontinuities, and contradictions are accounted for.

In the case of the pentateuchal sources, compositional analysis results in the identification of works shaped to stand alone and characterized by a high level of internal cohesion, that is, a robust internal field of reference. Though their compositeness has diminished their literariness, it is clear that they originated as literary works, and they retain the markers of such. Indeed, this is the basis of their identification.

This is not the case for the Pentateuch as a whole, however. The explanations for its duplications, discontinuities, and contradictions leave nothing in their wake that resembles a literary text at all.[55] Nearly all of its text can be assigned to one of the pentateuchal sources, and what cannot be assigned to one of these works is best explained as late supplementation. When that material is isolated, it exhibits no autonomy or closure; neither does it create autonomy or closure for the texts that it augments. In other words, what is missing from the Pentateuch is *the possibility* of an internal field of reference. The principle of its organization—its sequentially ordered plotline—cannot overcome its multiple, conflicting details. Any semblance of an internal field of reference that might be identified within the Pentateuch is thus partial and imprecise. This textual combination does exhibit a variety of literary features, but, as noted already, the presence of such features is insufficient to identify it as literature. Moreover, given the compositional history of the Pentateuch, the presence of these literary features in it is readily explicable: in almost every instance, they stem from the underlying literary works combined.[56]

As considered briefly in the Introduction and as I discuss in more detail in Chapter 4, the early reception history of the Pentateuch attests the development of reading practices that respond to its distinctive features by redefining this text as nonliterary, namely, as (what would become known as) Scripture. The analysis offered here suggests that such developments are in no small part a response to the nature of the compiled Pentateuch itself. In other words, when confronted with a nonliterary text, early interpreters of the Pentateuch developed new, *nonliterary* methods for reading it.[57] And, of course, the problems that these early readers encountered have persisted and are perhaps even most vexing for those who would attempt to read the Pentateuch as literature. This is because the reading practices required by literary texts simply cannot be applied successfully to the compiled Pentateuch.

Etiology and Allegory

If the foregoing discussion secures the literary nature of D, the question remains, what is the character and aim of this literature? Scholars regularly understand D as an elaborate story whose details, though set several centuries before its composition, were meant to point to the political, social, and religious circumstances of their authors' present(s) and not just depict those of the past. Yet the correlations observed are not, according to this view, simple reflections of the author's compositional context. As constructions of the past, these accounts present legitimate difference, that is, something other than the present, yet they are fashioned for maximal explanatory value. In this way, D's historiographic work is explicitly *etiological.* It seeks to account for the origins of its authors' and audiences' contemporary conditions and, in so doing, makes a claim to historical verisimilitude beyond the story world. Such etiological ambition is a common feature of ancient Near Eastern depictions of the past, including those found in the Hebrew Bible.[58]

Crucially, however, and as I discuss further below, this claim to external referentiality is ultimately subordinated to D's internal field of reference.[59] This is not least because D's authors sought to challenge and reshape their contemporary conditions to new, different ends. In other words, D does not simply recount a past that explains a present *that is;* its account stands as a basis for a present *that should be.* As such, D's etiological discourse is one that Barbara Herrnstein Smith might deem "marginal":[60] it stands at the edge between the fictive and the natural, but its allegiance is finally to—and its resonance is with—the story world.

In service of their aims, D's authors also moved beyond etiology. They did so by encoding in their work a set of symbolic meanings, namely, specific correlations between the text's story world and the real world of its composition.[61] Without denying, then, the primacy of D's internal referentiality—its internal field of reference—and alongside the purported external referentiality that D's etiology entails, it is possible to explore the question of literary intent in D's additional, external reference to its present. That is, it is possible to consider the question of *allegory.*

As noted, D's use of allegory—like that of the other pentateuchal sources—is widely endorsed. Yet its identification has often been treated more intuitively than theoretically. For this reason, I focus here especially on D's allegory, attempting to situate it and its interpretation within a broader theoretical framework, even as I show the ways that it functions alongside D's etiology. Such theorization promises greater insight into what D is and how it works; it can also provide a basis for critical engagement with the scholarly claims that have been made concerning D's external referentiality.

Theorizing Allegory

In characterizing D as allegory,[62] it is important to clarify both the various ways that allegory manifests in literature and how it can function, for D does not employ certain features, such as symbolic names, that are sometimes viewed as the hallmark of allegory. Literary theorists have helpfully observed that allegory is properly a *mode* rather than a *genre.* That is, allegory appears in a variety of different literary genres and can be used in limited or extensive ways within a particular work. Angus Fletcher has observed:

> In the simplest terms, allegory says one thing and means another. It destroys the normal expectation we have about language, that our words "mean what they say." When we predicate quality *x* of person Y, Y really is what our predication says he is (or we assume so); but allegory would turn Y into something other (*allos*) than what the open and direct statement tells the reader. Pushed to an extreme, this ironic usage would subvert language itself, turning everything into an Orwellian newspeak. In this sense we see how allegory is properly considered a mode: it is a fundamental process of encoding our speech. For the very reason that it is a radical linguistic procedure, it can appear in all sorts of different works, many of which fall far short of the confusing doubleness that made Orwell's newspeak such an effective brainwashing device.[63]

Northrop Frye has similarly emphasized the flexibility of allegory and its varied expression in literature: "An author is being allegorical whenever it is clear that he is saying 'by this I *also* (*allos*) mean that.'" To characterize this complexity and variability of expression, Frye has proposed a "sliding scale" of literary allegory that moves from the most explicit to the most elusive, even as the full range continues to fall within the bounds of literature and is thus governed by literary norms.[64] Building on Frye's insights, Joel Rosenberg has drawn a distinction between works that "use" allegory but are not obviously identifiable as allegories themselves and works that "are" full-blown allegories. The former are, in his words, "complex and hybrid in nature" and may function identifiably within their literary genre even as they employ the allegorical mode.[65]

It is this complex style of allegory, or partial allegory, that I suggest characterizes D.[66] As noted already, this work is a richly imagined historical narrative with a robust internal field of reference. At the same time, it advances and endorses a set of corollaries with its contemporary context whose referentiality extends beyond its story world.

In light of these observations, it is possible to relate D's etiology and allegory with greater precision. The internal referentiality of D's history of the Israelites is meant to be real *for the past*. In this sense, though imaginatively wrought, D's etiology presents itself as corresponding straightforwardly with an external field of reference, even if this correspondence is incomplete or even illusory. Alongside this etiology D carries a second set of external references that are meant to be real *for the present*. This external referentiality is its allegory. What differentiates the two is the temporal gap between them: the "history" that D presents significantly predates the time period of its authors and audiences. This disparity between "then" and "now," between the circumstances depicted and commanded in D and those of its compositional context, creates the possibility of two external referentialities.

Notwithstanding their differences, D's etiology and allegory should both be understood as *political*. Each is a presentation of events in particular, value-laden ways that, by drawing correlations between D's story world and the real world, seeks to influence and persuade readers. The conceit of divinely revealed law is perhaps the strongest expression of political ambition in D. Yet throughout its presentation, D's narrative is an attempt to wield such power.[67]

Interpreting D's Allegory: Theory and Text

Critical scholars offer a range of interpretations for D's allegorical symbols. One of the most common understands Deuteronomic texts to point to the exilic/postexilic religious community's attempts to reestablish itself after the destruction of Jerusalem and the loss of the Judean kingdom. One factor driving this interpretation is the paucity of explicit Deuteronomic references to the monarchy and its temple cult, features presumed to be central to a monarchic era composition.[68] In other words, the apparent *lack* of symbolic reference to one historical context drives these scholars to identify another in its place.

Other factors that suggest that D's allegorical symbols index an exilic/ postexilic setting are specific claims in the text, including its differentiation between Israelite generations. Commenting on the famous reference to Israel's generations in Deut 5:3, for example, Eckart Otto contends that the distinction that Moses draws between his addressees and their ancestors is meant as an historically and theologically significant division between the Judeans before the destruction of Jerusalem and those after it: "The generation of the Exile distances itself in Deut 5:3 from its predecessors before the catastrophe. Those who survived the catastrophe are the addressees of Deuteronomy, and it is with them that the covenant is concluded."[69] Some have likewise identified Moses's exclusion from the land on account of the Israelites (Deut 1:37, 3:26, 4:21) as a reference to the audience's own experience of collective punishment in spite of individual innocence.[70]

As part of this reading, the Deuteronomic allegory has even been identified in the basic setting of the work. It is commonly argued that the Israelites' imminent entry into the land indexes the Judeans' return from the Babylonian exile and that Deuteronomic threats of future exile are reflections of their previous experiences. The account of Israel's first settlement of the land thus provides an explanation of and model for a second one.[71] The Deuteronomic rhetoric itself can also be understood as participating in D's allegory. For example, D's repeated references to the present ("today," *hayyôm*) are sometimes understood to draw together the Israelites of the story world and the putative exilic/postexilic audience (or any other readers in their present; see below for further discussion).

For some who identify this exilic/postexilic allegory in D, there was at least one prior stage of composition in D—and one that did not include any allegory at all. A number of scholars have reconstructed a highly truncated, early version of D that, they claim, did not include any of the Mosaic framework found in later, augmented versions.[72] In these proposed reconstructions, the early, non-Mosaic versions normally do not employ the allegorical mode. They are instead a preexilic collection of laws whose main concern is real cult centralization in ancient Judah; for many scholars, they are to be associated with the cultic reform of Josiah described in Kings and Chronicles.[73] According to this theory, it was only when this real law collection was resituated within a Mosaic framework that the work became an allegory. This is because only the existence of a story world can make references beyond the story possible. I return to each of these proposals below in the discussion of D's second- and first-person address.

Those who date both D's Mosaic framework and its laws to the late pre-exilic period likewise understand the text to contain allegorical symbolism, though they often find fewer external referents for D's story elements than do those who place the text in the exilic or postexilic periods. For example, many scholars identify the singular cultic place that is to be established in the land as Jerusalem.[74] Some construe D's insistence upon a narrowly defined Yahwism, including the elimination of the Canaanite nations and their religious practices, as a response to the religious policies of the Judean king Manasseh.[75] Some also view the warning to the king against multiplying horses and returning the people to Egypt against the backdrop of the seventh-century BCE politics of the southern Levant.[76] Yet these scholars do not necessarily find particular, external referentiality in D's depiction of the Israelites' position outside of the land. Diachronically speaking, the latter story element (and others like it) may be understood simply as a feature of D's literary inheritance; synchronically, it functions unproblematically as part of D's internal field of reference.

In the end, almost all scholars understand D to use the allegorical mode *to some extent,* and they do so on more or less the same basis: D's fictive descriptions of the past (i.e., the basic elements of D's story—its setting in the plains of Moab, its presentation of Mosaic speeches, its recollection of Horeb, etc.) and normative claims for the future (in the main, D's laws—but again, situated in its fictive setting) are meant to correspond with, apply to, and intervene in circumstances and concerns contemporary with the text's composition. Yet the differences between assessments of D's allegory can sometimes be significant, not least because they are often tied up with other features of the analyses of which they are a part. As the alternatives considered above attest, both dating and compositional history are closely related to identifications of allegorical symbols.[77]

These circumstances prompt the question, What is the critical control for assessing D's allegory (or any literary allegory, for that matter)? In other words, what is the basis for preferring one identification of allegorical symbols over another? This issue is all the more pressing—even beyond the complications already noted—because of the special risk of distortion by readers as they interpret allegory. As Frye has observed, because allegories actively attempt to guide their own interpretation, they can generate resistance in their readers, who are prone to favor their own interpretations over those recommended by the allegory.[78] In such instances, readers would substitute their own creativity for the creative symbolism that the allegory seeks to advance. In instances of partial allegory, it is likewise possible for readers to move from *the interpretation of allegory* into the realm of *allegorical interpretation (allegoresis)*, that is, reading narrative elements as allegorical symbols that were never so intended or reading them against the text's interpretive guidance.[79] This is an especially pressing issue when dealing with texts so far removed from readers temporally and culturally, and it is a feature that I identify in some of the interpretations I present at the end of this chapter.

The bulwark against such risks, and the measure for any interpretation of literary allegory, must be the text's internal field of reference. Addressing precisely these issues in relation to D's texts, Jean-Pierre Sonnet has argued:

> The involvement of the reader should not be achieved at the expense of Deuteronomy's historiographical claim, that is, "in the wilderness, in the Arabah, . . . the fortieth year, on the first day of the eleventh month" (Deut 1:1–2 [*sic*]). Nor should the hermeneutic process dismiss the narrative consistency of the history in question. . . . In Deuteronomy, like in the rest of the Hebrew Bible narrative, there is no hermeneutic shortcut; the reader has everything to gain by playing by the historiographical and narrative rules of the work.[80]

As Sonnet suggests, a work's allegory is *procedurally* secondary, even as its intent is primary. The same observation of sequence appears in the definitions of allegory noted above:

> "Allegory <u>says</u> one thing but <u>means</u> another." (Fletcher)

> "By <u>this</u> I also (*allos*) mean <u>that</u>." (Frye)

Each of these definitions proposes a two-step process of encoding that applies equally to interpretation: (1) what is present in the literary text (says; this) is the key to (2) what is not (means; that).[81] Accordingly, Maureen Quilligan concludes:

> Readers of allegory . . . gain in sophistication only as they follow the narrative . . . the experience of reading allegory always operates by a gradual revelation to a reader who, acknowledging that he does not already know the answers, discovers them, usually by a process of relearning them. If the reader begins with a presumptuous sense that he already knows how to interpret, the narrative will first teach him that he does not.[82]

These observations highlight two additional features of the internal field of reference relevant for the interpretation of allegory. First, though allegory may interact with both the internal and the external fields of reference of a work, the work's attempt at persuasion is located in and depends upon its internal field of reference. This is because a work's allegory is fundamentally an element of its creative expression, and the internal field is the central, creative domain of a literary work. Second, as Harshav observes, in the interaction of internal and external fields of reference, the internal field of reference prioritizes itself, subordinating and even subsuming within itself the external field of reference. It is only *after* this relegation of the external field of reference that allegory may emerge: "Any modes of discourse, ideas, norms, or semantic 'frames' brought in from the outside are individualized and framed in this particular work of literature. On the secondary level, of course, this individualized text and individualized Field of Reference may be projected onto External Fields and perceived as 'symbolic' or 'representative.'"[83] Harshav here highlights the difference between a text's external field of reference and the external referentiality of its allegory. The latter is not a field of reference that appears explicitly in the text (as the internal field of reference does) or is otherwise available to the reader as an orienting element (as is the case for the external field of reference). Allegory instead functions through implication and, as such, is properly absent from the text. It is in this sense that it is a *subsequent projection*, a set of correspondences between the text's fictive world and the outside world drawn by the reader at the text's guidance. In his comments on the interpretation of literary allegory, Joel Rosenberg describes this complex absence and projection: "There is every reason to avoid dispensing with the mythological 'charm' of the narrative. We must travel its trajectory before we try to offer any exegesis. We must understand the tug on our attention exercised by myth and fancy, then politely disengage ourselves from it, and reconstruct the concrete, if textually absent, social setting to which the story 'refers,' and in the presence of which it dissembles."[84]

Interpretation of D, then, as of all of the pentateuchal sources, requires constant estimation and evaluation of primary and secondary reference to explain the text's *partial* allegory. The persistent questions to be posed are, which elements of the text belong strictly to its story world, and which elements also have secondary, symbolic reference beyond the story? And, what is the *correlation between* (but not *equation of*) story world and real world? The nonspecificity and even imprecision inherent in the external referentiality of partial allegory suggest in the case of D that this work's ambition is ideational and programmatic. It simply does not offer a detailed, prescriptive blueprint for religious practice in its author's contemporary context.

Is It Law?

This literary analysis—and, in particular, its characterization of D as etiology and allegory—prompts anew the perennial question posed of biblical law, including Deuteronomic legislation: *Is it law?* As noted already, scholarly identifications of real legislation in D entail the differentiation and reconstruction of individual laws as well as of larger legal collections. Accordingly, they rely on a theorization and description of that process— different from, but serving the same purpose as, the theorization and description I have offered in this chapter. When such an analysis is performed along the lines proposed above, the following observations emerge: (1) the evidence for identifying an earlier, nonliterary legal corpus in D that once stood apart from its literary framework is quite tenuous, if not absent; and (2) the Deuteronomic laws are well-integrated in their literary framework and its plotline.

These observations together point to a conclusion: the Deuteronomic laws may be understood as an integral and original part of the fictive work of D. This is not to suggest that D's author invented all of its legal ideas de novo; judging by the cuneiform evidence of legal practice, for example, it appears that D probably mimicked real legal content and reasoning in its composition.[85] Yet in assessing the genre of D's legislation, if it is to be understood as law, it can be so construed only *within D's story world.* This is, of course, not what scholars usually mean when they claim that the rules in Deuteronomy are (or have been) legislation. Their claim is instead that these rules served—or were meant to serve—as law in the real world.[86] What I have argued here is that D's compositional history and its literariness rule out this option. In other words, D is not law and does not contain real law; it is instead *a story about law.*

Compositional History, Allegory, and Moses's Addressees in D

As the foregoing discussion suggests, the idea of language embedded in and accountable to a literary work's internal, constructed world is immediately applicable to some of D's most prominent features. Analysis of these features illuminates not only the literariness of the text; it also sheds important light on the text's genre(s) and compositional history—precisely those questions that have preoccupied critics in their analyses of Deuteronomy. To further exemplify these features and their interconnections, I conclude this chapter with examinations of a major question in the interpretation of D: how to understand its second- and first-person address, both in its legal and nonlegal sections.

D's second-person address (and, to a lesser extent, its first-person plural address) has been a special concern of modern critics. As noted already, the alternation in D between second-person singular and plural (*Numeruswechsel*) is a peculiarity that has long funded attempts to differentiate strata in this text. The "if you . . ." formulation of some of D's laws as well as its larger discourse has likewise been the focus of specialized, form-critical and literary study.[87] Yet an even more significant aspect of this address in the history of research has been the identification of the addressee in D's second-person formulations. As a deictic element, second-person address is underdetermined; that is, it depends on contextualization (i.e., definition of the speaker and addressee) for its specification.[88] Accordingly, scholars have raised questions concerning the proper contextualization of the second-person address in D, especially (though not exclusively) with respect to its laws and their compositional history, in order to determine its indexicality.[89]

It is useful to survey briefly the use of second-person address in D before considering its implications. Across the D corpus, second-person address is very common: "Do not add to this word that I am commanding you, and do not subtract from it" (4:2a); "You shall not steal" (5:19); "Hear, O Israel, Yahweh is our god, Yahweh is one!" (6:4); "Remember—do not forget!—that you enraged Yahweh, your god, when you were in the wilderness!" (9:7a); "Watch yourself lest you offer up your burnt offerings in any place that you see" (12:13); "Because there will never cease to be needy ones in the land, I am therefore commanding you, you shall certainly open your hand to your brother, to the poor and needy in your land" (15:11). In each of these examples—and the many others like them—the text's second-person address is voiced by Moses and aimed at a fictive Israelite audience who are characters in the work, not toward the text's reader(s) (real or intended). This definition of the addressee is repeatedly made clear, as the foregoing examples themselves demonstrate: 6:4 employs the vocative "Israel," which, as defined in the text, is Moses's fictive audience (cf. 5:1); the Israelites who are adjured in 9:7a are, according to this verse, those who experienced the wilderness wandering; those who must offer charity to their fellow Israelites in the land, according to 15:11, are those about to enter Canaan, as the foregoing verses describe (cf. 15:4, 7).

Defining the Speaker

There are at least two manners by which scholars have sought to re-contextualize the address in D and thus redefine the addressee away from the fictive Israelite audience depicted as Moses's audience in the text. These recontextualizations each have significant implications for the interpretation of D, including its genre, compositional history, plotline, characterization, and allegory. To begin with the issues of genre and compositional history, a mainstay of modern scholarship has been to assign D's legal and nonlegal sections to different hands. In his 1805 dissertation, Wilhelm Martin Leberecht de Wette, the so-called father of modern biblical criticism, correlated Deuteronomic law with the discovered law book in the biblical account of Josiah's cultic reform (2 Kgs 22–23).[90] This view, which has come to be known as "the de Wette hypothesis," became firmly fixed in biblical studies more than a half century later when Julius Wellhausen made it integral to his reconstruction of Israelite religion.[91] Wellhausen argued that it was specifically the central legal section of Deuteronomy—chapters 12–26, which he isolated as the earliest layer of this composition—that was the Josianic law book "found" in the Jerusalem temple.[92]

Part of this compositional theory is a genre claim, which in turn entails a reanalysis of the second-person address in D's laws. Plucked from their literary context, the genre of D's laws is defined as real legislation, even if these laws were not practiced as such (though such a claim is sometimes made). This analysis thus amounts to an evaluation of D's legal *discourse:* it eliminates the fictive setting of D's legislation as Mosaic speeches to Israel in the plains of Moab and, in so doing, redesignates their speaker as the deity and the text's reader/audience as their addressee. These changes thus orient D's legislation toward the real world (and real Judeans) instead of a story world (and its characters), reconstructing from D's fictive discourse a putative, earlier stage in which this text was real discourse.[93]

More recent scholarship has regrounded this analysis of D's laws (and the dating of D that attends it), foregoing the strongest claims of historicity for the biblical account of Josianic reform in favor of a complex, form-critical argument that focuses on D's origin as a revisionary composition (topics to be discussed in detail in the following chapters). It is well-illustrated in the reconstruction of Eckart Otto, who contends that the earliest form of "the book of Deuteronomy" attested no Mosaic framing narrative (and thus also no Horeb or Moab covenants). This work was, in his view, a revision of and supplement to the preexilic Covenant Code, which by this time was framed by divine "privilege law" (*Privilegrecht*) that cast the whole of the Covenant Code (itself admitting of a complex compositional history) as divine legislation.[94] Thus, for Otto, D's reliance upon the Covenant Code and the latter's own compositional history are determinative for understanding D's voicing and address: because the Covenant Code that was received and revised by D was divine law in which the deity addressed the readerly audience directly, so too was D. It was only later that a fictive, narrative framework was added to this early D work and, with it, a new voicing (Moses's) and audience (the Israelites whom Moses leads) for its laws.[95] In this scenario, the second-person address of D's laws, situated in its hypothesized, older textual framework, is understood very much along the lines of the fictive presentation of the Decalogue in D (Deut 5:6–21)—namely, as divinely voiced law directed to its recipient (in this case, the reader) without mediation.[96]

Though they are presented with considerable sophistication, what is missing from analyses such as these is clear evidence to support the specific historical reconstructions offered or even their underlying assumptions. In the case of the de Wette hypothesis, there is insufficient evidence external to the biblical text to corroborate the claim of a Josianic book find, even as there is considerable evidence for the invention of historical details in biblical historiography, including in the biblical Josiah accounts.[97] Evidence for an early form of Deuteronomic legislation shorn of its Mosaic framework, whether understood in relation to the de Wette hypothesis or to a Covenant Code *Privilegrecht* or otherwise, is similarly lacking.[98] Even the basic assumption concerning the genre of the reconstructed text can be questioned: there is no evidence that Deuteronomic law originated in real Israelite or Judean legal practice. Indeed, the strong similarities that have been identified between pentateuchal legislation and the cuneiform legal collections, the literary relationships observable among biblical laws (especially between Deuteronomic law and the Covenant Code), and the literariness of the text discussed above together suggest that biblical laws are not examples of real, practiced law, even as they seem to reflect real legal reasoning and probably resemble in some instances real legal practice. Attempts to reconstruct earlier forms of Deuteronomic law in many instances have not dealt sufficiently with the relevant literary and comparative evidence, relying instead on problematic trajectories of existing scholarship as the frameworks for their analyses. In many cases, we may ask whether the hypothesized, earlier texts produced are indeed *reconstructed* or simply *constructed*, that is, modern creations only characterized as ancient ones.

Defining the Addressee

In the nonlegal portions of D, instances of second-person address cannot be reoriented away from the story world: these instances are straightforwardly voiced by Moses, who addresses the Israelite characters who are his audience. As noted already, it is this fictive framework that makes possible an identification of the text as allegory. Yet here, too, scholars have sometimes resisted the literariness of the text, favoring an analysis of D's second-person address as directed, at least to some extent, toward its reader, not the text's characters. Some have even argued that an explicit aim in D is to blur the distinction between the story's characters and the text's reader.

Examples from two scholars illustrate the point. In a section titled "The Literary Fiction of Deuteronomy," Thomas Römer has stated: "By directly addressing their audience, the Deuteronomists in a way made them contemporaries with Moses, and this fiction corresponds to the actual situation of the group in Babylonia to which the Deuteronomists address their history: as at the time of Moses, they find themselves outside the land and wait for instructions about the possibility of entering this land."[99] Advocating a similar perspective, Brent A. Strawn has extended the imagined temporal horizon of this address: "Deuteronomy's rhetoric traffics in the 'back then,' to be sure, but primarily and ultimately so as to address the audience in the eternal 'now,' which is an eternal now-*cum*-then."[100] For Strawn, this temporal rhetoric is directly connected to Moses's second- and first-person address in D in a process that he terms the "inscription" of the reading/hearing audience into the text in their own present ("today").[101]

While these statements rightly distinguish, at least to some extent, D's story world from the real world of its readers, their characterization of D's readers as "addressees" creates confusion, particularly when these readers are correlated with Moses's addressees in the text's story world. This is straightforwardly observable in Römer's characterization just cited: "*By directly addressing their audience* . . ." It also features in Strawn's description: "*so as to address the audience* [i.e., the readers]." In D's speeches, neither the second- nor the first-person address is ever directed toward the reader. Moreover, the work's third-person narrator, though sparsely attested, never "breaks the fourth wall" by addressing the reader directly.[102] Arguments such as Römer's and Strawn's, though hardly uncommon, risk truncating the two-step process for interpreting allegory discussed above.[103] They effectively rely upon the reader's misapprehension or neglect of the text's story world and its details in favor of an ill-defined metalepsis—ironically, even as the story world, with its differentiation from the real world of the reader, is reinforced at nearly every turn.[104]

As a response to such telescoped interpretation, it is useful to observe both the limits of interpreting the second-person address in D and the manner in which Moses's rhetoric of contemporaneity in his speeches functions within the story world. To begin with the former, an example such as Deut 4:3 illustrates how a general claim to external referentiality in D's second-person address proves problematic: "Your eyes saw what Yahweh did at Baal Peor—that Yahweh, your god, wiped out from your midst every person who went after Baal Peor." This line works uncomplicatedly within D's internal field of reference: the character Moses addresses his audience, the Israelites, within the story world and in relation to that world and its events. It is the Israelite characters whose "eyes saw" and from whose "midst" the Baal-followers were struck. To claim that somehow readers are directly addressed in these second-person references is nonsensical. The readers were not at Baal Peor; accordingly, they cannot recall any such experience.[105] Their "fellow Israelites" certainly were not eliminated there from any group to which they belonged. While readers can learn a lesson from this story—for instance, about Yahweh's passion for his people—it is difficult to understand its details as instances of allegory with any specific external referentiality.[106] It seems better to conclude that the reference to an incident at Baal Peor experienced by the text's characters, as well as the second-person address within it, are simply parts of Moses's speech that exemplify his concern for religious fidelity among his fictive addressees. As noted, readers may learn from this account, but the claim that it has specific, intended symbolic reference to D's compositional present is difficult to sustain.

A second example appears in Deut 5:2–3, a case that uses first-person plural address rather than second-person address. In these verses, Moses famously recounts the Israelites' Horeb experience: "Yahweh our god made a covenant with us at Horeb. It was not with our ancestors that Yahweh made this covenant, but with us—we, the ones here today—all of us living." Read in relation to the tradition of Israelite generation change in the wilderness (Num 13–14), v. 3 poses an obvious issue: if Moses is addressing the Israelites in the plains of Moab at the end of the wilderness period, they must be *the children* of the Exodus and Horeb generation, not that generation itself. Such apparent imprecision in characterization, coupled with its prolix formulation, has led a number of interpreters to read this verse as an intentional rupture in D's internal field of reference and one that specifically invites readers to identify with the Israelite characters addressed by Moses. Bernard M. Levinson articulates the argument clearly: "The insistent staccato of repetition [in Deut 5:3] suggests that the authors' true appeal is to their own contemporaries in late-seventh-century Judah and, with them, perpetually to every subsequent generation of the text's readers: 'us, we—these here today—all of us living.'"[107]

This interpretation, of course, is reminiscent of the well-known rabbinic tradition that all Jews were at the mountain and participated in the covenant ratified there.[108] Yet as I show in detail in the next chapter, Deut 5:3 is best understood straightforwardly within D's story world. In service of its distinctive perspectives and in response to its source material, I argue that D rejected Israelite generation change in the wilderness, imagining this period as one of miraculous preservation of the Exodus generation and not as one of punishment by extirpation. This preservation, according to D, was for the purpose of Israel's training. If this explanation is correct, the plain sense of Deut 5:3 is unproblematic: within D's story world, Moses addresses the Exodus generation, which is the same generation that heard Yahweh speak at Horeb and that is about to enter the land of Canaan. The clever interpretive acrobatics that many have attempted, including their redefinition of the first- and second-person address in Moses's speeches, actually introduce problems rather than solving them.[109]

As for D's rhetoric of contemporaneity, Deut 5:3 is also a good example of the regular invocation of the present moment in Moses's speeches. This instance, like all instances of "today" in Moses's Deuteronomic speeches, functions straightforwardly within D's story world. The accent that Moses puts on the contemporary moment and experience of his audience stands in contrast to the experience of the ancestors in their own era. It also underscores the gravity of the occasion. The ancestors did not have the Horeb experience and thus were not bound by its covenant rules. In D's presentation, the imposition of new rules at precisely this moment in Israel's history makes good sense: D's laws are for the Israelites once they take up residence in the land (e.g., Deut 6:10, 7:1, 11:29, 17:14, 26:1). This legislation would have been meaningless for the ancestors of Moses's audience. D's emphasis in 5:3 upon the living correlates with its characterization of the Israelites' miraculous preservation across their wilderness trek (Deut 2:7, 8:4, 29:4); it also accords with D's claims concerning Israel's future welfare, which the work associates with legal observance (e.g., Deut 4:1, 5:33, 16:20, 30:19). Indeed, Moses insists in D that nothing is more important than Israel's legal observance, and it is this legal observance that will result in prolonged life in the land. Finally, coming as they do at the end of Israel's desert journey, Moses's speeches in D serve as a culminating event, both for the Israelites' experience in the wilderness and in Moses's lifetime (Deut 1:37, 3:27, 4:22, 31:27). In view of each of these details, then, the weight placed on the contemporary moment in D's speeches is fully explicable within the story world.

The irony in the example of Deut 5:3 is that in many cases scholars who seek to identify an address to the reader in D do so *not* by treating that address as a feature of D's allegory—namely, as one with secondary, external referentiality. They instead define the reader as its *primary referent*. In so doing, these interpreters redefine D's fictive discourse as real discourse, much like what is done in the case of a reconstructed *Privilegrecht*, as discussed already. In Deut 5:3, it is usually interpreters' struggle to make sense of Moses's address in the story world (specifically, in relation to assumed Israelite generation change in the wilderness) that prompts their claim that a different, symbolic reference is intended.[110] If, as I have suggested, the generation that heard Yahweh speak at Horeb in D is the same generation that listens to Moses in Moab, and if this detail is fully accounted for in the text's internal field of reference, the search for an alternative explanation outside of the story world may be abandoned. A case such as the reference to Baal Peor in Deut 4:3 only buttresses this argument: its use of the second person is difficult to understand as a meaningful address of D's reader at all, whether construed as primary or secondary. In each of these instances, like the many others that could be adduced, the story world is primary, and the text can achieve its didactic function without negating this story world or adding secondary reference beyond it.

These examples from D accord well with the theoretical observations already presented. If literary allegory operates on a sliding scale, it is likely that some of its features will have secondary reference beyond the story world while other features will not. Judged against the history of D's interpretation, I am suggesting that, while it does sometimes employ the allegorical mode, D is rather less allegorical than many have argued. By moving too quickly to allegory, or even insisting upon a *direct* or *primary* address of the reader in D, scholars have short-circuited the priority and guidance of the text's internal field of reference in the process of interpretation. Such reading practices tend toward overreading or, put more precisely, the move referenced above from *interpretation of allegory* to *allegorical interpretation*. It is likely that the assumptions of scriptural reading described in the Introduction, and especially the basic assertion of the relevance of the biblical text for the real world at every moment of reading, have contributed to such claims; in some instances, such appeals to scriptural models are explicit.[111] Even so, the argument here suggests that scriptural reading practices must be resisted if D is to be appreciated in the context of its composition, which is to say, as the literature that it is.

Conclusion

The interpretive approach outlined here both accords with and differs from other contemporary approaches to the interpretation of Deuteronomy, both literary and nonliterary. Like others, I have argued for the contribution of multiple hands in the composition of D and have done so on literary-critical grounds. Yet in view of the strong evidence for D's literariness, I have also eschewed what others regularly attempt, namely, to interpret D, or parts of it, as nonliterary—for example, as real legislation or as Scripture. As I have argued, to identify D as nonliterary—to find its referents first outside of its story world—at turns decontextualizes and recontextualizes this text and its constituents, without sufficient evidence. Such an approach tends also to ignore, excise, or distort literary features that it cannot explain in service of ends that are ultimately different from the literary-historical. In the face of such approaches, this chapter has sought to demonstrate the importance of understanding D fully as literature, both for the analysis of its compositional history and for the interpretation of its various parts. With the literary nature of D more firmly established, I turn to the details of D's revisionary composition.

2 Literary Revision in Deuteronomic Composition

Some biblical texts, both in their self-presentation and (apparently) in fact, are highly original compositions. In the main, D is not. It instead exhibits extensive interaction with, dependence upon, and revision of both biblical and nonbiblical sources. D may thus be termed a "learned text."[1] Yet close inspection reveals that D's revisionary method of composition is itself remarkably creative, if in a different manner: its authors borrow specific language, ideas, and plot elements from their sources while at times contravening those sources' details. The result is a substantially new work that at turns sustains, reframes, builds upon, and/or reimagines its literary precursors. This compositional method also provided a model for authors who came after D; in fact, as I discuss in more detail in Chapter 4, later authors revised and reused parts of D, at times apparently drawing inspiration not only from D's content but also from its revisionary method.

The derivative nature of D's composition has been well recognized; indeed, significant aspects of it were perceived long before the modern period. One such example is found in the title of the Septuagint's translation of the Deuteronomy scroll. The Greek name *Deuteronomion*, meaning "second law" or "copy of the law," is drawn from Deut 17:18, which requires the Israelite king to make "a copy of this law" (Greek: τὸ δευτερονόμιον τοῦτο) for his personal study (v. 19). In its context, Deut 17:18 apparently refers to the legal teachings in Deuteronomy, not to the entirety of the D scroll (i.e., the story of the law).[2] Yet it is likely that the title *Deuteronomion* was chosen because it could also be applied to the full scroll, which rehearses a considerable amount of material also found in Exodus and Numbers, including the Decalogue and much of the legal content of the Covenant Code.[3]

The intent of this chapter, then, is not simply to show that D is a learned, revisionary work. It is also to demonstrate the far-reaching implications of this compositional approach for understanding D and its relationship to its forebears—especially those that are now also part of the Pentateuch. To do so, this chapter examines D's compositional method in both its legal and its nonlegal sections, considering both brief and more extensive examples that illustrate the conventions and complexities of this composition's creative reimagination of source material. Because many instances of D's revisionary composition are so well-known, the examples to which I give more extended attention (the war with Amalek and the Israelites' forty-year journey) are ones that have received comparatively less attention. They are also ones that emphasize the situation of D's legislation in the context of its narrated story world—what I have argued is the hallmark of the D work.

Legal Composition

Though D does not begin with law, legislation stands at its heart. Law is thus an obvious starting point for discussing its compositional method. A significant number of Deuteronomic laws allude to and, in some instances, even directly engage and rework the laws and historical narratives in the pentateuchal books of Exodus and Numbers and, in particular, those of the Elohistic (E) source. Though they are no longer preserved, it is likely that D also employed other legal sources in its composition.[4] Because E's laws are extant, then, their adaptation provides a special opportunity to observe D's learned style of revisionary composition. Moreover, because the Elohistic Horeb narrative inspired the fictive frame for all of D's legislation, the E text exerts a special, structural influence on D's reuse of all of its source material.

Scholars have long recognized that D employs a method of reuse that has been termed *lemmatic citation*. That is, D redeploys the precise language of its literary patrimony, though sometimes to new, distinctive ends.[5] Yet as the examples that follow show, this redeployment of language is not simply a shallow repetition of lexemes. Neither is it only a set of clever reorientations of language (though it is sometimes that). It is instead the most visible element of a much deeper engagement with the ideas of D's sources. Indeed, the frequency and density of D's reuse and revision of source material prompts global questions concerning this compositional method: Why does D salvage and redeploy so much source material? Why does it so often thoroughly reorient the thrust and claim of this inheritance? What does D mean for the afterlives of the sources it employs and revises, and what evidence is relevant for deciding this issue? In what follows, I first examine D's revisionary practice and then, in light of it, return to the questions that it prompts.

Reuse of Legal Material in Deuteronomic Legislation

As noted already, in its legislation, D regularly draws upon, interprets, and reformulates material from existing sources, in particular, from the Elohistic Covenant Code (Exod 20:22–23:19/33). Examples of such reuse and revision appear in a number of D's laws, including its legislation concerning cult centralization and nonsacral slaughter (Deut 12), debt release (15:1–11), manumission (15:12–18), cultic festivals (16:1–17), and asylum (19:1–13). In many instances, the revisionary thrust of these laws is coordinated, especially in relation to the centralization law, which stands at the head of D's central legal section. Indeed, cult centralization has implications for how D treats both the legal topics that it inherits and those that it introduces. This coordination across D's laws, and especially among those instances where D's legal patrimony is extant, sheds important light on D's larger ideological profile.

When addressing an inherited legal topic, D at turns reproduces the content and language of its source, interprets or otherwise clarifies its legal details, and/or makes both small- and large-scale modifications to it, including reorganizations, omissions, and supplements. In the midst of such alterations, however, conceptual and linguistic correspondences between D and its parent text, both in their density within single laws and in their repeated appearance across legal topics, confirm the direct, literary relationship between them. Beyond these basic contours, D's legal revision does not admit of an easily identifiable typology, nor does it show evidence of working systematically across the laws of the Covenant Code.[6] D can thus be distinguished from a work like Chronicles. Though Chronicles is another highly revisionary biblical text and, like D, one for which modern readers have access to (at least some of) its parent texts (namely, Samuel and Kings), its revision of its literary patrimony is more systematic and standardized than is D's. When D is compared with other revisionary compositions in the Hebrew Bible, then, it is better to argue for family resemblances among them rather than insisting that they share a singular or narrowly defined revisionary method.[7]

In place of a typology, then, I offer here a series of brief examples to demonstrate the style of Deuteronomic revision of existing laws. In Exod 20:24, E offers in legal form its vision for Israelite sacrificial worship:

> You shall make for me an earthen altar, and you shall sacrifice upon it your burnt offerings and your well-being offerings, your sheep and your cattle. In every place where you call upon my name I will come to you and bless you.[8]

Deuteronomy 12:13–14 draw upon this verse but also thoroughly reorient it. The revision is framed in cautionary terms:

> [13]Be careful lest you offer up your burnt offerings in any place that you see fit. [14]Rather, in the place that Yahweh will choose in one of your tribes— there you shall offer up your burnt offerings, and there you shall do all that I command you.

Amidst their significant correspondences, marked above, the contradiction between the instructions for Israelite sacrifice in these two laws is clear.[9] In Exod 20:24, Yahweh permits the Israelites to construct altars at sites that they choose and promises to visit those sites to interact with them.[10] Deuteronomy 12:13–14, by contrast, characterize the selection of the worship site as Yahweh's prerogative and insist that sacrifice be limited to a single site ("in one of your tribes"). Moreover, D's larger presentation suggests that once a single sanctuary where sacrifices will be offered is established, Yahweh will physically reside there; he will not simply visit it to receive offerings and bestow blessings, as E states.[11]

Anticipating the impact of its centralization provision, D also makes accompanying provisions for slaughtering animals and consuming their meat. D understands sacrifice as a regular accompaniment to the consumption of meat from domesticated animals. Yet if sacrifice could be performed at only a single site, such meat consumption would be very difficult for all but those living close to the central sanctuary. D thus allows for the nonsacrificial slaughter of sacrificeable animals. In order to underscore the nonritualistic nature of this slaughter, D requires that the Israelites pour out the blood of the slaughtered animal "like water"—in other words, in an unambiguously nonreligious manner and completely, so that it may not be used for any other purpose (cf. 2 Sam 14:14; for the sense of completeness, see also, e.g., Hos 5:10, Amos 5:24).

D's seventh-year laws similarly appropriate and reorient Elohistic leg-islation, employing E's ideas and language to new, distinctive ends.[12] In the case of debt release, D's use of the root *šmṭ*, drawn from Exod 23:11, demon-strates well its ability to reimagine its source material even as it maintains key elements of its legal patrimony. Exod 23:10–11 state:

> [10]Six years you shall sow your land and gather its produce. [11]But in the sev-enth, <u>you shall strip it off</u> (*šmṭ*) and leave it behind, so that the poor of your people may eat, and what they leave behind the beasts of the field may eat. Thus shall you do for your vineyard and for your olive grove.

Deuteronomy 15:1–11 contain D's seventh-year release law. The first three verses in particular highlight this law's reimagination of "release" (*šĕmiṭṭâ*):

> [1]At the end of seven years you shall enact a <u>release</u> (*šĕmiṭṭâ*). [2]This shall be the manner of the <u>release</u> (*šĕmiṭṭâ*): every debtholder shall <u>release</u> (*šmṭ*) what he holds against his neighbor. He shall not exact payment from his neighbor, his brother, for Yahweh's <u>release</u> (*šĕmiṭṭâ*) is proclaimed. [3]You may exact payment from a foreigner, but what is yours from your brother your hand must <u>release</u> (*šmṭ*).

The meaning of these seventh-year laws from E and D and their pos-sible relationship to each other have been the subject of extended debate among scholars, not least because of the apparent difference between the basic topics of each law. The E text has often been understood as a fallow law—a law commanding the agricultural practice of periodically leaving fields uncultivated for the purpose of restoring the soil's fertility. Yet there is no way to construe D's law as a fallow law; in fact, it has no discernable concern for agricultural practices at all. Its focus is straightforwardly the periodic release of debts.

Yet the difference between these laws is not as great as is sometimes claimed, especially when the E law is read as a charitable provision and not as a land fallowing prescription. The verb + object suffix *tišmĕṭénnâ* in Exod 23:11 is best understood as referring to a harvesting activity: *šmṭ* denotes a downward, stripping action, and the antecedent to the object suffix is the "produce" referenced at the end of v. 10.[13] Read in this way, the law intends Israelite farmers to cultivate their fields for their own use for six consecutive years. In the seventh year, what is planted is to be harvested and left for the poor to eat (v. 11aα). It is likely that the law anticipates that the landowner will do the harvesting in the seventh year himself—for pragmatic reasons:

this practice would preserve his fragile and valuable vineyards and olive groves (v. 11b).[14] So understood, Exod 23:10–11 follow quite naturally upon the laws that precede it, laws that are strongly oriented toward the vulnerable and their protection. This charitable orientation likewise accords with the immediately following Sabbath law, which explicitly allows servants and working animals to rest on the seventh day. A fallow law, by contrast, with its concern to maximize the profits of the farmer and its requirement that no planting take place in the seventh year, would make little sense contextually.

Viewed against this backdrop, D's seventh-year release legislation is a substantial innovation that nonetheless maintains key aspects of its legal patrimony, including its basic ethos. That is, though directing its focus toward debt rather than agricultural yields, it seeks, as E does, a regular provision for the Israelite poor through a redistribution of wealth. D achieves this end through its creative recasting of the verb *šmṭ*. Specifically, D capitalizes on the semantics of this root, redirecting the downward motion that it denotes from harvesting crops to forgiving debt. In each case, the owner is to release what he owns to the benefit of indigent Israelites (in E, "your people"; in D, "your brother").

D's legislation on city asylum offers another example of its creative revision of E's laws. Deuteronomy 19:1–13 represent an extended reorientation of the Elohistic altar asylum legislation in Exod 21:12–14. The latter text makes a provision for altar refuge in the case of manslaughter:

> [12]One who strikes a person who then dies shall surely be put to death. [13]But he who did not lie in wait, but rather God moved his hand—I will designate for you a place to which he may flee. [14]But if a man plots against his neighbor to kill him craftily, you shall take him from my altar to die.

As in the cases of centralization of the cult site and seventh-year release, D's asylum law draws on the precise language of its legal patrimony, including *nws šām* (Exod 21:13; Deut 19:3, 5, 11), *nky* H stem (Exod 21:12; Deut 19:4, 6, 11), *lqḥ* (Exod 21:14, Deut 19:12), *rēʿēhû* (Exod 21:14; Deut 19:4, 5, 11), and *mwt* (Exod 21:12, 14; Deut 19:5, 6, 11, 12). Yet it is the central term denoting the refuge in E's text, *māqôm* ("place"), that most affects D's reimagination of the law—even though D does not reuse the term itself.

D's legislation of cities of refuge builds upon the centralization law it already introduced. Given its severe restriction of cult sites, altar asylum, which relies on the ready availability of altars to those seeking asylum, is no longer tenable. D thus introduces city asylum in its place. As dictated by its practical concerns, D requires the distribution of these cities across the land so that the distance traveled to a refuge city is not too great, regardless of where the asylum seeker originates. Yet the idea of substituting cities for altars as places for asylum in D appears not to have sprung simply from pragmatic interests. It likely originated exegetically. Exodus 21:13 refers to the refuge place as a *māqôm*, a general term that denotes a physical location. Exodus 21:14 then defines this place further, clarifying that it is the site of an altar ("from my altar you shall take him to die"). D decontextualizes v. 13, reading its reference to a *māqôm* atomistically and thereby introducing the possibility of alternative connotations for this noun. As Deut 21:19 makes clear, one such connotation is "city." The latter verse, which prescribes the procedure for confronting the case of a rebellious son, states, "His (i.e., the rebellious son's) father and his mother shall seize him and take him out to the elders of <u>his city</u>, to the gate of <u>his place</u>." Through this creative exegetical act, D finds in E a basis not just for asylum but specifically for *city* asylum.[15]

Each of these examples of Deuteronomic legal revision—cult centralization, seventh-year release, and asylum—highlights the extent and detail of D's engagement with its parent text. Each example also demonstrates a certain cleverness in D's reuse of language: a locution once used to permit multiple sacrificial sites is redeployed for the purpose of cult centralization; *šĕmiṭṭâ* is transformed from an agricultural practice to a financial one, with apparent reference to its basic semantics; the cultic *māqôm* is reanalyzed as a noncultic, urban site and thereby coordinated with cult centralization, again through attention to semantic possibilities. This dexterous reorientation of E's language has suggested to some that D displays both deference and subversive intent toward its parent text: while borrowing E's prestige, it also seeks to undermine its legal claims. I will address this question of D's intent toward the texts that it revises, but before doing so, it is important to consider D's engagement of narrative alongside and in relation to its reuse of legal content.

Reuse of Narrative in Deuteronomic Legislation

D redeploys narrative content in both legal and nonlegal contexts. In its legal composition, it is important to differentiate between two basic approaches that D uses when it alludes to and revises narrative material. The first approach is to offer a brief allusion to a narrative, with either explicit reference to the story/event or implicit allusion to it through borrowed themes and language. The second approach is characterized by a more intensive rehearsal and even reformulation of the narrative invoked. In each case, D's use of story details contributes to its persuasive attempts. Yet the instances of D's extended renarrations result from its intent to reimagine and thereby reshape the events themselves in service of the laws to which it connects them. In its brief allusions, by contrast, D leaves the narratives it references substantially intact.

Deuteronomic legislation attests numerous brief allusions to Elohistic narratives, both explicit and implicit. Some of these allusions are of a sufficiently general nature (e.g., "Remember that you were a slave in Egypt," Deut 5:15; 15:15; 16:12; 24:18, 22) that it might be claimed in such instances that D is not alluding to a specific text at all but instead to a more general cultural tradition. Yet as I show, the specific constellation and extent of at least some of these instances suggest that D's allusion is to a specific work and not merely a tradition.[16]

An example of brief, explicit allusion appears in Deut 24:9: "Remember what Yahweh your god did to Miriam when you were on your way out of Egypt." The narrative referenced in this instance is found only in E, in Num 12:10–15: Yahweh struck Miriam with skin disease in response to the challenge that she and Aaron raised against Moses's special prophetic status. D alludes to this narrative as part of its instruction to follow proper procedure in cases of skin disease: the Israelites must heed the directives of the Levitical priests (Deut 24:8). The allusion to Miriam in D's law seems to operate thematically on two levels: both texts address skin disease, and both texts perceive Miriam as a challenge to religious authority. D makes an implicit analogy between Miriam's opposition to Moses and the punishment that she endured and any would-be contestations with the Levitical priests. D's law thereby warns the Israelites of the consequences of defying the rulings that priests might offer regarding skin disease.[17]

An instance of brief, implicit allusion appears in Deut 15:13–14, which draw upon Exod 3:21. In describing the Israelites' departure from Egypt, Yahweh promises in the Exodus verse to favorably dispose the Egyptians toward the departing Israelites, who will despoil their masters: "I will put positive regard for this people in the eyes of Egypt; thus, when you depart, you will not depart empty-handed (*rêqām*)." D's use of the rare term "empty-handed" (*rêqām*), coupled with the rationale for the parting gift that it requires Israelite masters to provide to departing slaves—"Remember that you were slaves in Egypt" (Deut 15:15)—suggests that, alongside E's slave law in Exod 21:2–11, D also drew upon its narrative in Exod 3.[18]

Together with these brief allusions to preexisting narratives in Deuteronomic legislation, D contains a number of extensive rehearsals of and revisions to narrative in its legal presentation. The most prominent example is D's reformulation of E's account of the Horeb revelation. According to the categorization offered here, it might be objected that while such reformulation affects D's legislation, it does not technically fall within D's main legal presentation (chs. 12–26). Yet it is precisely D's revision of E's Decalogue that qualifies it for consideration here. D "upgrades" the Elohistic Decalogue from a nonlegal demonstration of prophecy to the status of legislation. Specifically, D rejects E's claim that the intent of the Decalogue revelation was only to provide the Israelites an experience of direct, divine revelation ("for it was in order to give you an experience," Exod 20:20) that would prompt them always to trust Moses ("in order that the people might hear when I speak with you and thereby always trust you," Exod 19:9a). In its place, D terms the Decalogue a covenant (běrît) in its own right—a set of laws to be observed in the wilderness, apart from the laws that Moses would later communicate to the Israelites in the plains of Moab (Deut 4:13; cf. 28:69). The explicit reformulation of the account of the Decalogue's revelation is thus integral to D's legislative claim, a point to which I return below in the treatment of Israel's forty years it the wilderness.[19]

Another instance of extensive allusion to and revision of Elohistic narrative appears in Deut 25:17–19, verses that present D's command to the Israelites to destroy Amalek and its historical rationale. Like the Decalogue example, this example is particularly striking for its detailed interpretive engagement with an E narrative and its deployment of that narrative for the purpose of specific legislation. Deuteronomy 25:17–19 state:

> [17]Remember what Amalek did to you on the way as you journeyed from Egypt—[18]what happened to you along the way when Amalek attacked you from the rear, all of those straggling at your tail end. Though you were worn and weary, they showed no fear of the divine! [19]When Yahweh your god gives you rest from all of your surrounding enemies in the land that Yahweh your god is giving to you to possess as an inheritance, you shall blot out the memory of Amalek from under heaven. Do not forget!

Significantly, D not only adjures its audience to recall the Israelite encounter with Amalek during the wilderness sojourn; it also rehearses and thereby establishes the specific details of this confrontation. As such, though formally comparable with its introductory command, "Remember!," this citation differs from the reference to Miriam's skin disease discussed already.

The details of Israel's encounter with Amalek that D describes result from its interpretive interaction with Exod 17:8–16 (E). Through this interpretation, D shapes a version of the Amalek encounter that more compellingly supports its law, which is itself also inspired by the E account but not actually contained in it.[20] Exodus 17:8–16 state:

> [8]Amalek came and fought with Israel at Rephidim. [9]Moses said to Joshua, "Choose men for yourself and go out to fight against Amalek tomorrow. I will stand on the top of the hill with the staff of God in my hand." [10]Joshua did as Moses instructed him in order to fight against Amalek, while Moses, Aaron, and Hur ascended to the hilltop. [11]When Moses would raise his hand, Israel would prevail, but when he would rest his hand, Amalek would prevail. [12]Now Moses's hands became heavy, so they took a stone and placed it beneath him, and he sat upon it while Aaron and Hur supported his hands, one on one side and one on the other, and his hands remained fixed until the sun set. [13]Joshua thus felled Amalek and his people by the sword. [14]Yahweh said to Moses, "Write this as a remembrance on the scroll, and place it in Joshua's ears: I will surely wipe out the memory of Amalek from beneath the heavens!" [15]Moses built an altar and called it, "Yahweh is my banner." [16]He said, "Victory is on my banner! The war against Amalek is Yahweh's from generation to generation!"[21]

As many commentators have noticed, D's command to wipe out the Amalekites reformulates Yahweh's statement that he will "surely wipe out the memory of Amalek from beneath the heavens" (v. 14). In the words of S. R. Driver, "The Divine purpose, declared in these words, is here impressed upon Israel as a duty."[22]

By consolidating this command with its Horeb legislation, D also provided a concrete fulfillment of Yahweh's command in Exod 17:14a that Moses write down a memorial of the Amalek event in "the scroll." D's Horeb legislation, couched in the adjuration to "remember" and "not forget," is not only an enactment of the deity's concern for memorialization; it serves precisely as the reminder (*zikkārôn*) that Yahweh instructs Moses to write. Deuteronomy 31:7–9 recount Moses's instructions to Joshua and his subsequent commitment to writing of the Horeb laws, including the instruction to destroy Amalek. Notably, the narrative of Moses's instructions in Deut 31 creates overlap and even conflation between Yahweh and Israel in its description of the conquest of the land and the military clashes that attend it. Such conflation accords well with the alternation of agency expressed in Exod 17 and Deut 25 between Yahweh and Israel vis-à-vis Amalek.

D's interpretive treatment of Exod 17:8–16 also engages the latter's basic plotline, and this plot revision plays a significant role in bolstering the persuasiveness of the encounter with the Amalekites as a rationale for D's command to annihilate them. According to Exod 17:9, Moses commanded Joshua to muster troops to fight Amalek in a battle that was to take place the following day. Yet the prior verse already reported that Amalek approached and fought with Israel at Rephidim ("Amalek came and fought with Israel at Rephidim"), a statement that might be taken as an introduction to the ensuing account (and thus contemporaneous with it), as an expression of Amalek's intent, or as a report of chronologically prior action. D's account in Deut 25:17–19 suggests that its authors understood Exod 17:8 as chronologically antecedent to vv. 9–16. Though Moses and Joshua had reached their camp and were thus not close to the Amalekite offensive, there were still stragglers on the march, and these were the Israelites whom Amalek assailed. If this explanation is correct, D transformed what E portrayed as a pitched battle (unnecessarily provoked by Amalek) into a massacre. Those attacked, according to D, were exhausted and, by implication, unable to defend themselves sufficiently.[23] Given Moses's instruction to Joshua to engage in battle on the following day, D infers that Amalek slaughtered the stragglers. It is an act that D labels, in good Elohistic parlance, unconscionable: "they did not fear God," that is, they did not have any regard for anyone outside of themselves—even a deity who might retaliate against them.[24]

Yet D's authors did not stop there. Having fixed their interpretation of the E story—an interpretation that took into account both the first and second days that E describes—D's authors omitted the second day entirely from their retelling. That is, D's account sets aside E's claim that Joshua achieved battlefield success against Amalek (as well as the striking details of Moses's raised arms and the subsequent altar building and naming). D's narration suggests instead that Israel had no immediate victory. This interpretation of D's silence is confirmed by the stated temporal horizon for its command in v. 19: only after Israel would achieve stability in the land—once it had overcome the vulnerable state in which it found itself during its wilderness sojourn—should it take its revenge upon Amalek. By means of this interpretation and renarration, D heightens the Amalekites' wrongdoing and, with it, their culpability.[25] In so doing, it also more clearly accounts for Yahweh's stated intent to destroy Amalek and confers agency upon Israel to achieve this end.

Nonlegal Composition

As suggested already, though D's legal speeches are central to its project, a significant portion of D does not present legislation. Beyond its relatively brief third-person, omniscient narrations, D contains a significant amount of parenetic speech in which Moses recounts the experiences of the Israelites in their exodus from Egypt and across the wilderness period, normally as part of his adjurations to them to obey the deity's commands. These Mosaic recitations of Israel's past regularly reformulate narrative material from E, and to a lesser extent J, and include such events as the appointment of judges in the wilderness (Deut 1:9–18), the battles with Og and Sihon (2:24–35, 3:1–11), the golden calf incident (9:7–21), and the larger set of occurrences at Horeb. Scholars have examined each of these examples in detail, showing the extent of D's revisions of its narrative sources in constructing its own account of Israel's wilderness experience.

Forty Years in the Wilderness and the Exodus Generation

A particularly instructive example of revision of nonlegal source material in D, and one that has gone largely unappreciated by scholars, relates to the Israelites' forty-year sojourn in the wilderness.[26] This example underscores the integral connection between D's historical and legal presentations. It also demonstrates just how dramatic D's recasting of its source material can be and how well that source material can be integrated across the D composition. Finally, the forty years example sheds light on the ways that the Deuteronomy scroll attracted interpolations that sought to harmonize the distinctive views it contained with those found elsewhere in the Pentateuch. In this way, this example anticipates the discussion in Chapter 4 of Deuteronomy's early reception and, in so doing, demonstrates the ways that the issues of composition, textual transmission, and history of interpretation are sometimes closely tied to each other.

The source material that served as the basis for D's account of Israel's extended wilderness sojourn is the Yahwistic account of the spies' reconnaissance mission in Canaan. According to J's account, which is interwoven in Num 13–14 with a corresponding account from P,[27] the Israelites exhibited a basic lack of faith in Yahweh when they sided with those spies who gave a negative report after their scouting mission. In response, Yahweh became infuriated, and though Moses successfully intervened to save Israel from immediate destruction, the deity insisted that with the exception of Caleb, none of the generation of Israelites who experienced the exodus from Egypt would possess the Canaanite land (Num 14:22–24). Deuteronomy 1:19–45 retells this event and includes several verbatim or near-verbatim parallels with its J counterpart. The nature of these correspondences makes clear that the D text here has borrowed directly from J.[28]

Yet even as the inspiration for D's extended wilderness period is the J spies account, D makes significant changes to it. Foremost among them are its rejection of Yahweh's verdict against the Exodus generation in J and the latter's view of the purpose of Israel's wilderness wandering, which J relates directly to this verdict. Yet D does not develop its alternative view in its retelling of the spies episode. It is instead in its reimagination of another J episode, the story of the manna (Exod 16:4–5, 26–30), that D offers its rationale for Israel's extended wilderness trek.[29]

In Deut 8:2–5, Moses commands the Israelites:

> [2]You shall remember the entire journey upon which Yahweh, your god, led you these forty years in the wilderness in order to try you with hardships, that he might know what your will was—to keep his commands or not. [3]He afflicted you with hunger and then fed you with the manna that you did not recognize and your ancestors had never known in order to teach you that a human does not live by bread alone but by every issuance of Yahweh's command. [4]Your garments did not wear out, nor did your feet swell these forty years. [5]You are thus able to recognize by your own reflection that Yahweh your god has been disciplining you as a man disciplines his son.[30]

Both the specific language ties between Deut 8:2–4 and the J manna episode and their shared conceptualization of the manna procedure as an obedience test confirm D's dependence upon J in these verses. Particularly instructive is Deut 8:2,[31] which includes the testing motif and evinces both direct and near-direct linguistic correspondences with Exod 16:4:

> Yahweh said to Moses, "I am about to rain down bread from heaven for you, and the people shall go out and gather each day one day's portion, in order that I might test them: will they follow my direction or not?"

D reimagines two specific elements of J's manna episode, both of which concern J's conceptualization of the manna as a test. The first is the scope of this test. J does not correlate the testing motif with the entire wilderness experience; it instead limits it to the manna. Yet as Deut 8:2–5 make clear, D conceptualizes the entire wilderness period as a test. This generalization of the testing motif is part of D's larger reorientation of the wilderness era's purpose. Israel's protracted journey is not a *punishment* for prior bad acts, as it is in J. It is instead a period oriented toward the Israelites' future and dedicated to their *preparation* and *training* for it.[32]

This reorientation of the wilderness era also highlights D's second modification to the J testing motif, namely, its redirection of the semantics of the verb *nsy*. The semantic range of *nsy* in biblical Hebrew is relatively broad and includes such senses as "to test," "to tempt," "to attempt/try," "to have/give an experience of," "to be familiar with," and "to train."[33] In the J manna account, the nuance of the verb is clearly "to test": as noted already, Yahweh's concern was to learn whether the Israelites were willing to obey him.

Deuteronomy 8:2 reflects the same testing idea, even stating explicitly that Yahweh's attempt was to learn what was in Israel's collective "mind" or "will" (*lēbāb*).[34] But in the following verse, D introduces an additional, *pedagogical* element: the manna was intended "to teach" (*yd'*, H stem) Israel about the sustaining quality of Yahweh's commands.[35] D argues that by means of the manna, Yahweh "gave Israel an experience" of the benefits of obedience and meant for the Israelites to generalize this lesson, learning thereby the importance of submitting to the deity's plan rather than following their own way (cf. Deut 8:16–17).[36] The lesson "that a human does not live by bread alone but by every issuance of Yahweh's command" (v. 3b)[37] is thus a specific instance of the adjuration repeatedly put to Israel in D—including in 8:1—to follow Yahweh's commands "so that you may live!" (cf. Deut 4:1, 5:33, 16:20, 30:19).[38] The continuation of Moses's speech in Deut 8 maintains the future orientation developed in vv. 2–5, emphasizing that the bounty of the land of Canaan should not lull Israel into a complacency and self-reliance that might lead to apostasy.[39]

In this reconceiving of the wilderness period, the fact that D would make a connection between J's manna and spies accounts is not entirely surprising. In the J manna account, after Yahweh introduced the manna as an obedience test, Israel promptly failed it (Exod 16:27–28). The manna episode thus foreshadows the Israelites' subsequent wilderness defiance in J, including their faithless response to the spies' report. In fact, J depicts Yahweh's exasperation in response to Israel in the manna and spies episodes in notably similar ways:

Exod 16:28
Yahweh said to Moses, "How long will you refuse to observe my commands and teachings?!"

Num 14:11
Yahweh said to Moses, "How long will this people act contemptuously toward me?! And how long will they continue to fail to put their trust in me—in all of the signs that I have done in their midst?!"

Yet unlike D, J makes no direct connection between Israel's extended wilderness wandering and its manna test. Indeed, it is not at the time of the manna test (Exod 16), but only later, in the spies incident (Num 13–14*), that Yahweh condemns the Exodus generation to die in the desert. At the time of the manna test, according to J, Yahweh had not yet decided to destroy the Exodus generation.

Consistent with D's reorientation of the wilderness as a training ground is its emphasis in texts such as Deut 9:7 and 29:1–3 upon Israel's persistent rebelliousness and even dimwittedness across the forty years:

Deut 9:7b
Remember—do not forget!—how you enraged Yahweh, your god, in the wilderness. From the day you left the land of Egypt until your coming to this place (namely, Moab) you have been rebellious against Yahweh![40]

Deut 29:1–3
[1]Moses called to all Israel and said to them, "You have seen all that Yahweh did before your eyes in the land of Egypt to Pharaoh, all his servants, and all his land—[2]the great trials that your eyes saw, those great signs and wonders—[3]but Yahweh did not give you a mind to know or eyes to see or ears to hear until this day."

In view of such claims, an extended period of discipline and training was fully warranted: from the start Israel was both degenerate and daft; it did not quickly learn to obey.

Yahweh's miraculous sustenance of the Israelites likewise accords with D's recasting of the wilderness era. According to D, not only were the Israelites fed with supernatural provisions and thus never in want; they also enjoyed exceptional health, and their clothing and footwear were extraordinarily durable (Deut 2:7, 8:4, 29:4). This provisioning is what made it possible for the Israelites to undergo such a protracted period of training.[41]

Through such reimagination of the wilderness era, D was able to eliminate Israelite generation change in the desert. This revision is visible in several instances in D and has led many readers to puzzle over the discrepancy between D's presentation of the wilderness period and that expected from Num 13–14. For example, August Dillmann already noted that texts such as Deut 1:22ff. present Moses as addressing the same generation of Israelites who experienced the departure from Egypt and the Horeb revelation.[42] Other scholars have similarly noted occasional inconsistency between D on the one hand and J and P on the other with regard to generation change. What they have not noticed is the consistency of D's perspective on this issue and its significance for understanding D's various parts.

A particularly striking expression of D's view appears in Deut 11:2–7. This text not only assumes but *insists* that there was no generation change in the wilderness:

> [2]Know this day that <u>it was not your children</u>, who did not experience or witness the instruction of Yahweh your god—his greatness, his strong hand, and his outstretched arm. . . . [7]<u>Rather, your eyes are the ones that saw</u> all the great work of Yahweh that he did.

Responding to the implications of this text for the wilderness generation, Moshe Weinfeld diagnosed a "blurring of generations" and discounted the literary claim of the text: "The author stresses the fact that the signs and miracles done by God at the Exodus were experienced, not by the sons of the listeners (who are the ones actually being spoken to), but by the listeners themselves (11:7; cf. 29:1)."[43] A. D. H. Mayes also noted that this text emphasizes that its addressees are the Exodus generation and not the second generation of J and P; he thus saw a connection between these verses and 5:3 (see below). Yet, like others, Mayes minimized this discrepancy and concluded, "The contradiction should not be over-emphasized."[44]

Moses's adjuration to the Israelites in Deut 6:21–24 to teach their children to obey Yahweh contains a claim much like that in 11:2–7. Having experienced all of Yahweh's miraculous deeds on Israel's behalf, including their preservation throughout their wilderness trek, the Exodus generation can credibly conclude that the god who has given them the elaborate laws of the covenant does intend the best for them and is thus to be obeyed (cf. Deut 29:1–3). Deuteronomy 6:24 articulates this view precisely: "Yahweh commanded us to keep all of these statutes, to fear Yahweh, our god, for our good, for all time, in order to preserve us alive, as today."

The most widely recognized Deuteronomic challenge to generation change is in Deut 5:3, which emphatically states that it was with the hearers of Moses's Moab speeches that Yahweh struck a covenant at Horeb:

²Yahweh made a covenant <u>with us at Horeb</u>. ³It was <u>not with our ancestors</u> that Yahweh made this covenant <u>but with us—those of us here today, all of us who are living</u>.

Though many have attempted to explain these verses' reference to the Horeb generation's presence in Moab as a rhetorical flourish or an oversight,[45] in light of the evidence outlined here, there is no reason to depart from its plain sense: Moses's audience in Moab is the same generation that was at Horeb.[46] In fact, the insistent quality of both Deut 5:3 and 11:2–7 suggests that these texts may be responding directly to and rebutting the (J) claim that the Exodus generation perished in the wilderness.[47]

An important implication of D's presentation of the wilderness period—and a further discrepancy between its view and those of both J and P—is that the Israelites' wandering is not a divine punishment in response to a particular sin. Yet Yahweh does impose their wilderness sojourn as a response to sin: specifically, it is the deity's measured response to the reality that he observed in Israel ever since its departure from Egypt, namely, Israel's consistent *disposition* toward sin (Deut 9:7, 24). For D, however, this sinful disposition is not a fatal flaw. It is instead an occasion for divine beneficence: Israel's training is meant to enable its obedience to the covenant that it would receive in the plains of Moab. Within such a framework, the death of the Exodus generation makes little sense, for it would mean that this generation's preparation could never bear its intended fruit.

Interpolations in Deuteronomy 1–2

In light of D's otherwise consistent depiction of the Exodus generation's perdurance across their wilderness trek, Deut 1:35 and 2:14–16 create literary fractures that require explanation, for these texts each envision some sort of extirpation of (some) Israelites in the wilderness. Indeed, these are the verses that are regularly cited to support the claim that D imagines generation change in the wilderness, as J and P do. Deuteronomy 1:39 presents a similar problem in D, for it claims that the children of the Exodus generation were to inherit the land, not their parents. However, there is reason to suspect that each of these texts is, in its entirety, an interpolation into a preexisting D narrative. This is especially the case for 2:14–16, which combine elements distinctive to each of the Torah sources—a strong indicator of postcompilational interpolation.[48] At the same time, evidence suggests that portions of these verses belong to D (or at least accord with

D's views) and that the interpolations in them were introduced in stages. These texts thus offer important insight into the impact of D's integration into the Pentateuch in the early stages of its interpretation, particularly with regard to the issue of wilderness generation change.

In MT Deut 1:35, Yahweh swears that the entire Exodus generation will die in the wilderness: "No one from among these men (*'ănāšîm*), this evil generation, shall see the good land that I swore to give to your ancestors." Yet the words "this evil generation" (*haddôr hārā' hazzê*) are not reflected in the LXX. Moreover, as scholars have noted, the appositional reference to "this evil generation" in the MT is awkward and even disruptive in its present position. Taken together, these details suggest that "this evil generation" is a late interpolation meant to clarify that the entire Exodus generation *did* perish in the wilderness.[49] The inspiration for this interpolation was likely Num 14:26–35 (P; cf. Num 32:13),[50] where Yahweh refers to Israel as "this evil community" (14:27) and explicitly targets the entire Exodus generation (14:29).

Additional evidence for this claim emerges from the wider literary context. The immediately following verse, Deut 1:36, states, "Only Caleb, the son of Yefunneh, may see it: I will give to him and to his children the land on which he trod, for he remained true to Yahweh." The distinction drawn here is between Caleb and the other Israelite spies.[51] As such, it confirms that the men (*'ănāšîm*) mentioned in v. 35 should be understood as the spies, a conclusion that accords well with the account of the selection of these men (*'ănāšîm*) in Deut 1:22–23. This interpretation is also fully consistent with the Deuteronomic claims concerning the Exodus generation reviewed above: though the faithless spies were to die in the wilderness, the rest of the Exodus generation—faithless as they themselves were—were preserved.[52]

The evidence recommends a similar, if more complex, analysis for Deut 2:14–16:

> [14]The length of time that we walked from Kadesh Barnea until we crossed the Wadi Zered was thirty-eight years: until the death of the entire generation (*kol haddôr*), the warriors from the midst of the camp, just as Yahweh swore to them. [15]Indeed, the hand of Yahweh was against them to sweep them from the camp until they died. [16]When all of the warriors had died off from amongst the people . . .

Verses 15–16 unambiguously differentiate "all of the warriors" (*kol 'anšê hammilḥāmâ*) from the remainder of the Israelites and identify these warriors as the target of Yahweh's anger. Verse 14, however, refers to the death of *kol haddôr 'anšê hammilḥāmâ*, "the entire generation, the warriors," in the wilderness. In this noun phrase, the definite article attached to *haddôr* requires that the phrase be analyzed as two contiguous construct chains; as such, they are most naturally read in apposition to each other ("the entire generation, namely, the warriors"). Yet v. 16 suggests that the entire generation and the warriors should *not* be equated: the warriors alone perish from amidst the people. In light of the textual evidence already observed for Deut 1:35 and the reference to "all of the warriors" in Deut 2:16, it appears that "the generation" (*haddôr*) in 2:14 is an interpolation. If so, 2:14 and 16 originally corresponded precisely, each attesting "all of the warriors." Additional support for this conclusion is found in the reference to Yahweh's oath in 2:14. This oath appears in 1:35, and, as argued above, 1:35 originally made no claim for Israelite generation change in the wilderness.[53]

Yet it is noteworthy that, in contrast to the case of Deut 1:35, LXX Deut 2:14 does reflect a *Vorlage* that included "the entire generation" (*kol haddôr*). If *haddôr* in 2:14 is an interpolation, then, it should not be attributed to the same hand that introduced *haddôr* in 1:35. The LXX rendering of 2:14 is instructive nonetheless, for it suggests that the Greek translator struggled to make sense of his Hebrew text.[54] Specifically, it appears that the LXX strained to translate the noun phrase *kol haddôr 'anšê hammilḥāmâ*, rendering it πᾶσα γενεὰ ἀνδρῶν πολεμιστῶν, "the entire generation of men, warriors." The genitive case of ἀνδρῶν suggests an underlying Hebrew text of **kl dwr 'nšy hmlḥmh*, that is, with no definite article attached to *dwr*.[55] However, there is no manuscript evidence to suggest that such a variant existed or served as a *Vorlage* for the LXX. It is instead more likely that the translator had a *Vorlage* identical to the MT but also knew well the text of Deuteronomy. He thus attempted to harmonize v. 14 with vv. 15–16 and with the several other texts in Deuteronomy that presume the Exodus generation's survival throughout their wilderness sojourn.

There is also evidence, however, that 2:14–16 as a whole—and not just the word *haddôr* in 2:14—should be identified as an interpolation.[56] These verses offer a unique combination of material that is otherwise distinctive in the individual Torah sources: the reference to Wadi Zered (E, Num 21:12; cf. Deut 2:13), the use of *tmm* to describe the extirpation of the Israelites in the wilderness (P, Num 14:33, 35), generation change (J, P), and the reference to thirty-eight years (2 + 38 = 40, matching P's chronology of the wilderness, Exod 40:17; Num 1:1, 10:17). Note, too, that 2:16 employs the temporal construction *wayĕhî ka'ăšer* + *qātal,* a grammatical formulation otherwise unattested in D. Deuteronomy 2:14–16 also appear to be consciously integrated into their present location. The reference to Wadi Zered in 2:14 follows closely upon its appearance in 2:13, and, as noted already, the oath referenced in 2:16 corresponds with 1:35–36. Also noteworthy is the fact that 2:14–16 may be excised entirely without any damage to the surrounding text.

These observations combine to suggest that 2:14–16, minus *haddôr* in v. 14, were inserted as a block in their present position. Notably, this interpolation reflects elements of J, E, and P but, in conjunction with the preinterpolation (=/≈ LXX) version of 1:35, maintains the perspective of D regarding the Exodus generation. This interpolation thus offers a partial harmonization of D with the other pentateuchal sources: it integrates relevant non-D material into D's narrative framework without blatant contradiction. The subsequent interpolation of *haddôr* into v. 14, however, is different: it sought a more thoroughgoing harmonization and thus introduced generation change into D (or, more precisely, Deuteronomy), prioritizing to an even greater degree the pentateuchal context of these verses and, in so doing, creating significant contradiction with original D texts. On the basis of the evidence adduced here, the stages of this textual growth are as follows:

1. Deut 1:35 minus "this evil generation" (= LXX)
2. Interpolation of Deut 2:14–16, minus *haddôr*
3. Interpolation of *haddôr* in Deut 2:14 (= LXX, MT)
4. Interpolation of "this evil generation" in Deut 1:35 (= MT)

Finally, the case of Deut 1:39 follows a similar trajectory. In its assertion that the children of the Exodus generation will enter the land, it seems to suggest, as do MT Deut 1:35 and 2:14, that the adult Exodus generation will perish. As others have noted,[57] 1:39 also corresponds very closely with Num 14:31, a P text that asserts generation change (cf. also Num 14:3):

Deut 1:39 (MT)
Your children, whom you have said will become plunder, your children who today do not know good from evil—they are the ones who will enter there, and to them I will give it, and they are the ones who will inherit it.

Num 14:31
Your children, whom you have said will become plunder, I will cause them to enter, and they shall know the land that you have spurned.

Yet the text of Deut 1:39 is highly variable, with the LXX and the SamP (and perhaps also 4QDeut[h]) each attesting a shorter text than the (rather prolix) MT.[58] In the case of the LXX, the minuses there vis-à-vis the MT eliminate almost entirely the ties between Deut 1:39 and Num 14:31. When considered alongside LXX Deut 1:35, the differences between LXX and MT 1:39 raise the question of whether 1:39 originally endorsed Israelite generation change. It seems more likely that the similarities between MT 1:39 and Num 14:31—similarities that suggest reading 1:39 as endorsing generation change, as the P text does—are the result of a late interpolation.[59] If this interpolation does endorse generation change, it may find inspiration not only in Num 14:31 but also in the additions already identified in 1:35 and 2:14 (if they predate MT 1:39). In any case, Deut 1:35, 1:39, and 2:14–16 each attest interpolations intended to achieve harmonization at the level of the Pentateuch as a whole,[60] and it is this harmonizing effort that accounts for the introduction of generation change in the wilderness in Deuteronomy.

Rationalizing the Wilderness and the Deuteronomic Project

Why do the D authors eliminate Israelite generation change yet insist upon a prolonged wilderness trek? How do these revisions fit into D more broadly? These questions may be posed with an eye toward both the authors' religio-political ambitions and the text's story world. Beginning with the former, D's revision of the wilderness serves its larger reimagination of the Elohistic Horeb lawgiving. Its chief concern was to recast the legal content of the Elohistic Book of the Covenant (Exod 20:23–23:19), but attending this concern was an anxiety regarding similar, future revision of its own laws (Deut 4:2; 13:1). D thus delayed Moses's delivery of the covenant laws he received from Yahweh at Horeb until the end of his life, which is to say, until the end of the wilderness period. Such a delay represents an attempt to prevent any further, post-Deuteronomic "Mosaic" revision.[61] Including an extended wilderness wandering thus served D's interests well.

The unique combination of extended wilderness sojourn and persistence of the Exodus generation in D also represents some measure of compromise between its source materials. In E, it is the Exodus generation that receives the covenant at Horeb, and the same generation enters the land of Canaan. J's extended wilderness period and generation change are thus in direct conflict with E's claims. Seeking to maintain the basic storyline of E, D jettisoned J's extirpation of the Exodus generation but incorporated its prolonged wilderness journey by transforming the latter into a catechetical period. This change then rationalized the delay of Moses's delivery of the second covenant, which corresponds with E's single covenant, to the end of the wilderness era. Yet because in E the Israelites are not forced to endure a prolonged desert trek, the moment in which Moses delivers the covenantal laws to them is functionally equivalent in E and D: in each case, this legal conveyance occurs shortly before the Israelites enter into the land. The result of D's combination of wilderness traditions is a striking amount of consistency with its source material even as its finished product also represents a substantial innovation.

Within its story world, D integrates its depiction of the wilderness era into its larger characterization and plot and, in particular, its elevation of the Decalogue to the status of law (Deut 4:13, 28:69). D claims, as does E, that the Israelites heard the Decalogue directly from Yahweh at Horeb (Deut 5:22–24), but in E the Decalogue serves as a demonstration of Mosaic prophecy, not as covenantal law (Exod 19:9a, 20:20).[62] D's upgrade of the Decalogue is explicable as part of its portrayal of the wilderness wandering as a training period. The Decalogue serves in D as a brief, elementary version of the much more extensive set of laws that Israel would receive at the end of the forty years.[63] It is, in effect, a "trainer law" that Yahweh employs in his pedagogical effort.[64] D's transformation of the wilderness into a period of preparation, its elimination of generation change, and its upgrading of the Decalogue to the status of law thus all work together as part of a single, cohesive story.

D's conceptualization of the wilderness period, as hinted at already, also plays a central role in its characterization of Yahweh, the Israelites, and their interactions with each other. D casts Israel's relationship with Yahweh in explicitly familial terms and accentuates the paternal quality of Yahweh's wilderness training program. Deuteronomy 8:5 states, "Yahweh your god has been disciplining you as a man disciplines his son." This parental image complements the characterization of Yahweh as Israel's caregiver throughout their desert trek:

Deut 1:30–31
[30]Yahweh, your god, is the one who went before you. He himself will fight for you, just as he did for you in Egypt, before your eyes, [31]and in the wilderness,

> where you saw that Yahweh, your god, carried you as a man carries his son, on the whole path you walked until your coming to this place.

In each instance, D portrays Yahweh's parental acts as not only benevolent but persistent, even as they are ostensibly directed toward different stages of Israel's maturation. Yahweh's conveyance of the Israelites imagines their infancy, while the wilderness training depicts their childhood and perhaps adolescence.[65] Moreover, D presents Yahweh's actions in Egypt and his transport of Israel in the wilderness as themselves instructional: they were done in such a way that the Israelites could observe them and learn from them—even if they did not, in fact, learn quickly or well the lesson that Yahweh intended (Deut 1:32, 29:3).

Though D's explicit references to the parent-child relationship between Yahweh and Israel are few (Deut 1:31, 8:5, 14:1), comparison with descriptions of parental instruction elsewhere in the Hebrew Bible demonstrates the extent to which this familial framework informs D's presentation. Proverbs, for example, underscores the (potential) unpleasantness of parental discipline and training (Prov 13:22, 22:15, 23:12). It also emphasizes the extended temporal horizon envisioned (Prov 19:20, 22:6) and the consequences for accepting or rejecting such instruction (Prov 5:23; 8:33; 10:17; 13:1; 15:5, 10, 32; 19:20).[66] Deuteronomy 8 insists that Yahweh's gift of manna was not first a response to Israel's hunger and complaint. It was instead a lesson that Yahweh staged: he himself caused the Israelites' hunger pains *so that* he could provide them with food and thereby teach them a lesson (cf. Deut 29:5).[67] According to Deut 8:16, this catechesis was intentionally arduous because it aimed at lasting results, and the following verses make clear how high the stakes were: even after their training, the Israelites would be able to abandon their covenant responsibilities, and should they do so, destruction was assured (Deut 8:19–20).

Yet this training was not all "tough love." D portrays Yahweh as having brought Israel along slowly, employing the full forty years of the wilderness period. Though, as noted above, this lengthy duration accords with D's view of Israel's recalcitrance, D's familial metaphor suggests an additional purpose for this extended timeline. As an insightful and generous parent, Yahweh gave the Israelites only what they could handle at each stage. He recognized that as he inaugurated a new social and religious program for his people—one governed by divine laws—he had to help them adjust gradually. Doing so would prepare the Israelites for optimal success in their new reality. Yahweh's parental instruction in D thus offers a powerful, plot-level explanation for its reorganization of the timeline of legal revelation: the Israelites did not—indeed *could not*—receive the main body of Deuteronomic laws until the end of the forty years because they were not ready for them. As suggested already, the law that Yahweh does give the Israelites directly at Horeb, the Decalogue, is a brief, elementary version that is manageable for them and from which they could learn.

This model of preparation for covenant obedience is comparable to that described for the new covenant in Jer 31:31–34.[68] In this text, as part of a future covenant with his people Yahweh promises to write his teaching within them, namely, *on their minds*. This internal inscription, it is imagined, will relieve the Judeans of any need to learn Yahweh's covenantal requirements, for they will all already know Yahweh and his will. This treatment of the Judeans' minds (*lēb*) corresponds closely with Yahweh's concern to condition Israel's mind (*lēbāb*) in Deut 8:2–5. Yahweh undertook his training program in the wilderness to ensure that the Israelites would obey him. In each case, Yahweh's actions are portrayed as a benevolent treatment of his covenant partners' minds that seeks to position them to fulfill their covenantal responsibilities. The difference between Deut 8 and Jer 31, of course, is that in the latter case, the treatment of the Judeans' minds seems to preclude any possibility for future covenant violation. In D, Yahweh's covenant preparation does not rule out such an option, even if its aim is to avoid such violation.[69] In view of Jeremiah's reliance upon D, it is likely that the prophetic text is a specific response to the pedagogical program that D describes and one that reflects a pessimism regarding Judah's future teachability. The wilderness experiment in D, in Jeremiah's view, failed, and this failure motivates the "hardwired" alternative that it imagines.

Loose Ends?

For all of D's achievement in creatively combining the traditions it inherited, its reimagination of the wilderness period features at least two possible loose ends. The first concerns the forty-year duration itself. In J, a protracted duration serves an eminently logical purpose: it functions to eliminate the entire Exodus generation, as forty years represents the stereotypical extent of a generation.[70] Yet with its elimination of generation change, D's reimagination of the wilderness lacks such a rationale for its forty-year timespan. Indeed, though D claims that Israel was particularly stubborn and rebellious and thus in need of an extended period of instruction, it is unclear why this training should last forty years instead of, say, twenty or thirty (or any other sizeable number), each of which would represent a substantial training period in its own right.[71]

The second potential loose end concerns the transformation accomplished by the wilderness instructional period. D offers no explicit indication that the Israelites demonstrated any behavioral improvement across the forty years. In fact, Deut 9:5–6 state the opposite:

> [5]It is not because of your righteousness or moral fortitude that you are coming to inherit their land. It is instead because of these nations' wickedness that Yahweh your god is dispossessing them before you and in order to fulfill the promise that Yahweh swore to your fathers, to Abraham, to Isaac, and to Jacob. [6]You shall thus know that it is not because of your righteousness that Yahweh your god is giving you this good land to inherit, for you are a stiff-necked people!

Yet even if D does not detail its realization, it does anticipate Israel's successful maturation. Deuteronomy 8:11–18 imagine a scenario in which, once the Israelites are settled and finding economic success in the land, they might forget what they learned during their wilderness sojourn and revert to their former ways. Moses commands Israel in v. 18: "You shall remember Yahweh, your god—that it is he who gave you the ability to accumulate wealth, in order to fulfill his promise that he swore to your fathers, a promise that remains in effect." D's omission of any lengthy description of the effectiveness of Israel's forty-year training program is thus best understood as a rhetorical choice. D instead emphasizes Israel's past rebelliousness, the importance of continued obedience to Yahweh's commands, and the agency of its audience to keep or disregard those laws.

What Was the Goal of D's Revision?

In response to such extensive literary reuse in D, the question naturally arises, what is the purpose of this distinctive compositional method? Such a question is not (first) a question of why D simultaneously exhibits a substantial fidelity to and freedom with the story elements of its literary patrimonies. The answer to such a question is arguably straightforward: D challenges, at least on some level, the accounts offered by its sources. The issue is instead why D reproduces the language of its sources in near verbatim fashion while also, in the midst of such close imitation, sometimes cleverly reorienting that language to substantially new ends. Strawn has put the issue plainly: "The *fact of revision* in Deuteronomy is incontrovertible. The primary question that remains, however, is *what is the revision meant to do?*"[72] The debate thus ultimately concerns the relationship between D and the texts that it revises and the ongoing existence of each.[73]

Different possibilities can be imagined, of course, and scholars have offered several explanations for D's revisionary method of composition. In each case, the arguments require moving beyond a simple comparison of Deuteronomic texts with their literary patrimonies to a larger historical, social, and literary contextualization of D. Within this study, then, the question of why D employs its revisionary compositional method is, at least in certain respects, premature, for this question cannot be answered without considering some issues that are the subjects of the following chapters. What can be considered here are the options that have been proposed for understanding D's rewriting and revision, their attendant claims, and the contribution of the foregoing examples toward answering this question.

The Subversion Theory

A first option for understanding D's revisionary composition may be termed the *subversion theory*. Articulated most forcefully by Bernard M. Levinson but building on a long scholarly tradition,[74] the subversion theory focuses specifically on D's method of lemmatic citation in its revision of laws from the Covenant Code, as highlighted above. Levinson argues that D's careful reuse of language in the midst of its sometimes stark reorientations of legal content is part of a two-part strategy: D sought to borrow the prestige and authority of the Covenant Code, even as it undermined the latter's legal claims. In Levinson's words:

> Precisely at the points of conflict between their agenda and the conventions of the Covenant Code, the authors of Deuteronomy appropriated the problematic laws in question and reworked them in order to erase the conflict and to further their own program. The authors of Deuteronomy employed the Covenant Code, in other words, not merely as a textual source but as a resource, in order to purchase the legitimacy and authority that their reform agenda otherwise lacked. The reuse of the older material lent their innovations the guise of continuity with the past and consistency with traditional law. The authors of Deuteronomy cast their departure from tradition as its reaffirmation, their transformation and abrogation of conventional religious law as the original intent of that law.[75]

A strength of the subversion theory is its single explanation for both the persistent content contradictions between D and its literary patrimonies and D's seemingly clever replication and adjustment of its sources' language. As noted above, in the subversion theory, these two elements explicitly work in tandem. D's reuse is conceptualized as an instance of a broader and well-documented phenomenon in religious practice and discourse, namely, the negotiation between tradition and innovation.

The subversion theory also avoids any special pleading in service of harmonization. The eventual combination of D with those texts that it used and recast is understood to have blunted the individual distinctiveness of each work. As I discuss in Chapter 4, the harmonistic interpretations that arose very soon after this compilation attest to this loss of each work's determined perspectives. Yet the considerable effort required to produce unifying interpretations of the combined pentateuchal text also highlighted the disparate content of the underlying works. D's intent to replace its literary forebears need not be undermined by its subsequent reception.[76]

A challenge to the subversion theory is the paucity of evidence to support its attendant claim that the Covenant Code was an authoritative or prestigious text at the time of D's composition.[77] Scholars who argue for subversion sometimes assume the real practice of biblical laws, including the laws of the Covenant Code, in ancient Israel/Judah.[78] It is this real practice that constitutes the authority to which D responds. Others have assumed widespread knowledge of the Covenant Code and other texts that D rewrites. According to this argument, such widespread knowledge created a prestige for these texts that D sought to co-opt. Some scholars have assumed both.[79]

Neither of these assumptions, however, can be sustained.[80] There is no evidence for the real practice of biblical law in ancient Israel and Judah. Moreover, comparative evidence suggests that biblical law, like other examples of legal texts from the ancient Near East, did not function as real, practiced law but instead served other sociopolitical ends. The likelihood that D's laws are something other than real, practiced law only increases in light of their situation in a literary work. As shown in Chapter 1, these laws, as they appear in D, are part of a fully realized fictive discourse, and they can be extracted from their richly imagined narrative world only through extensive, speculative reconstruction.

The Supplementation Theory

An alternative to the subversion theory is one that views D's recasting of its literary forebears in more irenic (or at least less starkly oppositional) terms. Like the subversion theory, it focuses especially on D's legal revision and understands this activity as a more modest challenge to the Covenant Code, meant not as a mutually exclusive alternative to existing legislation but as a supplement intended to stand alongside and guide understandings of the parent text. This view may thus be labeled the *supplementation theory*, and it exists in a number of variations.

Because its treatment of revision differs in certain respects from the analyses offered above, an example is useful to illustrate this theory. To return to the topic of asylum, Otto has argued that Deut 19 demonstrates well not just D's revision of the Covenant Code but also its supplementary intent. He identifies in the nonoverlap of key elements in the two laws an attempt by D's authors not only to revise but to complement the existing law. Specifically, the law in the Covenant Code explicitly refers to altar asylum, but the law in D never refers to altars or to the central sanctuary site. Perceiving the Deuteronomic law's silence regarding the central cult site as problematic,[81] Otto suggests that D's authors meant the "place to which he may flee" in Exod 21:13 to be understood as a reference to the central sanctuary. In this way, not only could the two asylum laws be read together, but the D law *required* that the Covenant Code law be retained. In Otto's view, then, Exod 21 was reimagined by D to apply to the central sanctuary, and Deut 19 was written to supplement it with rules for asylum cities. Finally, the connection between these laws was meant to be perceived by readers, in part through specific hints. Otto suggests that the distinctive sequence of *'ăšer* followed by *wĕkî* in the legal introductions in Exod 21:13–14 was intentionally mimicked in Deut 19:4b and 5 (each with *'ăšer*) and 11 (*wĕkî*) as a signal to readers that these laws should be read as complementary.[82] Otto has summarized his larger view as follows: "The concept of 'revision' does not entail the abolition of the revised laws. Such a view would lead to the difficulty that the part of the Covenant code which was subject to a process of revision became invalid, while the part which was not subject to such a process remained valid. Rather, the process of revision maintained the validity of the revised laws within the horizon of the revising laws."[83]

In some of its articulations, the supplementation theory extends beyond Deuteronomic law to its frame, often in posited stages. As such, it can accord with and draw upon redaction-critical arguments for accretive growth in Deuteronomy and even larger combinations of pentateuchal materials. This is the case in Otto's reconstruction. As discussed in Chapter 1, Otto suggests that D's early, legal core, with its revision of the Covenant Code (including the asylum example just discussed), was later extended and reframed by situating D's laws in their fictive, Mosaic framework. Within this framework, Deut 1:5b is an especially transparent indicator of revisionary intent. Otto interprets Deut 1:5b as a self-conscious depiction of Moses as the first commentator on pentateuchal law: "Moses began *to interpret this (i.e., the foregoing) law.*"[84] I treat this issue in detail in Chapter 4.

Other scholars have argued along similar lines. Kevin Mattison has recently argued that D's revisionary composition should be characterized as "amendment." In his view, this model acknowledges the legal reorientations in D vis-à-vis its forebears while also accounting for "the combination of cross-references, verbal echoes, and substantive and rhetorical gaps that pervade D's legal corpus," particularly in relation to the Covenant Code.[85] The category of amendment allows Mattison to equate the revisionary process in D's modifications of Covenant Code laws and those of later D strata that revised earlier D legislation. Mattison's argument thus ends up being very similar to Otto's: each suggests that D's authors engaged repeatedly in the same activity with the same intent, first subjecting the Covenant Code to revision and expansion and then revising and augmenting those revisions further.[86]

Additional arguments have been offered in support of the supplementation theory. Hindy Najman has suggested that Deuteronomy should be understood in relation to Jewish texts from the Hellenistic period that participate in what she has termed a "Mosaic discourse." Texts such as Jubilees, the Temple Scroll (11QT), and the works of Philo, rather than replacing (or displacing) the Mosaic laws they each interpreted, worked together with them, providing "authentic exposition" for (biblical) Mosaic legislation. According to Najman, Deuteronomic law should be considered the first instance of this Mosaic discourse. In support of this argument, she points to the close language correspondences between the Covenant Code and Deuteronomy, the latter's selective revision of Covenant Code laws, and Deuteronomy's inclusion of references to stories and events that are not narrated in Deuteronomy but that appear elsewhere in the Pentateuch. Najman frames the question ultimately in terms of the text's authority: "Should a contemporary conception of textual authority be attributed to the Deuteronomists? What alternative could there be?"[87]

Working mainly in the opposite direction chronologically, Joshua Berman has focused especially on Mesopotamian and Hittite legal materials to ground his supplementation argument. Inspired by his ancient Near Eastern comparisons, he has proposed a theory of biblical legal corpora as common-law traditions rather than statutory legislation. This means that biblical laws are legal only in form. Together with the nonlegal materials of the Pentateuch, they compose a repository for jurisprudential consultation. At the same time, however, pentateuchal texts that take a legal form do still constitute "law collections" for Berman. Moreover, they are (somehow) still separable from their narrative settings. Berman states: "The law collections of the Pentateuch, like the law collections of the ancient Near East, were prototypical compendia of legal and ethical norms, rather than statutory codes. Their inclusion in the Pentateuch served to publicize digests of the divine requirements for 'justice and righteousness.'"[88] Because these laws were nonstatutory, they were not subject to strict construction, and their content contradictions were unproblematic, at least with respect to textual authority. Berman avers, "As authors revised the collections, they certainly intended to invalidate former normative practices—but that did not entail a rejection of the authority of that text."[89]

One potential strength of the supplementation theory is the simplicity of its analysis: it identifies a single intent across the stages of literary growth in both D and the larger Pentateuch. In the literary interactions identified, what is envisioned is not the creation of separate and independent works but repeated expansions of a single work or compendium. In instances where redactional activity is considered, individual strata with distinctive content can be identified and assigned to different hands, but later strata are consistently understood as accretions to and/or interpretations of the earlier material with which they are combined.[90]

For some readers, another strength of the supplementation theory is its consistency with a scriptural model. Discordant texts are read together as part of a (repeatedly augmented) single work. A principle of harmonization thus adheres, much as it does in scriptural reading. This consistency with the scriptural model actually goes hand in hand with the single intent just highlighted. Whatever these texts were before they became Scripture is largely carried forward to their scriptural existence.

Of course, the tendency toward harmonization in supplementation approaches is also a potential weakness, particularly if pentateuchal texts should be theorized as literature, as argued in Chapter 1. Sacrificed by the supplementation model is almost any semblance of a work's internal field of reference. This is even the case for those, like Berman, who gesture toward keeping the pentateuchal laws together with the narratives within which they appear. Berman characterizes the Pentateuch's contents, at turns, as "collections," "compendia," and "resources from which future norms could be worked out."[91] He never addresses the issue of the Pentateuch's plot-driven stories in which laws appear within character speeches as part of larger fictive discourses.[92] The literariness of these texts is thus lost. In this respect Berman's analysis ends up resembling Najman's: each characterizes pentateuchal texts in ways that make them particularly amenable to the scriptural interpretive strategies of Hellenistic and Roman period Jewish texts—and even resemble those texts themselves.

Many articulations of the supplementation theory also suffer from a shortcoming already discussed is relation to the subversion theory, namely, an assumption of the authority of the legislation revised. As observable in the various articulations of the supplementation theory reviewed above, this issue often manifests itself in characterizations of the "validity" of biblical legislation, however vaguely defined. What is clear is that this authority/validity is understood as part of the real world, not the text's story world. As such, its identification here too runs afoul of D's literariness.

The Resuscitation Theory

A third option, and one that shares some features of each of the foregoing theories, may be termed the *resuscitation theory*. According to this view, D was written to stand alone as an alternative to E, but its stance toward the latter was not subversive.[93] It instead sought to recast, update, and thereby revitalize ideas from an E composition that it deemed outmoded, untenable, or otherwise unsuccessful. In this sense, the resuscitation theory is similar to the subversion theory: each theory suggests that D sought to replace E. Yet the resuscitation theory posits that D's stance toward E is irenic and even committed to E's basic theological perspective and aims. In its identification of a positive stance in D toward its literary forebear, the resuscitation theory resembles the supplementation theory.

As this description implies, the resuscitation theory understands D's substantial reuse of E's language differently from the ways that the subversion and supplementation theories understand it. Rather than seeking to borrow E's prestige, surreptitiously undermine its laws, or build upon and extend them, D's extensive imitation and adaptation of E's language can be explained as a feature of its authors' strong familiarity with E and esteem for it. Even Elohistic content judged inadequate could be updated within the linguistic and theological framework in which D's authors found it. This suggests that D's position toward E is different from that suggested by the subversion and the supplementation theories. As the label "resuscitation" makes clear, this theory understands D as a revitalization project and explains its revisionary compositional method accordingly.

One strength of the resuscitation theory is its ability to acknowledge the competing internal fields of reference of D and its literary patrimonies, including their implications for understanding these texts as independent works, while prescinding from any claim about the authority or prestige of D's forebears. As noted already, articulations of both the subversion and supplementation theories have regularly asserted the prestige and/or authority of the Covenant Code (including, in some cases, the real practice of its laws) without sufficient warrant. Yet these claims prove unnecessary: as the resuscitation theory suggests, D's literary revision can be explained on the basis of the extant evidence without recourse to such speculations.

Another strength of the resuscitation theory, especially in light of the foregoing analysis, is its ability to account for both legal and nonlegal revision in D. Though articulations of the subversion and supplementation theories sometimes gesture toward the nonlegal materials in D, they tend to focus mainly (if not exclusively) on law. The resuscitation theory, by contrast, gives sustained attention to the nonlegal speeches and narration in D and accounts for both its legal and nonlegal parts as integral components of a single revisionary project. As such, it foregrounds the literariness of D. D's ambition to replace E is construed as a *literary* ambition. It is a feature of its literary autonomy, not an attempt to exploit and subvert the Covenant Code's legal authority. Legal contradictions can be treated not as real jurisprudential disputes but as narrative inconsistencies—conflicting details in the story of Yahweh's revelation at Horeb. Accordingly, this theory aligns with the view laid out in Chapter 1 that the pentateuchal legal collections, including D's legislation, are not "law codes" but instead parts of complex narratives with well-developed story worlds. These narratives feature divine legal revelation *to and for the characters in their stories*.

Finally, the resuscitation theory can be paired with the available historical and material culture data in a compelling historical reconstruction of D's compositional context. As I detail further in Chapter 5, it is possible to understand D's reorientation of E and in particular its focus on cult centralization in relation to the Assyrian devastation of Judah at the end of the eighth century BCE. According to Exod 20:24, Yahweh endorsed a proliferation of altars at local cult sites. The preservation of Jerusalem and its temple in the face of Sennacherib's onslaught in Judah (especially in the Shephelah) suggested a different divine preference—a single worship place. D thus reimagined E in line with this new reality. According to this reconstruction, D had no need to challenge E's authority or to borrow from its prestige. History itself had undermined E.

In light of the foregoing, then, I would suggest that the resuscitation theory offers the most persuasive account of the evidence of D's revisionary method. It accounts for D's reuse and revision within a framework that fully endorses this work's literariness. It also avoids the shortcomings of the subversion and supplementation theories identified above.

Conclusion

The foregoing discussion has demonstrated the extent to which D interacted with both narrative and legal material from J and E and recast it in service of its own distinctive ends. D is indeed a "learned text." Yet its authors were not bound by their source material. In D's revisionary composition, the legal and nonlegal materials are integrally related. Like the main source material that D drew from—source material in which narrative and law were part of a single composition—D comprises legal material, presented as speeches, within a narrative framework. Given the integral connection between narrative and law in D's literary patrimony, the simplest conclusion is that D exploited legal and narrative source material concurrently.

This observation adds weight to the argument concerning D's genre already presented in Chapter 1. That is, the evidence of D's revisionary method of composition aligns with the evidence of this work's internal field of reference: D's laws work together with its narrative as part of a single, fictive framework. Moreover, it is this fictive framework, with its distinctive narrative and legal perspectives, that underscores D's literary intent, namely, to stand apart from its literary forebears as an autonomous work.

Another implication of the analysis here is that the material in the Tetrateuch that corresponds closely with D need not be judged Deuteronomi(sti)c simply because of its affinity with D's language and style. The direction of dependence in the case of D's correspondences with texts in Exodus and Numbers is consistent: D reused and adapted Tetrateuchal (J and especially E) material. In most cases, texts that have been identified as Deuteronomi(sti)c in the Tetrateuch are actually Elohistic and serve as source material for D's revisionary composition.[94]

Finally, D's revisionary method, and in particular its close mimicry of the language and content of E, is explicable as part of what I have termed a rehabilitation project. While also drawing from J in a limited way, D sought to resuscitate E in the context of new circumstances that had shown that E's religio-political outlook—and thus its story of the past—was untenable. According to this view, D's reuse of the specific language of its Judean literary patrimonies—its style of "lemmatic citation"—can be understood as a feature of its esteem for them and need not be deemed subversive.

3 Ancient Near Eastern Influence in Deuteronomic Composition

The 1950s and 1960s witnessed an initial engagement with the question of cuneiform treaty influences upon D, in relation to both Hittite sources and the then-newly discovered Esarhaddon's Succession Treaty (EST, referred to originally as the Vassal Treaties of Esarhaddon). More recent decades have seen renewed and broadened attention to such influences and especially the possibility of EST's influence upon D.[1] A number of factors have contributed to this focus, including what is known more generally about the time frame for the development of ancient Israelite and Judean polities in the southern Levant and of their scribal cultures.[2] Yet most significant for recent studies has been the 2009 discovery of a new exemplar of EST at Tel Tayinat, a site located in the Amuq Valley near the modern Turkish-Syrian border. This find has been especially important for the information it provides concerning the distribution of EST tablets, their deposition, and the broader sociohistorical context of this text's use. All of this new data have specific relevance for any posited dependence of D upon EST and for what this dependence might mean for D's own sociohistorical situation.

Yet investigation of EST's possible influence upon D—or the influence of any text upon another—properly begins with the form and content of each respective work. This is both because such data are available to be examined and because it is only on their basis that a possible connection between texts would ever be suggested. Without such ties, it would be possible to make comparisons between D and other ancient Near Eastern treaty materials—especially at the level of genre but also otherwise—but there would almost certainly be no scholarly proposals of direct influence.

In this chapter, then, I investigate the possible influence of various ancient Near Eastern treaty materials upon D, first from the second millennium BCE and then from the first millennium. I pay special attention to the content-related correspondences between the texts compared. In so doing, I treat the question of the relationship between D and treaty texts in much the same way as I treated D's relationship with E and J material in Chapter 2. In this juxtaposition of D's revisionary reuse of different source materials, a significant difference emerges: while D's reliance upon E and (to a lesser extent) J is extensive and provides an orientation for the work overall, its adaptation of material from EST is much more circumscribed. These quantitative and qualitative discrepancies reflect D's main focus and priority. While D draws upon nonnative ancient Near Eastern treaty materials and Neo-Assyrian content in particular, its major concern is more local—namely, a revised portrayal of Israel's wilderness experience and especially the Horeb revelation. Accordingly, D integrates the limited material it draws from other ancient Near Eastern sources into this framework.

Though I consider in this chapter D's content correspondences with other ancient Near Eastern texts and its direct borrowing from EST, I postpone a detailed discussion of the context for D's reuse of EST until Chapter 5. There I address this issue as part of a larger discussion of the historical and social circumstances of D's composition. While not directly connected to the claim of EST's influence upon D, such historical contextualization for D's adaptation of EST provides important corroboration for the arguments presented here.

D and the Second-Millennium Hittite Treaties

Though scholars have largely rejected the claim for the direct influence of Hittite treaties upon D, it is important to address the similarities between D and the Hittite vassal treaties that have been identified and why arguments for influence should be rejected. Similarities identified between D and Hittite materials relate to both genre and content, though the former ties have proved more influential in the history of scholarship and continue to endure, if often in modified form. That is, even among those who have rejected direct Hittite influence in D, the possibility that D's genre is nonetheless informed by the same broad ancient Near Eastern treaty tradition to which the Hittite texts belong is still acknowledged. In this general sense, it is claimed that D and the Hittite treaties participate in a common ancient Near Eastern social milieu. Yet this is a very different argument than one of direct Hittite influence in D. As I discuss here, the extent of the differences between D and the Hittite treaties has not been fully recognized. One of the benefits of reexamining this comparison, then, is to sharpen a description of D's distinctives. It also underscores important methodological issues that arise again in evaluating the possible influence of EST upon D.

The discussion of cuneiform treaty influences upon biblical material was set in motion by George E. Mendenhall, who in 1954 published a study of the formal features of biblical and other ancient Near Eastern covenant/treaty texts that included an extended discussion of similarities between Hittite treaty materials and hexateuchal covenant texts.[3] On the basis of the formal similarities he identified, Mendenhall argued for the influence of the Hittite treaty genre in the Hebrew Bible. As I discuss below, this study inspired subsequent scholars who sought to apply Mendenhall's work more systematically to Deuteronomy.

In his comparison of biblical and Hittite materials, Mendenhall drew especially from Viktor Korošec's analysis of the Hittite treaty form. Korošec identified six elements of this genre: (1) Preamble, (2) Histori-cal Prologue, (3) Stipulations, (4) Provisions for Deposit and Public Read-ing, (5) List of Divine Witnesses, and (6) Curses and Blessings Formula.[4] Mendenhall isolated three examples in the Hebrew Bible that he identi-fied as comparable to the Hittite suzerainty treaty type: the Decalogue, Deuteronomy, and Joshua 24. In a highly positivistic historical reconstruc-tion, he characterized the Decalogue as the paradigmatic covenant of this type in Israelite history.[5] Mendenhall focused especially on the Decalogue found in Exodus and identified in that scroll its Historical Prologue and Stipulations in accordance with the Hittite treaty form. In his view, the account of the Israelites' deliverance from Egypt was the Historical Pro-logue, and the Decalogue's commands constituted the Stipulations. Men-denhall also identified one or more enactment ceremonies in Exod 24:3–8, 11bβ, which he viewed as reflecting the ratification events that necessar-ily attended Hittite treaty making (even if evidence for such events was lacking). At the same time, he acknowledged that formal elements 4–6 (Deposit and Public Reading, Divine Witnesses, Curses and Blessings) do not appear alongside the Decalogue; neither is there an oath, which Men-denhall asserted must have been part of the Hittite treaty procedure. Yet he downplayed these missing elements, arguing that they are otherwise important parts of Israelite religious tradition, as attested elsewhere in the Hebrew Bible.[6]

In the same publication, Mendenhall also commented at some length on Josh 24, but his treatment of D was cursory.[7] In the few observations he did offer, Mendenhall characterized "Deuteronomy" as a compromised version of the suzerainty covenant model—one that was innovative in its ability to accommodate monarchy but whose "philosophy or theology of history became in popular thought at least a caricature of the original structure of religion."[8] Potentially against his form-critical thesis, he also stated, "As the tradition in Deuteronomy indicates, the curses and blessings may not have been regarded as an element in the text of the covenant, but as an *action* which accompanied the ratification of the covenant."[9] With regard to Divine Witnesses, Mendenhall initially entertained an interpretation of the geographical features in Deut 32:1 as demythologized treaty witnesses, but he ultimately disparaged their effectiveness: "Later materials [= Deuteronomic texts] do make poetic use of this legal pattern in spite of the fact that they really do not succeed in walking on all fours, so to speak."[10]

If Mendenhall's form-critical assessment of D was equivocal and underdeveloped, scholars subsequently sought to apply Korošec's identification of the Hittite suzerainty treaty genre to Deuteronomy more systematically. For example, scholars such as Meredith G. Kline and Peter C. Craigie characterized all or nearly all of the Deuteronomy scroll according to the Hittite treaty form. Kline's analysis was comprehensive: Preamble (1:1–5), Historical Prologue (1:6–4:49), Stipulations (chs. 5–26), Sanctions (chs. 27–30), and Succession Arrangements or Covenant Continuity (chs. 31–34).[11] Craigie's delineation was only slightly less so: Preamble (1:1–5), Historical Prologue (1:6–4:49), General Stipulations (chs. 5–11), Specific Stipulations (chs. 12–26), Blessings and Curses (chs. 27–28), and Witnesses (30:19, 31:19, 32:1–43).[12]

Less ambitious, in relation to both Deuteronomy and the treaty form, were the claims of Moshe Weinfeld and Dennis J. McCarthy. Even as he identified in Deuteronomy the treaty elements found in the Hittite texts, Weinfeld argued against any direct Hittite influence, preferring instead a first-millennium borrowing via the Assyrian tradition and EST, in particular.[13] For his part, McCarthy limited his identification of the treaty genre to three elements in Deut 4:44–28:68: Introduction (4:44–11:32), Stipulations (12:1–26:15), and Conclusion: Oath, Rite, Blessing, and Curse (26:16–19, 28:1–68).[14]

A major factor in the more modest claims of Weinfeld and Mc-Carthy—and the persistent challenge to any claim of Hittite influence upon Israelite/Judean texts—is the question of vectors of transmission for such influence. Mendenhall sought to discount this problem already in his initial study, even if he could not solve it. He argued (correctly) that the Hittite treaties were almost certainly examples of a wider ancient Near Eastern genre. As an "international form," this genre could have reached Israel/Judah in a number of ways. Mendenhall also noted that some Hittite treaties were concluded with people groups in Syria/northern Mesopotamia, a region where Israelite ancestors (i.e., the patriarchs) had known ties. Finally, he pointed to connections that other scholars had posited between biblical and Hittite materials.[15]

More recently, Joshua Berman has advocated strongly for Hittite influence in Deuteronomy. Yet he has also been forced to admit that any claim for specific cultural contact is conjectural. His conclusion thus ultimately mirrors Mendenhall's: "It may be that in due time we will unearth more treaties from other periods and locales and that the treaty elements in Deuteronomy may represent a highly refracted reworking of a tradition that we witness today only in Hittite material."[16]

Berman's speculation is an attempt to address what Meir Malul has labeled "the test for coincidence *versus* uniqueness" in evaluating possible ancient Near Eastern influence upon biblical texts.[17] A major aspect of this test relates to the means of and opportunity for influence: "If the similarity [between texts] is the main proof of foreign influence, then it is not sufficient proof. One has first to prove *the possibility of influence or connection,* and only then may he proceed to check the significance of the similarities and differences."[18] Malul's concern for methodological rigor aims to redress the occasional tendency in modern biblical studies toward what Samuel Sandmel famously labeled "parallelomania"—in this case, uncontrolled and unsubstantiated identification of ancient Near Eastern influence in biblical texts.[19]

Aaron Koller has recently attempted to rebut the argument that insufficient evidence of contact between Hatti and Israel/Judah undermines claims of Hittite influence in D.[20] To this end, he has highlighted that some comparisons between biblical and other ancient Near Eastern materials are so compelling (he cites the case of Lamentations and Sumerian city laments) that they recommend a conclusion of borrowing even without evidence of transmission.[21] He also notes that Bernard M. Levinson and I have endorsed this conclusion, citing the goring ox laws in Exod 21:35 and Laws of Eshnunna §53 as such a case. Yet Koller then goes a step further: on the basis of such extraordinary cases, he argues that insistence upon an explanation for vectors of transmission can be set aside in all instances of posited influence.

A closer consideration of Exod 21:35 and Eshnunna §53 demonstrates why Koller's suggestion cannot be accepted. Most important is to recognize what makes a case extraordinary and why on that basis it is possible to deviate from a requirement to identify possible vectors of transmission in claims of dependence. Briefly stated, what is determinative are the *kinds of evidence* and, in its accumulation, its *corroborative value.*

Eshnunna §53 and Exod 21:35 read as follows:

> Eshnunna §53
> If an ox gores another ox and kills it, both ox owners shall divide the price of the live ox and the carcass of the dead ox.

> Exod 21:35
> If the ox of a man knocks the ox of his neighbor and it dies, they shall sell the live ox and divide the resulting silver, and also divide the dead ox.

As can be seen readily, the parallels between these texts are unusually precise. Moreover, among known texts, only Exod 21:35 and Eshnunna §53 share their extensive similarities. The correspondence between Eshnunna §53 and Exod 21:35 also exhibits linguistic features that are peculiar to Akkadian (and potentially even the Neo-Assyrian dialect) and otherwise anomalous in Hebrew.[22] These details make it difficult to explain Exod 21:35 except by recourse to some hypothesis of direct influence, even without a secure explanation of transmission.[23]

Lacking in the comparison of Hittite treaties and D are the sorts of detailed, extended, or otherwise distinctive similarities that exist for Exod 21:35 and Eshnunna §53—a point that Koller himself concedes. Koller's methodological argument thus proves self-contradictory. It is extraordinary evidence that makes a case *extraordinary.* Such cases, characterized as they are by extraordinary evidence, cannot serve as the basis for dismissing the need for such evidence where it is absent, that is, in *ordinary* cases. If the charge of parallelomania is to be avoided, claims of influence require such corroboration. As Malul has rightly argued, evidence of plausible transmission vectors serves precisely this corroborative function. Accordingly, the need for transmission data may be set aside only in instances in which equally strong corroboration is found in other (usually multiple) forms of evidence. Taken together, the distinctive features of Exod 21:35, as described here, provide such corroboration for its likely dependence upon Eshnunna §53. Without similarly distinctive features in the case of D and the Hittite vassal treaties, and without a plausible account of the transmission of these Hittite texts to Israel/Judah, the claim that they influenced D directly cannot be sustained.[24]

Another major challenge encountered by those comparing Hittite treaties and D is the compositional analysis of D that scholars have offered apart from any comparison with ancient Near Eastern treaties. The kinds of internal discrepancies in D discussed in Chapter 1 call into question the possibility of a single composition that could include the full set of formal treaty elements often identified in Hittite comparisons— at least at any point prior to the text's final (canonical) form.[25] For this reason, Kline and Craigie each formulated their analyses in relation to the question of Deuteronomy's unity and explicitly sought to discount the compositional analyses of nineteenth- and twentieth-century biblical scholarship, which they polemically described as "negative critical studies" (Kline) and operating on a principle of "radical doubt" (Craigie).[26] The Hittite comparative evidence provided an alternative, structural basis for Deuteronomy's compositional unity and one that aligned with (some aspects of) religious belief, traditional views of the dating of Deuteronomy, or both.[27]

Less appreciated have been the significant formal differences that obtain amidst otherwise apparent similarities between D and the Hittite treaties. Indeed, D's story world and third-person, omniscient narrative frame stand as equally problematic features for many such comparative claims— and in ways that are reminiscent of the challenge that these features present to evaluations of D's second-person address, as discussed in Chapter 1. The questions that have so often been overlooked are deceptively simple: Is D itself a covenant, or is it a story about covenant making? Is D's discourse real or fictive? And is D accountable to the external world or only to its internal field of reference?

Those who have sought a comprehensive and precise correspondence between Deuteronomy and the Hittite treaty genre have sometimes recognized, at least in part, the problem that queries such as these present. Yet their analyses have not successfully addressed the issues—or the differences between the Deuteronomic and Hittite texts to which they point. Such differences, it should be noted, did prompt Mendenhall to characterize the Deuteronomic text as a hybrid form. He observed that even as the Hittite treaties attest first-person voicing of the king who imposes the treaty, D recounts Mosaically voiced speeches in which Moses relays the deity's messages. In these speeches, the first person is employed by Moses the mediator, not the divine treaty-maker. For Mendenhall, this change reflected the melding of the old covenant tradition with the monarchy, with Moses representing the royal lawgiver and relying upon a divine footing.[28] Kline similarly gestured to the story details in D, which he sought to validate as accurately described historical events.[29] In his view—a view that others have followed—D describes an actual covenant renewal ceremony for the second generation of the Israelites after their departure from Egypt.[30]

Yet ultimately unexplained by those who have argued in favor of Hittite influence in D/Deuteronomy is the difference between D's third-person, omniscient narration, with its fictive discourse and constructed world, and the real discourse of the Hittite treaties and their form. The evidence suggests that the Hittite vassal treaties were actual utterances in real historical situations and that their addressees were the real-world parties upon whom they were imposed. In D, an anonymous narrator addresses the narratee and depicts Moses's speeches to the Israelite *characters* within the story world. Accordingly, Moses's orations are *represented* speech, not real speech.[31] Moreover, if D were taken to be real speech, the other pentateuchal sources create significant—even insurmountable—problems for its evaluation. Notwithstanding attempts to serialize or otherwise harmonize D with E or P, D's story cannot be so reconciled with these other texts. The evidence instead suggests that D bears no accountability beyond its own internal field of reference. It is a literary work and must be treated accordingly. The Hittite treaties, by contrast, are nonliterary.

Finally, it should be observed, especially in response to those who have argued for direct Hittite influence in D, that D's extensive interaction with the Covenant Code and the larger E composition should be judged the primary source of its covenantal framework and storyline (see further below). In this respect, a return to Mendenhall is partially in order. As noted already, Mendenhall argued for the primacy of the Exodus account of covenant making and viewed D as a later development that drew upon its tradition. At least for the native Israelite/Judean material, this sequence and direction of influence proves correct. What is tenuous, however, is the

Hittite connection with the Exodus (i.e., E) materials that Mendenhall endorsed.[32]

The foregoing observations do not by themselves rule out the possibility of Hittite influence in D. They do, however, undermine the particular claims of those who have advocated for it. In the absence of more distinctive correspondences and/or better evidence of cultural contact between Hatti and Israel/Judah, claims of the influence of Hittite texts upon biblical texts should be rejected. Renewed consideration will be possible if new evidence comes to light.

First-Millennium Ancient Near Eastern Treaty Influence in D

A different scenario obtains in the Neo-Assyrian period. Scholars have observed that D exhibits a number of content correspondences with other ancient Near Eastern materials of the first millennium—especially treaty texts and loyalty oaths—and they have subjected these similarities to repeated investigation. The details of these comparisons are relatively well-known—especially in the case of so-called Esarhaddon's Succession Treaty, a text that is not properly a treaty but an example of the closely related loyalty oath genre (Akkadian: *adê;* I maintain the scholarly convention and refer to it here as EST).[33] Because the history of the scholarly debate has moved from arguments in favor of D's direct dependence upon EST to critiques of this thesis that have sometimes advocated in its place a more general reliance upon ancient Near Eastern treaty traditions, I follow this sequence in the ensuing discussion. In each case, I review the main points of comparison before offering new arguments in support of D's creative adaptation of EST.

Esarhaddon's Succession Treaty

Though limited instances of correspondence between D and EST do exist outside of Deut 13 and 28,[34] these two chapters have been repeatedly identified as loci of D's creative adaptation of material from EST. Already in his 1958 editio princeps of EST, which he labeled "the Vassal Treaties of Esarhaddon," Donald J. Wiseman noted the similarity between the curses in Deut 28 and those of the Neo-Assyrian text.[35] Other scholars, including Riekele Borger and William Moran, soon expanded on Wiseman's initial observations.[36]

Two studies that appeared independently in 1965 probed the details of these curse correspondences further, and their findings remain the backbone of claims for D's dependence upon EST. Among other similarities, both Moshe Weinfeld and Rintje Frankena observed the striking parallels between the curses in Deut 28:26–33 and EST §§39–42 (= SAA 2 6 419–30; see Table 2). Weinfeld argued, moreover, that in the midst of this curse cluster, the particular order of D's curses—and especially the ordering of curses in vv. 27–29—has no native Israelite rationale but instead corresponds with the order of the Assyrian curses, whose sequence is traceable to the stereotypical hierarchy of the Assyrian pantheon and its conventional pairing of the deities Sin and Shamash.[37] Both Weinfeld and Frankena suggested a direct literary connection between D and EST and outlined plausible historical conditions for such borrowing during the reign of Manasseh.

Spencer L. Allen has offered additional analysis of the ordering of the gods in the curses of EST and, in so doing, has corrected some details of Weinfeld's analysis, especially concerning traditional Mesopotamian divine hierarchies and groupings.[38] Yet he has also confirmed and even added weight to the importance of the Sin/Shamash pairing in EST as a diagnostic feature of D's reuse of this text. This is because, as Allen has noted, the Sin/Shamash ordering (as opposed to Shamash/Sin) is idiosyncratic in curse contexts: "Despite the general variability of whether Sîn or Šamaš is listed first when these two gods appear side-by-side in Mesopotamian inscriptions, the Sîn/Šamaš sequence in ll. 419–424 remains anomalous among our extant witnesses to the set of traditional curses."[39] Thus, if D were dependent in this case on a traditional Mesopotamian curse ordering and not EST, its skin disease (v. 27) and blindness (vv. 28–29) curses would likely appear in reverse order. These observations serve as a challenge to scholars such as Christoph Koch, who has argued against the uniqueness of the similarities between the curses in Deut 28 and EST, suggesting instead that the list of Assyrian gods reflected in the curses in this section is conventional in Neo-Assyrian treaties and thus not tied directly to EST.[40]

Hans Ulrich Steymans has subjected the curse materials in Deut 28 and EST to further, detailed scrutiny. In so doing, he has extended the claim of D's direct literary dependence upon EST, observing not only the sequential clustering of parallel curses in Deut 28 and EST but also additional, nonsequential parallels between them and a shared thematic and sequential structure between EST §56 (SAA 2 6:472–93) and Deut 28:20–44.[41] Recently, Nicholas O. Polk has provided additional refinement to Steymans's

Table 2. Parallel curse clusters in Deut 28:26–33 and EST §§ 39–42 (SAA 2 6 419–30)

Curse Topic	Deut 28:26–33	EST §§ 39–42
Carcasses as carrion	[26]May your corpse become food for all the birds of the sky and for the beasts of the earth, with none to scare them off!	[§41]May Ninurta, the foremost of the gods, fell you with his furious arrow! May he fill the steppe with your blood and cause the eagle and vulture to eat your flesh!
Skin disease	[27]May Yahweh strike you with the boils of Egypt and with hemorrhoids and scab and itch from which you cannot be cured!	[§39]May Sin, the light of heaven and earth, clothe you with leprosy! May he not permit you to enter before gods or king! Roam the steppe like an onager or gazelle!
Blindness	[28]May Yahweh strike you with madness and blindness and mental tumult, [29a]so that you grope at noontime as one who is blind gropes in the dark, and so that you do not navigate your paths successfully!	[§40]May Shamash, the light of heaven and earth, not judge you justly! May he take away your sight! Walk continuously in darkness!
Rape of wife	[30aa]May you betroth a woman and another man ravish her!	[§42a]May Dilbat (Venus), the brightest of the heavenly bodies, make your wives lay in the lap of your enemy before your eyes!
Loss of household and possessions	[30ab–b]Should you build a house, you will not dwell in it. Should you plant a vineyard, you will not make use of it. [31]Your ox will be slaughtered before your eyes, but you will not eat from it. Your ass will be robbed from before you and not return to you. Your flock will be given to your enemy, with none to rescue it. [32]Your sons and daughters will be given to a strange people, and though your eyes see and long for them continually, you be powerless. [33]A people whom you do not know will eat of the fruit of your land and of all of your labor, and you will only ever be oppressed and crushed.	[§42b]May your sons not take possession of your house but instead a strange enemy divide your possessions.

analysis, even as he has confirmed the likelihood that D engaged EST in its curses beyond the curse cluster in EST §§39–42.[42] With these studies, Steymans and Polk have only strengthened the case against the claim that a common ancient Near Eastern curse tradition can account for the similarities between D and EST.

Correspondences between Deut 13 and EST have similarly led scholars to posit a direct literary relationship between these texts. Most ambitious are the claims of Steymans and Otto that the base texts of Deut 13, together with portions of Deut 28, amount to direct translations of sections of EST. Steymans has argued at length for this position,[43] and Otto has followed it closely, stating plainly, "Die Texte Dtn 13,2–10*; 28,15*.20–44* sind *Übersetzungen* aus den VTE [= EST]."[44] As I discuss further below, this assessment overstates the case. Even so, substantial evidence suggests that the author(s) of Deut 13:1–10 did creatively adapt material from EST §§4 and 10 (SAA 2 6:108–22).[45]

The details of D's reuse in this instance relate to both shared themes and brief strings of parallel wording. Especially striking is the similarity between EST's adjuration to report any negative word concerning Assurbanipal, "whether from the mouth of a prophet, an ecstatic, or one who inquires for a divine message" (*lū ina pī raggime maḫḫê mār šāʾili amāt ili*, SAA 2 6:116–17), and the case of "a prophet or dream diviner" (*nābîʾ ʾô ḥōlēm ḥălōm*) who encourages apostasy in Deut 13:2–6. Though the correspondence in this case is not exact, it is notable that this EST line is the only known instance in which religious figures appear in a treaty text as potential rebels against the king.[46] Moreover, the specific locution used in Deut 13:6, "to encourage rebellion" (*dbr sārâ*), is a likely Akkadian borrowing and may derive from EST (SAA 2 6:502).[47]

Among these parallels, as scholars have observed, the dream diviner in Deut 13:2–6 is of special note. Such a figure is not attested elsewhere in the Hebrew Bible, even within lists of prohibited divinatory practices and practitioners (e.g., Deut 18:9–14). It is thus questionable whether dream divination (oneiromancy) was a feature of ancient Israelite/Judean divination, either at the time of D's composition or at other times. These contextual details suggest instead that this figure's appearance in Deut 13 constitutes a so-called blind motif, that is, a feature that is disconnected from its immediate literary and cultural contexts. Such disconnection, however, can be accounted for if the dream diviner is borrowed from EST and, in particular, its reference to the *šāʾili amāt ili* ("one who inquires for a divine message").[48]

There is ample evidence for dream divination in Mesopotamia, and, as Martti Nissinen has observed, "*šā 'il(t)u*, a rare word in Neo-Assyrian, is usually—though not exclusively—connected with dream interpretation and thus comes near to the designation *šabrû* [dream specialist]."[49]

D's reuse of EST in this instance, it should be observed, amounts to a substantial expansion of a brief reference in the Assyrian text. Mention of three diviners in the midst of a litany of potential instigators in EST is taken up by the D authors and developed as part of the lead case (vv. 2–6) among three hypothetical cases of sedition in Deut 13. Within D's literary and sociopolitical worlds, however, this expansion is readily explicable. D's story centers on Moses's recitation of the prophetic message of law that he received directly from Yahweh at Horeb (Deut 5:31). Yet D's laws also represent a substantial revision of prior formulations—most notably, those of E. As such, its new version of Moses's mediation of divine law is a challenge to its forebears. That D would be especially mindful of the possibility of future prophetic utterances that could call its religious vision into question is thus foreseeable. Prompted by EST's brief reference to prophetic sedition, D developed a larger treatment of a topic that was especially salient in its own context. Unsurprisingly, D returns to the topic in its laws of offices (Deut 16:18–18:22), which include rules for future licit prophecy that substantially limit the function of post-Mosaic prophets (18:15–22).[50]

The same concerns inform the apparent borrowing of EST's "canon formula" in Deut 13:1. This verse states:

> The entire message that I am commanding you, you shall be careful to carry out. Do not add to it, and do not subtract from it.

EST includes a similar admonition (SAA 2 6:57–60):

> You shall not alter or change the word of Esarhaddon, the king of the land of Assur. You shall heed this very Assurbanipal, the great crown prince designate whom Esarhaddon, the king of the land of Assur, your lord, has presented to you.

D's admonition accords well with its interest in securing its larger revisionary project. It also relates directly to the specific hypothetical scenarios of instigation that it presents in 13:2–6, 7–12, and 13–19.

It is precisely in view of the similarities to EST identifiable elsewhere in Deut 13 that the correspondence between these texts' canon formulae can be identified as another instance of D's creative adaptation of EST.

Levinson has highlighted this parallel and, in response to the relatively frequent appearance of such canon formulae in ancient Near Eastern texts, emphasized the significance of the contrasting sequences of the respective Hebrew and Akkadian formulations.[51] The Hebrew text begins with an adjuration to obey the ruler's command (single underline, above) and is followed by a double prohibition against altering it (double underline). The Akkadian text begins with the double prohibition against alteration (double underline), which is followed by an adjuration to obey the ruler (single underline). As in other instances of Judean revision, Levinson identifies the D text as an instance of the scribal practice of marking reuse through inverted citation (Seidel's law).[52]

Finally, the lines in EST that immediately precede its references to diviners contain another distinctive parallel with D. These lines enumerate family members who might speak an untoward word concerning the crown prince and, in so doing, provoke disloyalty toward him. The family members listed are "your brothers, your sons, or your daughters" (SAA 2 6:116–17). As Levinson and Steymans have emphasized, this collocation of family members finds a close parallel in Deut 13:7a, which includes as potential instigators "your brother, the son of your mother, or your son or your daughter." The combination and sequence of brother-son-daughter is notable, for the inclusion of a daughter distinguishes these two instances from other examples. Steymans has raised this point in response to Berman, who suggested that the second-millennium BCE Hittite treaty with the men of Išmerika offers a better parallel to Deut 13 than does EST. This Hittite text also lists family members as potential instigators, but its list includes father-mother-brother-sister-relative (*CTH* 133:23), with no mention of a daughter.[53] Yet when set in the context of the other correspondences already enumerated, the brother-son-daughter parallel between D and EST is suggestive of further borrowing.

Other Ancient Near Eastern Treaty Influences

Though the evidence for D's creative adaptation of EST is compelling, this reuse hardly accounts for all of D's content or its distinctive literary shape. This is the case not only for D generally but also for its specifically covenantal elements. Indeed, scholars have long recognized resonances with non-Assyrian treaty/covenant in D. Most significant among them, of course, are native Israelite/Judean influences. As discussed in Chapter 2,

D's authors interacted extensively with the covenantal traditions of the pentateuchal E source. Owed to this interaction are the basic storyline of covenant making in D, much of the content of its covenantal stipulations, and even its conceptualization of its covenantal requirements as legislation. Notably, neither EST nor any other nonnative treaty source posited for D frames its requirements as law; neither do those texts' instructions treat the broad range of topics that D addresses. Such features and, in particular, the combination of covenant and law in D can be traced exclusively and directly to E. By comparison with this far-reaching dependence, D's reliance upon other materials, while identifiable, is much more restricted.

D's substantial reliance upon native covenantal traditions, combined with the notable differences observable between its presentation and that of EST, has prompted some scholars to question whether D used EST at all. For example, in 1978, Christianus Brekelmans called into question the strength of the connections between D and EST and the validity of privileging EST as a partner for comparison with D. With special focus upon structure, Brekelmans highlighted several differences between D and the ancient Near Eastern treaty/loyalty oath tradition in general and between D and EST in particular. Most significantly, he argued that the substantial native covenant tradition from ancient Israel cannot be traced directly to the ancient Near Eastern treaty tradition. Brekelmans thus suggested that scholarly claims of D's reliance upon EST were overstated, concluding that he was "much in doubt about the treaty background of *Dt* [Deuteronomy]."[54] While the evidence reviewed above does suggest that D drew upon EST, Brekelmans's emphasis upon the extensive native covenantal influence in D is well-founded. EST serves as a relatively minor resource for D in comparison with its reliance upon the pentateuchal E source.

Scholars have also noted that some covenant/treaty details in D that do not align with EST or other Mesopotamian texts do find analogues in non-Hebrew Levantine traditions.[55] This is particularly the case in the curses of Deut 28. Even as there are clustering, shared sequences of curses, and other patterns of correspondence with EST in this chapter, there is also curse content in it that corresponds only with Levantine Aramaic curse texts. Laura Quick has recently made this claim forcefully: focusing especially on futility curses (i.e., those that promise that little or no success will result from efforts expended), she argues that the Levantine curse traditions rather than EST or any other text provide close analogues to the curses in

Deut 28. She even observes instances in which EST's curses were developed by D through the incorporation of Levantine traditions within them.

This is not to suggest, however, that any particular Levantine text served as a source for D. Quick instead advocates a shared cultural context for similarities between D and other Levantine curse traditions (and potentially also Mesopotamian ones). In her view, it is likely that transmission of such traditions and in particular Levantine curse structure and themes occurred orally rather than in a textual medium. Quick concludes that D's curses represent a distinctive combination of Mesopotamian and Levantine traditions: "Even as the scribe references the curses from a treaty that subjugated his homeland, these are buttressed with curses that display the literary artistry of his native tradition: a new covenantal agreement between Yahweh and Judah has replaced the treaty imposed by the Assyrian overlords, borrowing from that treaty tradition but at the same time still creating a consciously Northwest Semitic product."[56] Even if this argument for D's subversive intent is questionable (see below), Quick's observations buttress the long-articulated claim that D's authors were influenced by a variety of ancient Near Eastern treaty and curse traditions.

Contextualizing Deuteronomic Revision of EST

Though I offer in Chapter 5 a fuller reconstruction of the historical context of D's composition, including the sociopolitical circumstances of its adaptation of EST material, it is important here to address a number of specific contextual issues related to the claim that D drew upon EST. This is not least because the argument I am making differs in some respects from those of other scholars who have also observed such reuse. Addressing these contextual issues, then, provides an opportunity to characterize further the nature of D's creative adaptation of content from EST.

Was D's Reuse of EST Subversive?

In the assessment of possible Deuteronomic revision of EST, a significant point of debate has been the intent of this alleged adaptation. In some respects, this debate mirrors the debate discussed in Chapter 2 concerning the intent of D's revision of the Covenant Code's laws. Several scholars have suggested that the Deuteronomic authors' creative redeployment of aspects of EST represents a subversive theopolitical response to Assyrian imperialism. A clear articulation of this position is that of Bernard M. Levinson: "In the process of reworking VTE [= EST] for its own legal and literary purposes, Deuteronomy also subverted its source by replacing Esarhaddon and Assurbanipal with Yahweh as the object of the demand for exclusive loyalty. The instrument of Neo-Assyrian imperialism, as transformed by the Judean authors of Deuteronomy, thereby supported an attempt at liberation from imperial rule; the literary reworking came in the service of a bid for political and cultural autonomy."[57] Literary appropriation, according to this analysis, was thus meant to deflect the ideology expressed in EST and redirect it against the Assyrian overlord.

Carly Crouch has recently addressed in detail the subversion thesis in its various forms, focusing especially on D's posited subversive adaptation of EST. Central to her analysis is a detailed consideration of what subversion is—including motivations for it, contexts in which it is regularly found, its specific mechanics, and, particularly important for Crouch, what subversion requires of its audience. Crouch insists that because an audience must recognize subversive allusion for that allusion to be successful, if it cannot be established that such signaling of source text/tradition would have been recognizable (e.g., through extensive similarity, distinctive formulation, and widespread knowledge of the source), it likely did not occur.[58] In her review of the correspondences between D and EST, she finds too loose of a connection to recommend the sort of subversive appropriation that scholars have proposed. Crouch thus concludes, "The lack of specificity, distinctiveness, and frequency in the supposed similarities between Deuteronomy and VTE means that Deuteronomy is not recognizable as an adaptation of VTE."[59]

Crouch's critique of the subversion thesis is instructive.[60] While more complex audience scenarios might be proposed to accommodate at least some of her concerns (e.g., multiple audiences, with subversive intent recognizable only among a relatively small, scribal elite), it is the case that D lacks specific reactionary features that would make an ostensibly subversive stance within it clear. Moreover, even those who argue that D creatively adapted EST acknowledge that it engaged this Assyrian text in a limited way (primarily in Deut 13 and 28). This restricted redeployment of material from EST suggests that this text—and, in particular, countering it—was not D's primary concern. The latter observation is only strengthened when D's engagement with EST is compared with its much more extensive reuse of native Judean materials, as discussed already.

These observations suggest that if a connection between D and EST is to be observed, its intent should be understood as something other than subversive. Too often, however, scholars have considered only two alternatives: either D adapted portions of EST in an attempt to subvert Assyrian religio-political aims, or D did not draw on EST at all. Yet the question must be posed: Could D have appropriated material from EST without subversive intent?

There is another option for understanding D's reuse of EST. Rather than seeking to subvert Neo-Assyrian imperial policy and propaganda, D's adaptation of EST can be understood as an opportunistic engagement, both in light of D's use of other source materials and in line with the political Zeitgeist of the seventh-century BCE Levant. In several respects, this option for explaining D's dependence upon EST is akin to scholarly arguments for a more general correspondence between D and the ancient Near Eastern treaty tradition. In other words, rather than countering EST specifically, D drew from what was at its disposal in service of its literary aims.

In this scenario, reuse of EST comes in the context of D's exploitation of multiple treaty/covenant sources that differ in significant ways from each other. D appears to have drawn from each of them, albeit to different extents and with different levels of fidelity. The guiding framework of all of this reuse, however, is discernable. It is the pentateuchal E source and D's revision of it.

That EST is particularly concerned with the possibility of sedition and contains a robust litany of curses made it an attractive resource for D's authors, who incorporated each of these elements into their Horeb covenant framework. Notably, the E material that D revised contained no formal curse section. Yet the concluding section of its Covenant Code (Exod 23:20–33) does gesture toward blessing and curse (especially vv. 22, 25–26), making the incorporation of curses from EST a logical supplement to the E material that D reimagined. Introducing Levantine curse traditions into this hybrid text appears to have worked similarly.

D's Reuse of EST and Judean Knowledge and Use of Akkadian and Aramaic

Another point of debate in the scholarly discussion of D's possible reuse of EST has been the prospect of Akkadian literacy (proficiency in reading and writing) among Judean scribes of the seventh century BCE and, in its absence, potential alternative vectors of content transmission. Several scholars, including William Morrow, Carly Crouch, and Laura Quick, have raised concerns over the extent and even possibility of such Akkadian literacy in the Neo-Assyrian periphery. They have also noted the substantial shift from Akkadian to Aramaic in Neo-Assyrian diplomacy and governance that was occurring during this period, further reducing the likelihood of Akkadian literacy among local populations at the empire's far reaches.[61] In light of these details, Quick has even concluded that "an Aramaic translation of Esarhaddon's Succession Treaties is a necessary hypothesis for any positive assessment of the connections between the Succession Treaties and Deuteronomy 28."[62]

Such scholarly caution is well-founded, insofar as it calls into question a claim for widespread cuneiform literacy in Judah. Indeed, there is good reason to doubt substantial Judean literacy not only for Akkadian but also for Aramaic and even Hebrew.[63] Yet a total disavowal of Akkadian literacy is only possible if a significant, if limited, body of evidence is suppressed. It should be noted, moreover, that widespread cuneiform literacy in Judah is hardly required by the claim made here that D drew upon and adapted portions of EST. But perhaps even more important is testing the assumptions that have often accompanied scholars' appeals to Aramaic as a prevalent language of seventh-century BCE Judah.

To address first the question of Akkadian literacy, there is compelling evidence within biblical texts that substantial facility with Akkadian existed among at least a small number of Judean scribes of the late eighth and seventh centuries.[64] Scholars have observed specific, detailed interactions between Akkadian and Hebrew texts. Examples include Exod 21:35, discussed above, and several Isaianic texts, including Isa 1:7–8, 2:5–21, 8:7–8, 10:13, 37:24 // 2 Kgs 19:23, 37:26b // 2 Kgs 19:25.[65] On the basis of distinctive correspondences identifiable in First Isaiah, the prevalence of the parallel locutions and images in Neo-Assyrian materials, and their appearance in Isaianic texts that specifically target Assyria, Peter Machinist concluded, "What we have found in the way of a general image and specific motifs is enough to raise the distinct possibility that Isaiah's knowledge of Assyria was gained not merely from actual experiences of the Assyrians in Palestine, but from official Assyrian literature, especially of the court."[66]

In at least some instances, moreover, it has been shown that an Aramaic intermediary/translation for what appears to be a Hebrew borrowing from an Akkadian text is unlikely or even precluded. The clause "you shall cover it . . . with pitch," which appears in the deity's instructions for the ark in Gen 6:14b, is one such instance. Scholars have long observed that the noun *kōper* ("pitch/bitumen") is likely a borrowing from Akkadian *kupru*.[67] Yet as Samuel L. Boyd has observed, there is important, additional evidence of Akkadian influence in the larger clause in which *kōper* appears. Specifically, the verbal formulation in this verse, with the cognate verb *kpr* in the G stem, is found only in this single example in Hebrew, even as the G stem of *kpr* is well attested in Akkadian, both by itself and in combination with the cognate accusative. This attestation pattern suggests that even if a specific parent text for Gen 6:14 cannot be identified,[68] the line "you shall cover it . . . with pitch" was likely borrowed.

At the same time, the linguistic evidence recommends against an Aramaic intermediary for this borrowing. In no period does the G stem of the Aramaic verb *kpr* carry the semantics "to wipe on," as required by Gen 6:14. It is unsurprising, then, that even as some ancient Aramaic translations of Gen 6:14 render the noun *kōper* with a cognate formation, *kwpr'*, they do not employ it with the cognate verb. In the case of Pseudo-Jonathan and Neofiti, even the noun *kōper* is rendered with an unrelated root (*ḥmr*).[69] Taken together, these details suggest that the non-Hebrew features present in Gen 6:14 are readily explicable if they stem from an Akkadian text but are highly anomalous if derived from an Aramaic one. Accordingly, a claim for an Aramaic intermediary for the borrowing of "you shall cover it . . . with pitch" in Gen 6:14 is dubious, if not impossible.

A key component of Quick's argument against cuneiform literacy in Judah and preference for Aramaic in its place is the scarcity of Akkadian epigraphic evidence from the Judean region.[70] This basic observation, namely, that there is a general absence of Akkadian texts from the Neo-Assyrian period in Judah, is correct. Yet, as suggested already, a theory of D's dependence upon EST need not be built upon a claim of widespread cuneiform literacy in Judah or even the prevalence of Akkadian texts in the region. The biblical evidence for cuneiform literacy in Judah is both limited *and* significant, and its relative paucity actually aligns well with the small amount of epigraphic evidence that has been uncovered.[71]

At the same time, holding up the extant epigraphic evidence as the measure for non-Hebrew literacy in Judah creates a significant impediment for the claim that Aramaic was in use in Judah during the Neo-Assyrian period, either on its own or as the language of translation for EST. Notwithstanding Aramaic's status as a burgeoning lingua franca in the latter part of the Neo-Assyrian period,[72] there is no epigraphic evidence of Aramaic from seventh-century Judah.[73] Moreover, with the label "lingua franca," the precise distribution, function, and even definition of Aramaic during the eighth and seventh centuries have sometimes been taken for granted. Recent studies have demonstrated that although its use was on the rise, particularly in certain regions, Aramaic hardly took over as the official administrative language of the Neo-Assyrian empire in the Sargonid period, and there was no standardization across Aramaic dialects during this period.[74] Commenting on the scholarly discussion in relation to the evidence for the southern Levant, Peter Zilberg has observed: "The idea that during the time of Sennacherib and Esarhaddon, most of the administration of the province and the correspondence were done in Aramaic emerged because we do not have many documents that describe the western correspondence of Sennacherib, Esarhaddon, and Ashurbanipal. Although writing boards and papyri were widely used, we can still see the use of cuneiform tablets for correspondence on the periphery of the empire during 611–12 BCE."[75]

The details that are known of Aramaic and Akkadian use in the Neo-Assyrian period shed additional light on the issue. Scholars have observed that by the seventh century, Aramaic was employed administratively, especially in legal texts, both in the Assyrian heartland and in the empire's peripheries.[76] Yet it was not employed by the Assyrians across all genres. For the present discussion, especially important is the fact that Assyrian adê texts apparently were not composed in Aramaic; nor were Aramaic or vernacular translations of these texts produced.[77] As Kazuko Watanabe and Boyd have observed, the Assyrians did incorporate in their adê texts elements related to their subjects in an attempt to appeal to local concerns. Thus, for example, versions of EST included Babylonian dialectical variants, particularly in their curses, to appeal to Babylonian audiences. The inclusion of Levantine deities, as attested in the Tayinat exemplar, were similarly meant to appeal to local populations in the western periphery of the empire. Yet as Assyrian adê texts, exemplars of EST were invariably written in Akkadian.[78]

Contemporary Aramaic treaty texts, such as the Sefire inscriptions, have sometimes been referenced as support for posited Aramaic translations of EST or other Akkadian texts. Yet these Aramaic texts actually provide a helpful contrast with their Assyrian counterparts. The Aramaic treaty texts originated in non-Assyrian contexts and addressed nonimperial interactions. Accordingly, their authors freely deviated from Assyrian norms and practices, including in their language choice.[79]

With regard to Judah specifically, scholars have sometimes supported their claim that Judean scribes had the ability to employ Aramaic through appeal to the biblical account of Sennacherib's blockade against Jerusalem, which depicts the Judean officials as proficient in Aramaic (2 Kgs 18:26 // Isa 36:11). Some have also observed the closeness of the Aramaic language and writing system to those of Hebrew, sometimes in contrast to the Akkadian language and the cuneiform writing system. On the latter point, James Barr's comments are representative. Weighing the likelihood of Aramaic versus Akkadian influence in Hosea, he surmised, "Contact with Accadian is also a possibility; it is somewhat less likely than Aramaic influence, because Accadian must have been to the average Israelite a much more strange and difficult language than Aramaic."[80]

The discussion above suggests that such arguments, when deployed in relation to the question of Judean interactions with EST, fail to address the most salient data. If the evidence suggests that EST, like other Assyrian *adê* texts, was not translated into Aramaic (or other languages), there is no reason to entertain the possibility that Judeans encountered this text in Aramaic. Indeed, even if Aramaic would have been easier for Hebrew scribes to learn and use than Akkadian, this does not mean that Aramaic was employed widely in Neo-Assyrian-period Judah, either generally or as a translation language for texts originally composed in Akkadian.[81] Though it is hardly complete, the known evidence suggests the opposite, namely, that Aramaic probably was not common in late-eighth- and seventh-century Judah (an observation, incidentally, that would align with the claim of 2 Kgs 18:26).[82] Finally, given that there is good evidence of Akkadian proficiency among at least a small number of Judean scribes, insistence upon the need for an Aramaic translation of EST in Judah can be set aside.

Creative Adaptation versus Translation

As noted already, scholars have occasionally mischaracterized the nature of D's reuse of EST, labeling it a Hebrew "translation" of the Akkadian text. This exaggerated claim has been met repeatedly with objection.[83] It has also spurred more precise descriptions of D's revision as "creative adaptation" and even detailed, theoretically and contextually informed consideration of what translation entails and whether any part of D's interaction with EST should be so characterized.[84]

Each of these concerns hearkens back to a perennial issue in the evaluation of reuse in biblical and other ancient Near Eastern texts and especially in D, namely, the question of the extent of similarity in posited cases of influence. To return once again to the goring ox laws, Malul addressed this issue in his rebuttal of Adrianus Van Selms's rejection of a direct connection between the Covenant Code laws pertaining to goring oxen and the similar cuneiform laws. Van Selms argued that the differences between the biblical and cuneiform laws are too great for a claim of direct influence to be plausible. Malul responded by noting that differences should be expected when a source text is used and that precisely what is *not* being claimed is verbatim reproduction of the source material:

> It should be emphasized that as the factual existence of similarities is not in itself a sufficient reason for reaching the conclusion of some connection between the sources under comparison, so also the existence of differences does not constitute a sufficient reason for a priori rejecting the possibility of such a connection. In fact, differences are by nature an inevitable aspect of the problem, and had they not existed, no problem would have arisen in the first place, for then the sources would have been virtually identical.[85]

Put differently, the question that is regularly addressed in instances of apparent influence in works such as D is not the *replication* of a text (i.e., a new copy) or its *translation* into another language. It is instead *recasting* and *creative adaptation*. Such instances of revisionary reuse are, by their nature, more difficult to demonstrate than replications and translations because they are less extensive and precise. They might even be, as Crouch has termed them in the case of D and EST, "sloppy allusions."[86]

This style of revision raises a question, then, about whether revisionary authors always intended their reuse to be observed by their audiences. Such a query is especially pertinent in cases of relatively limited dependence—cases such as D's reuse of material from EST. If D's adaptation of elements from EST is, as argued here, not subversive but opportunistic—a symptom and reflection of the cosmopolitan world of the Near East in the Neo-Assyrian period—its significance may be greater for modern scholars than it was for D's authors or their audience. Identifying EST as a source exploited by D's authors sheds important light on the context of their composition and, as such, suggests options for understanding various details within that work. Yet its greatest contribution, as I discuss in Chapter 5, may be the information it offers for dating D. In the final analysis, reliance upon EST in D is quite limited. It certainly does not serve as an orienting framework for the whole of the D work.

Conclusion

Building upon a substantial body of scholarship that has been produced over the past few decades, I have reexamined here the question of ancient Near Eastern treaty influence in D. I have endeavored to show both the promise and limits of the relevant evidence and to contextualize it more broadly within D's literary project. Claims for the direct influence of second-millennium Hittite treaty texts upon D, once popular and recently reinvigorated, cannot be sustained. This is not simply because of the absence of plausible vectors for the transmission of texts between Hatti and Israel/Judah. It is also because the arguments in favor of identifying parallels between Hittite and Deuteronomic texts, with respect to both content detail and form, have at turns misconstrued the evidence or ignored its implications. The final form of the Deuteronomy scroll, characterized as it is by significant compositional complexity, cannot serve as the basis for comparison with Hittite treaties; nor can the form of D (or Deuteronomy) be aligned with that of the Hittite texts. Likewise, alternative scholarly explanations for internal discrepancies in D that draw analogies to Hittite materials fail to withstand scrutiny.

The situation in the first millennium, particularly with regard to EST, is different. There is good evidence for D's adaptation of material from EST. The curse cluster in Deut 28:26–33, with its correspondence with the distinctive ordering of EST's curses, is particularly compelling, as is the correspondence between the otherwise anomalous dream diviner in Deut 13:2–6 and its equivalent in EST.

Yet even as this evidence for dependence is persuasive, it also points to the limited scope of D's interaction with EST. D did not draw upon EST as a guiding framework; it already had that in the pentateuchal E source and its story of the Horeb revelation. Nor did D pitch a subversive attack against Assyria by turning its loyalty oath against the empire. D's authors instead seem to have drawn on several sources, interacting with them in different ways according to the varying contributions they made to their work. As I discuss further in Chapter 5, treaties and loyalty oaths were part of the Zeitgeist of the Neo-Assyrian empire's last century and an especially common political instrument of the Sargonids. Given the historical and political situation in which D's authors found themselves, it is little surprise that they produced a text with similar themes and ideas and that they drew selectively from an especially well-known and widely distributed Assyrian example.

4 Deuteronomic Reception and the Compiled Pentateuch

A major point of debate in recent discussions of Deuteronomy has been the interpretation of Deut 1:5—both the basic sense of the verse and what its implications are for understanding Deuteronomic law in relation to other pentateuchal legislation. Advancing a dubious lexical analysis of this verse's rare verb *bē'ēr*, some have argued that D self-consciously presents itself as an *interpretation* of preceding pentateuchal law. According to this view, Moses's legal recitations in Deuteronomy are a commentary of second rank, and their speaker is the first proto-rabbinic biblical commentator: "On the other side of the Jordan, in the land of Moab, Moses undertook *to explain* (*bē'ēr*) this law, saying ..." (Deut 1:5).[1]

The claim that Deut 1:5 characterizes Deuteronomic law as commentary is an extension of the argument for D's laws as a supplement to the Covenant Code. Indeed, for some scholars, Deut 1:5 belongs to a late stratum that learned from and specifically built upon the hermeneutics of innovation exhibited already in D's revision of Covenant Code legislation. Eckart Otto has advocated strongly for this view:

> The authors of the redaction of the Pentateuch [= those responsible for Deut 1:5] also knew very well the pre-exilic literary relations between the Covenant Code and the deuteronomic book of Deuteronomy as a revision of the Covenant Code. It is characteristic for the literary history of the Pentateuch that the legal hermeneutics of the narrative of the Pentateuch corroborates the modern exegetical results in the analysis of the literary relations between the Covenant Code and the book of Deuteronomy.[2]

For Otto, then, the compositional stance of D is largely one of *continuity*. The Deuteronomic work, across its compositional history and up to and including its incorporation into the Pentateuch, evinces a consistent relationship with what preceded it. In each case, it was meant as a revisionary supplement. The history of this text is thus conceptualized as one of steady, agglutinative growth.

I have suggested in the foregoing chapters that such an explanation cannot adequately account for D's literary nature, its relationship to its predecessors, or its distinctive socioreligious vision. In its place, I have offered a different analysis—one that identifies much more significant *discontinuity* in D's compositional history, particularly as this work relates to the rest of the Pentateuch. Yet the continuity thesis should not simply be discarded. It should instead be redirected temporally, from the period of D's *composition* to that of its *reception*—and in particular its reception as part of the Pentateuch. For the vast majority of its reception history, D has been understood, like all pentateuchal material, according to its *compilation*, namely, as part of the one Torah. This is the case even though, as I have repeatedly highlighted, the experience of reading D as part of the Pentateuch is disorienting and confounding—something like wearing a pair of corrective lenses with a prescription very different from one's own. Under such conditions, broad outlines are perceptible, but the details remain obscure.

This blurred experience easily could have resulted in the Pentateuch's obsolescence, with an incomprehensible text being discarded. Yet interpreters were not easily frustrated. They instead reacted with alacrity to the lack of cohesion in both Deuteronomy and the broader Pentateuch. Indeed, the early reception of the Pentateuch is remarkable precisely for its considerable creativity and dynamism, and much of this vitality is in direct response to the Pentateuch's recontextualization of the literary works of which it is composed.

As discussed in the Introduction, early interpretive efforts focused on constructing a unity from the Pentateuch's disparate parts. Yet as I explore below, the type of unity that early interpreters pursued actually differed from that created by the pentateuchal compiler's work. If the compiler was successful in achieving the *idea* of unity through story arrangement—a single, chronologically ordered plotline—early interpreters of the Pentateuch accepted this premise but substituted its substance. That is, in place of the unity of a sequentially ordered storyline, early interpreters preferred a *thematic* unity. Pursuit of this thematic unity is what informed their primary hermeneutical strategy, namely, *harmonization*. The implicit questions posed time and again by early interpreters were, How can this text be understood together with that one? How can each be part of a coherent whole?[3] Such harmonistic reading practice would become a hallmark of the *scriptural* reception of biblical texts; in view of the examples below, it is even possible to find the origins of scriptural reading in the early interpretation and deployment of the Pentateuch.

Yet it should also be observed that the reception history of D does not begin only after it was incorporated into the Pentateuch. Preserved instances of engagement with D material also exist from that time when D was still an independent work, namely, while it was materially situated as a separate composition and not yet part of the Deuteronomy scroll. In what follows, I consider such examples from the prophetic text of Jeremiah and from the Holiness (H) stratum of pentateuchal Priestly literature. I then turn to instances of D's reception in the late biblical texts of Ezra–Nehemiah and Chronicles, and then in two Qumran works, the Temple Scroll and 4QMMT ("Some Torah Rulings"). Unlike the Jeremiah and H examples, each of the latter texts engaged Deuteronomic content only once D was situated as part of the pentateuchal Deuteronomy scroll.

Comparing the reception of Deuteronomic material at these two stages of its development—before its inclusion in the compiled Pentateuch and after it—reveals a significant difference in what parts of D were influential and how they were used. Before pentateuchal compilation, both D's distinctive historiographic claims and its legal ones were loci of attention, interpretation, and revision. Yet they were not subject to harmonistic attempts. Thus, for example, Jeremiah could engage the D storyline alone, leaving aside (to the consternation of many previous interpreters) pentateuchal views that would (eventually) compete with D's. This is almost certainly because Jeremiah's authors knew an independent D work. Likewise, in their engagement with Deuteronomic legislation, H's authors offered determined legal perspectives that, while drawing on D's laws, were at significant odds with them. Moreover, H's interactions do not exhibit the irenic qualities of later harmonistic interpretive attempts, even when its laws take over elements of their forebears. As is the case in Jeremiah, the H authors seem to have known an independent D work and intended their work to stand apart from it.

After the creation of the Pentateuch, by contrast, when interpreters understood this text to be a single whole, they engaged mostly or even only with D's legislation and left aside its story details. When they did address D's distinctive story content, they usually incorporated it into the accounts of the same events that they knew already from Exodus and Numbers, using the latter as a controlling framework. This change, I would suggest, aligns with the thematic impulse identified already: what counted for early interpreters were the thematic similarities, legal and narrative, that could be identified across the Pentateuch and even within its single scrolls, not conflicting narrative details or the possibility of alternative stories.

To be sure, D's interpretive history is much longer and more varied than the texts considered in this chapter. I have chosen these examples because, situated on both sides of the Pentateuch's compilation, they highlight well the impact of D's inclusion in the Pentateuch. They also help to explain the origins of the scriptural reading practices discussed in the Introduction and the role that Deuteronomy played in their development.

Reception of an Independent D Work

Jeremiah 7:22–23

Scholars have long observed in Jeremiah extensive interaction with Deuteronomic material and have hypothesized on its basis detailed reconstructions of the connections between these texts.[4] Attempts to clarify the nature of these ties are complicated by the compositional histories of both Deuteronomy and Jeremiah. This is especially the case for Jeremiah, where not only multiple strata can be identified, but the delineation of these strata is bound up with the scroll's thorny textual history. Further complicating the analysis is the fact that D's influence appears to span originally distinct Jeremian strata. Accordingly, some scholars have argued that these strata reflect multiple, independent engagements with D. It is even possible to observe different conceptualizations of the Deuteronomic patrimony in the Jeremian strata—alternatively, as a prestigious source or as an authoritative guide.[5]

The reuse of Deuteronomic materials in Jeremiah is especially significant because this prophetic scroll is one of a relatively small number of extant texts that exhibit evidence of interaction with D before its inclusion in the Pentateuch. Jeremiah also preserves one of the only precompilational engagements with D's distinctive story of Israel's wilderness experience. As Nathan Mastnjak has observed, Jer 7:22–23 contains a subtle yet significant reorientation of Deut 5:33. In this revision, the Jeremian author sought to create space for new prophetic revelation through a revisionary reuse of D's Horeb revelation account:[6]

Deut 5:33
Walk fully in the way that Yahweh, your god, <u>has commanded</u> you in order that you might live and that it might go well for you and that you might lengthen your days in the land you will possess.

Jer 7:22–23
[22]For I did not speak with your fathers—nor did I command them when I brought them out of Egypt—concerning rules for burnt offering or well-being sacrifice. [23]It was instead this admonishment with which I commanded them: "Obey me, and I will be your god, and you shall be my people. Walk fully in the way that <u>I will command</u> you in order that it might go well for you."

Mastnjak has highlighted the important temporal difference expressed by the corresponding verbs of Yahweh's commanding (underlined above) in these two texts, a difference that also has implications for the mediation of these divine communications. According to Deut 5:33, Yahweh's directives were given *in the past,* that is, to Moses at Horeb. In Jer 7:23, by contrast, these directives would be given *in the future,* that is, after the Horeb revelation. As vv. 25–26 make clear, the Jeremian text envisions these divine commands as having been delivered by a number of Yahwistic prophets who followed after Moses.[7] Situated as part of Moses's Moab speech, Deut 5:33 articulates the Deuteronomic story's central claim concerning Yahweh's laws: all of the directives that the Israelites were to obey in the land were revealed to Moses already at Horeb. Particularly problematic for Jeremiah was the fact that included among those laws were warnings against prophetic innovations that might challenge Deuteronomic legislation (Deut 13:2–6, 18:15–22).

In relation to the story of the Horeb revelation, the reformulation of Deut 5:33 in Jer 7:23 was thus crucial for legitimating the prophecy of Jeremiah. Through a simple change in verbal morphology, the Jeremian authors reshaped Yahweh's Horeb revelation so that it would authorize future divine commands. Jeremian prophetic messages were thereby grounded in the Horeb revelation itself, and Jeremiah was made into a prophet on par with Moses. As Mastnjak has observed, the deft rewording of Deut 5:33 strongly suggests that the Jeremian authors understood the challenge that D's perspective posed to their project and introduced their alteration precisely to mitigate this challenge.[8]

To be sure, this change meant the diminution of D's legislative perspective, which D's account presents as decisive (Deut 4:2, 13:1). Yet within the story world into which Jer 7:23 inserted itself, the Jeremian claim to authority was also cleverly made to rest upon the Horeb revelation itself. It is perhaps significant, then, that Jer 7:23 does not name Moses explicitly.[9] This verse, voiced by Yahweh, instead refers only to what the deity spoke, not to the one who mediated that message. Within its etiology, D consistently aggrandizes Moses as a strategy of exclusivity. By redirecting focus to the divine message, the Jeremiah text was able to carve out license in Israel's past for subsequent prophecy, including its own message.

As noted already, a striking feature of this instance of Jeremian revision is its narrow focus on D's account of the Horeb lawgiving, to the exclusion of other pentateuchal perspectives. This is hinted at already in the direct engagement of Deut 5:33 in Jer 7:23. Yet it is even clearer in Jer 7:22, where Yahweh claims not to have given the Israelites commands concerning sacrifices when he delivered them from Egypt. This statement has confounded many interpreters,[10] for it stands in contrast with pentateuchal presentations of wilderness lawgiving. According to both E and P, the Israelites received detailed instructions concerning sacrifice while they were in the desert (E: Exod 20:24, 23:18; P: Lev 1–7, etc.). Yet Moshe Weinfeld observed that Jer 7:22 can be readily understood in relation to D's distinctive account of the Decalogue revelation.[11] As detailed in Chapter 2, according to D, Yahweh spoke only the Decalogue to the Israelites in the wilderness (Deut 5:22); the rest of D's laws Moses received in private and kept to himself until the end of their desert trek. Jeremiah 7:22 observes precisely this distinction: what Yahweh himself "spoke" and "commanded them"— the Decalogue—did not include any details concerning burnt offerings or other sacrifices. The topic of sacrifice appears only in the laws that Yahweh delivered to Moses alone (e.g., Deut 12 and 16), that is, in that legislation which the Israelites *did not hear* in the wilderness.[12] That Jer 7:22 is immediately followed by the explicit citation in v. 23 of Deut 5:33 confirms its reference to the Deuteronomic Decalogue, for D's Decalogue account immediately precedes Deut 5:33.

In their denigration of the temple cult, then, the Jeremian authors paid close attention to and capitalized on D's unique depiction of Israel's receipt of Yahweh's laws and in particular its temporal element. They could readily do so because they employed an independent D work. Yet it should also be observed that even as these authors built on D's distinctive, two-covenant story, they also quickly departed from that story in service of their own theological ends. Specifically, the conceptualization of the Decalogue in Jer 7:22 departs from D's view; this Jeremian verse also evinces a different judgment of the Israelites' wilderness experience than does D. As I argued in Chapter 2, D presents the Decalogue as a trainer law that serves the long process of Israel's catechesis. Jeremiah 7:22, by contrast, understands the Decalogue as a chief or ideal set of laws. A similar distinction can be drawn between each work's presentation of the wilderness era more generally. In D, this period is a time of preparation that is not romanticized; for its part, Jer 7:22 seems to align with Jer 2:2, which presents the wilderness period as an ideal.

In light of the distinction in Jer 7:22 between the Decalogue and the rest of the laws relayed to the Israelites by Moses in Moab, it is also possible to observe in Jer 7:23 another revision of D. Verse 23 depicts the divine message from Deut 5:33 as part of *Yahweh's* direct speech to the Israelites in the desert. Yet in D, Deut 5:33 is unambiguously part of *Moses's* Moab speech and not a rehearsal of any divine speech that Israel heard at Horeb. The third-person reference to the deity in Deut 5:33 ("all the way that *Yahweh* your god . . .") stands in contrast to the divine first-person speech that is quoted just two verses before. Recounting the Horeb event in Deut 5:31, Moses recalls Yahweh's words: "As for you, stand here with me so that I may deliver to you all of the commandment and the statutes and the judgments that you should teach them and that they should do in the land that I am giving them to possess."

It appears, then, that even as Jer 7:22 marks the distinction between those parts of D that rehearse what the Israelites heard directly from Yahweh in the wilderness and those parts that are Moses's speech in the Moabite plains, Jer 7:23 disregards this distinction. While it cannot be ruled out that this change represents an inattentive reading of D by the Jeremiah authors,[13] it seems more likely that it was intentional on their part. As discussed above, their revisionary redeployment of Deut 5:33 in Jer 7:23 inscribes (the likes of) Jeremiah into D's etiology, making it possible to read the Jeremiah scroll in concert with D's Mosaic speeches. Thus, even as Jeremiah here does not harmonize competing pentateuchal traditions, it does harmonize D in a different way, namely, with its own historical and theological aims. That Deut 5:33 appears in such close proximity to D's depiction of divine speech at Horeb probably helped facilitate this adjustment.

The Holiness Legislation

The pentateuchal Priestly source comprises two major compositional elements: a base layer (P) that provides its basic narrative structure and storyline, including an extensive set of legal speeches, and a supplemental layer (H) that at turns extends, challenges, and revises P's details.[14] H informed its supplementation and revision of P by drawing upon materials from E and D, materials that it also subjected to revision. A number of scholars have observed this interpretive revision in H and described it in detail.[15]

A particularly illuminating example of H's appropriation and recasting of D material is found in its tithe law in Num 18:20–32.[16] This is because, in this instance, H had no E content that it could use, for E did not include a tithe law. Likewise, P contained no tithe legislation for H to revise or augment. In the case of the tithe, then, D's law was an exclusive legislative resource.

Several important thematic correspondences between Num 18:20–32 and the Deuteronomic tithe law (Deut 14:22–29) confirm the direct literary tie between them.[17] Beyond their shared vision of a compulsory tithe for all Israelite laypeople and their common concern for the proper distribution and consumption of the tithe, Deut 14 and Num 18 both explicitly link the tithe with the Levites. Indeed, according to each tithe law, the Levites are to share in every tithe. Significant too is the analogous socioeconomic status of the Levites in the two legal corpora: in each case, the Levites occupy a place between priests and laypeople and are afforded no ancestral heritage like other Israelites (Deut 18:1, Num 18:24).

The holiness of the tithe is also at issue for both D and H. In Num 18, the Levites must desanctify the tithes they collect, which are holy "contributions" (těrûmôt), by tendering "a tithe from the tithe" to the priests (Num 18:25–32). This desanctification is described with two analogies: the "tithe from the tithe" to the priests is considered the Levites' "contribution," like that of the Israelite laity (Num 18:27). The remainder of the tithe retained by the Levites is accounted common agricultural yield like the produce retained by the Israelites after they surrender their tithe (Num 18:30). Analogous in D is the description of the third-year tithe as holy and the special procedures required for its treatment (Deut 26:12–15).

The significance of these thematic ties is bolstered by several key lexical and syntactic parallels. For example, both the D and H laws attest a tripartite agricultural list of grain, wine, and oil (Deut 14:23, Num 18:12). This list of foodstuffs is stereotypical of D, where it appears six times (7:13, 11:14, 12:17, 14:23, 18:4, 28:51)—more than in any other biblical work—and both in D's laws on tithes and in its laws on Levitical priestly service. By contrast, Num 18:12 contains the only instance of this agricultural list in all of pentateuchal Priestly literature; the list is also absent from the other pentateuchal sources.

But even more significant is the sequence of oil-wine-grain in Num 18:12. Of the twenty times these three agricultural products appear together in biblical texts, nineteen of them follow the sequence grain-wine-oil. H reversed this sequence, distinguishing its use of the tripartite list as an inverted citation of D.

A second incisive lexical parallel concerns the analogous use of the word pair "portion and inheritance" (*ḥēleq wĕnaḥălâ*) in Deut 14:27, 29; 18:1; and Num 18:20, as well as the repetition of *naḥălâ* alone in Num 18:21, 23, 24, 26. As a word pair, "portion and inheritance" appears only in this single instance in all of pentateuchal Priestly literature. By contrast, "portion and inheritance" appears six times in D (Deut 10:9; 12:12; 14:27, 29; 18:1; 32:9).

The corresponding use of "portion and inheritance" in D and Num 18:20 is especially important for understanding H's reaction to D's view of Levitical service and its reconceptualization of the tithe. The H author was careful to apply the "portion and inheritance" locution only to Aaron and the priests and not to the Levites, for whom only an "inheritance" is countenanced. By contrast, D applies the word pair "portion and inheritance" to the Levites generally. Normally understood as a hendiadys, Deut 18:1 reveals that the constituent parts of this word pair retain special nuance:

> The Levitical priests—all the tribe of Levi—shall have no <u>portion</u> or <u>inheritance</u> with Israel. They shall eat <u>the food offerings of Yahweh</u>, namely, <u>his inheritance</u>.

While "portion and inheritance" refers to land inheritance in the first half of the verse, its meaning is transformed in the second half. "Portion" takes on the specialized meaning *sacrificial portion,* evidenced by the explicit parallelism between "portion" and "the food offerings of Yahweh," and this meaning then governs the ensuing reference to "his inheritance."

The only pentateuchal Priestly attestation of "portion" outside of Num 18:20 is found in Lev 6:10 (P), which describes the priestly share of the most holy *minḥâ* sacrifice as "their (i.e., the priests') portion" (*ḥelqām*). Recognizing that both its Priestly predecessor and D specifically associated the term *ḥēleq* with sacrificial portions, the H author carefully assigned these sacrificial portions to the priests only and not to the Levites. H in turn employed the full word pair "portion and inheritance" in the context of priestly benefits (Num 18:20) but scrupulously avoided it in descriptions of Levitical perquisites, referring only to their "inheritance" (*naḥălâ*), a term that on its own never carries the connotation of sacrificial portion in pentateuchal Priestly literature or in D. Through such careful word choice, the H legislator directly challenged D's conception of the Levites and their due.

The example of H's tithe accords well with its larger engagement with D materials. In all such cases, H frames its laws not as updates, revisions, or addenda; in fact, H never acknowledges the existence of D's laws or its larger narrative at all. Had it done so—for example, through cross-references, explicit citation, and the like—it would be clear that H intended its work to stand alongside D. Yet H takes pains to frame its presentation in exclusivist terms, labeling its instructions as "a perpetual statute" or, in its expanded formulation, "a perpetual statute for your generations in all your habitations." It likewise makes no accommodation to D's distinctive storyline. In this way, H presents its laws as irrevocable and universally applicable among the Israelites and integrates them only into the P story world. In both its content and framing, then, H stands as a challenge to D and shows no signs of being written as a supplement to that work. Once it had borrowed its content, H could discard D, as it could its other non-Priestly source materials.[18]

Early Reception of the Deuteronomy Scroll

Chronicles

The Chronicler's engagement with pentateuchal texts is remarkable for both its harmonistic impulse and its determined chronological assertion. Insisting upon the unity of pentateuchal legislation, the Chronicler pursued a particular harmonizing procedure with respect to topically related laws. In so doing, the Chronicler was able to assert the strongest standard of adherence to pentateuchal legislation in the face of its inconsistencies. This task was important to the Chronicler because he situated pentateuchal law straightforwardly in Israel's history. Guided by the chronologically arranged plotline in both the Pentateuch and the Former Prophets, the Chronicler could not abide the apparent disregard for the Pentateuch's laws in the accounts of Israel's past that he found in Samuel and Kings—particularly in the cases of divinely favored Judean kings. If these kings were devout Yahwists, they must have observed the divine laws that were revealed already centuries before them. And in the case of royal scofflaws, they too should be judged in accordance with the pentateuchal legislation to which they were subject. The Chronicler thus set about to integrate a particular vision of pentateuchal law into the monarchic pasts of Israel and Judah.[19]

In some instances, the Chronicler's enactment of pentateuchal law is straightforwardly harmonistic. This is the case in his account of Josiah's Passover observance (2 Chr 35:1–19; cf. 2 Kgs 23:21–23),[20] where the Chronicler famously attempted to blend the pentateuchal rules for preparing the Passover sacrifice by piecing together the disparate rules in Deut 16:7a and Exod 12:9.[21] The corresponding elements in the source and revisionary texts are marked:

> Deut 16:7a
> You shall *boil* (*bšl*)[22] it and eat it in the place that Yahweh, your god, will choose.

> Exod 12:9
> Do not eat any of it raw or *boiled* (*bšl*) in water but rather <u>fire</u>-roasted (*Ṣĕlî ʾēš*), its head along with its legs and innards.

> 2 Chr 35:13a
> They *boiled* (*bšl*) the Passover sacrifice in <u>fire</u> (*bāʾēš*) according to the rule.

Beyond using specific language from each of these pentateuchal laws in order to combine them,[23] the Chronicler buttressed his amalgamation by claiming that the Passover celebration that Josiah initiated was done *according to the rule* (*kammišpāṭ*). Both the Chronicler and other biblical authors employed this locution to signal fastidious compliance with a single or consistent pentateuchal prescription (e.g., Neh 8:18, 1 Chr 15:13, 2 Chr 4:20). In 2 Chr 35:13a, however, "according to the rule" refers not to a single law but to two separate, conflicting laws. In this case, by virtue of the singularity of *kammišpāṭ* (*according to the* [*one*] *rule*), the Chronicler underscored his intent in reusing language from both Exod 12 and Deut 16: he sought to combine the conflicting pentateuchal instructions into a single rule.

Incidentally, the Chronicler likely learned the phrase "according to the rule," as he did the conflicting Passover rules, from his pentateuchal patrimony. This phrase appears several times in the Pentateuch, including in formulations precisely equivalent to those in Chronicles (e.g., Lev 5:10, 9:16; Num 15:24; 29:18, 21, 24, 27, 30, 37). However, it does not appear at all in D.[24] The use of this phrase in relation to Deuteronomic legislation is thus a further instance of harmonization in Chronicles.

This example, as well as the various others that can be adduced in Chronicles, suggests that the Chronicler overlooked the delimitation or autonomy of its literary forebears in favor of a single account that, abstracted on their basis, was construed as the real past. In the Chronicler's case, this is most clearly on display in his attempt to marry the Pentateuch and the Former Prophets to create a singular history of Yahweh's people, Israel. For the Chronicler, the discourse of his source texts (or, more precisely, the combination created from them) was not fictive; it was instead real, describing the real world of his ancestors and offering commands that were understood to apply to them. For this reason, when these texts' contents were historically unconvincing because of their theological implausibility, or when their characters acted in ways that suggested they were unaware of or inattentive to legal requirements, the Chronicler introduced changes. His goal was to apprehend the real world accurately, and treating his sources as literature was not conducive to this goal.[25]

Nehemiah 9:6–37

In Chapter 2, I argued at length that D depicts the Israelite generation addressed by Moses in the plains of Moab as the same generation that left Egypt forty years before. It is useful to return to this aspect of D's story because of the way that its features appear in an early example of the reception of the Deuteronomy scroll, Nehemiah 9. Specifically, the Levitical prayer in this chapter references Israel's preservation in the wilderness; moreover, it is suffused with Deuteronomic language.[26] Yet it includes nothing of D's distinctive view of the Exodus generation's perdurance across the wilderness era.[27]

Owing to its particular phrasing, a striking example of this omission appears in Neh 9:21. This verse states: "You provided for them for forty years in the wilderness. They did not lack. Their garments did not wear out, and their feet did not swell." The dependence of this verse upon Deuteronomic material has long been recognized.[28] Deuteronomy 2:7, 8:4, and 29:4 use nearly identical language in their references to provision during the forty years, the absence of want among the Israelites during this time, and the preservation of their clothing and health. Moreover, no other accounts of Israel's wilderness journey include these details.[29]

Yet even as Neh 9:21 redeploys D's description of Israel's miraculous preservation, this verse appears alongside explicit references to Israelite generation change. According to Neh 9:23–24:

²³You multiplied *their children* like the stars of the heavens, and you brought *them* (i.e., the Exodus generation's children) to the land *that you had commanded their fathers to enter to possess.* ²⁴*The children* came and took possession of the land. You subdued before them the land's inhabitants, the Canaanites. You gave them into their hand, their kingdoms and peoples, to do with them as they pleased.

Given its variance with D on the issue of generation change, it is all the more remarkable that the reference in v. 23 to the "stars of the heavens" also draws upon Deuteronomic texts (Deut 1:10, 10:22). The combination of the fathers, entry into the land, and possession of the land appears primarily in D (Deut 1:8, 4:1, 6:18, 8:1, 9:5, 10:11, 30:5; Josh 18:3; Jer 30:3). In one instance, Deut 1:8, this combination immediately precedes the stars motif.

The specific designation of which Israelites possessed the land in Neh 9:23–24 also suggests that v. 22 has the *second* wilderness generation in view: "You gave them kingdoms and peoples and apportioned them as shares. Thus they inherited the land of Sihon, the land of the king of Heshbon, and the land of Og, king of Bashan." This conclusion, in turn, has implications for understanding which characters are referenced in v. 21. The anaphoric reference to v. 21 in v. 22 ("you gave *them* . . . you apportioned *them* . . . *they* inherited") suggests that the authors of Neh 9 understood the miraculous preservation of Israel in the wilderness to be the preservation of the Exodus generation's children, not the Exodus generation itself. There is good pentateuchal precedent for this view, of course, in the J and P spies accounts (Num 13–14). Not surprising, then, is the reference to the spies incident among the specific acts of wilderness rebellion that Neh 9 cites. Alongside the allusion in v. 18 to the golden calf, v. 17 cites the spies incident directly: "They set a leader over them to return them to their enslavement in Egypt." This line draws from Num 14:4: "Let us appoint a leader and return to Egypt!" Likewise, the continuation of v. 17—"But you are a forgiving god, gracious and loving, slow to anger and abundantly merciful; thus you did not abandon them"—while likely drawing from more than one text, is prompted by another line in the spies episode, Num 14:18.³⁰ Thus, even though it does not mention it directly, the prayer assumes the outcome of the spies incident from Num 13–14 as it constructs its larger account of Israel's wilderness experience.

What complicates this analysis is the possessive pronoun in v. 23a: "*their* children." Its antecedent must be the Israelites described in vv. 21–22, in which case, vv. 21–22 should be understood as stating that it was the

Exodus generation that was preserved throughout the wilderness period and that dispossessed Sihon and Og.[31] In this case, then, it appears that the D storyline did have some impact upon the author(s) of Neh 9:5–36: in Deut 2:24–35 and 3:1–11, Moses recalls the defeat of Sihon and Og by the Exodus generation. Yet as the references in Neh 9:23 to the second generation and their possession of the land make clear, this impact was fleeting and resulted in an inconsistent combination of pentateuchal wilderness traditions—one that mimics the Pentateuch's own inconsistency.

The negligible impact of D's distinctive content can likewise be observed elsewhere in Neh 9. In the recollection of Neh 9:13–14, when the Israelites received the laws in the wilderness, they did not, as D claims, hear only the Decalogue directly from Yahweh and no other laws until they reached the plains of Moab. Instead, Israel received a larger set of commands—and from Moses, not only from Yahweh directly:

> [13]You came down upon Mt. Sinai and spoke with them from heaven; you gave them upright laws and true teachings, good statutes and commandments. [14]You made your holy Sabbath known to them, and commandments, statutes, and teaching you commanded them through Moses, your servant.

Though v. 13a likely has the Decalogue in view (as suggested by "with them"; cf. Exod 20:19, 22),[32] it might be argued that vv. 13b–14 do not *require* that Moses proclaimed the laws revealed to him while Israel was still in the wilderness. Verse 14 could instead accord with D's story of Mosaic legal proclamation in the plains of Moab. Yet the detailed reuse of the lawgiving narrative from Exod 19–24 in vv. 13–14 and the larger literary context surrounding these verses recommend that the author of Neh 9 did understand Moses's recitation of laws as having occurred in the wilderness. Specifically, vv. 13–14 draw directly from Exod 19:18, 20; 20:19, 22; 21:1; and perhaps 24:12. Moreover, even though the sequence of the lawgiving, manna, and water-from-the-rock events varies in Neh 9:13–15 when compared with the pentateuchal sequence of these events,[33] Neh 9:11–21 all describe wilderness events. It thus appears that, notwithstanding the integral tie in D between wilderness preservation and delayed legal proclamation, Neh 9 untethered these traditions from each other, denying Moses's delayed legal proclamation (v. 14) while affirming wilderness preservation (v. 21).

Given the apparent focus of v. 13a upon the Decalogue proper, there is another sense in which one might argue for D's influence. Like other Persian and Hellenistic era texts, this verse understands the Decalogue according to

D's view, which is to say, as law. It is not a demonstration of Mosaic prophecy, as E presents it. Yet it is unlikely that the authors of Neh 9 perceived themselves as preferring one view of *what the Decalogue was* over another. Guided by the compiled pentateuchal story (where the presentation of the Decalogue as prophetic authentication is decidedly muted) as well as the Decalogue's specific contents, these early interpreters probably never considered that the Exodus Decalogue could be anything but legislation.

The reuse of Deuteronomic material in v. 15b adds texture to this analysis. This line references Yahweh's command to the Exodus generation to take possession of the land that he had promised them and for which he had preserved them. The language it employs is strongly Deuteronomic: its combination of the verbs *bwʾ*, *yrš*, and *ntn* is found in the Pentateuch only in D texts (Deut 1:8, 39; 4:1, 38; 10:11; 11:29, 31; 17:14; 26:1). Yet because Neh 9 endorses generation change, its reuse of language that is directed in D toward an Exodus generation that does not die off in the wilderness creates a discrepancy in the prayer's larger historical retrospective. It appears, however, that in this case the Nehemian author engaged in further harmonization. In addition to drawing on D's language, v. 15b reuses material from Exod 6:8. Specifically, its reference to "the land that you (Yahweh) raised your hand to give to" the Israelites uses language that appears in the Pentateuch only in Exod 6:8 (cf. Num 14:30). In this case, then, the authors of Neh 9 again combined elements from D with language and ideas found elsewhere in the Pentateuch and, in the process, prioritized the non-D story.

The limited impact of D's distinctive story details in Neh 9 is likely due to its authors' interaction with the Pentateuch in its compiled state and ignorance of an independent D work.[34] These authors' conceptualization and use of Deuteronomic material thus assume the pentateuchal framework in which they found it. This is not necessarily to claim that the late additions that refer to generation change in Deut 1:35, 39 and 2:14–16 were already part of the Deuteronomy text used in the composition of Neh 9. (As discussed in Chapter 2, the text-critical data suggest that those additions probably came later.)[35] It is instead to recognize that a major and even controlling component of the pentateuchal framework is its chronologically sequenced storyline. In light of this arrangement, D rarely offers a first or independent narration. It is instead relegated to the position of *renarrating* events already known from Exodus and Numbers. Put differently, in its pentateuchal situation, D's presentation has regularly been experienced by readers as *belated*.[36] As such, it is easily preempted by the alternative presentations of J, E, and P—as is the case in Neh 9.

It is notable, too, that elements in Neh 9 that were drawn from Deuteronomy, such as the miraculous preservation of the Israelites in the wilderness, were easily imagined in service of different ends than they serve in D. Whether the Exodus generation survived the desert trek or only their children did, Yahweh could be credited with generously protecting and provisioning them across their forty-year journey. Moreover, none of the specific claims about the deity's care is exclusive to the Exodus generation, even in D. Given their pentateuchal perspective, then, it is possible and even likely that the authors of Neh 9 were unaware that D's alternative presentation of the Israelites' wilderness experience ever existed. Their creative reorientation of D's story was instead inadvertent, akin to that of subsequent interpreters—including even many in the modern period who endorse compositional analysis of the Pentateuch—who have overlooked D's distinctive storyline. The resulting account in Neh 9 is a classic instance of harmonistic interpretation.

The Temple Scroll

The Temple Scroll from Qumran contains an extensive revision of Deuteronomic laws (the "Deuteronomic Paraphrase") that, in many instances, seeks to harmonize D's distinctive perspectives with those found elsewhere in the Pentateuch.[37] One example that highlights the sophistication of this revision is this text's treatment of the status of Levites in relation to priests and the priesthood.[38] According to Deut 18:1–8, every Levite male was qualified to serve as a priest. Deut 18:6–7 state:

> [6]If a Levite should come from one of your towns anywhere in Israel, where he resides, coming of his own desire to the place that Yahweh will choose, [7]*he may serve the name of Yahweh his god like all of his brothers, the Levites, the ones presiding there before Yahweh.*

The Priestly text, Num 18, however, asserts that only the family of Aaron should have access to the priesthood. Other Levites are to serve as second-rank cultic functionaries, subordinate to the Aaronid priests. Num 18:1–2 state:

> [1]Yahweh said to Aaron, "You and your sons and the house of your father with you shall bear responsibility for the sanctuary; you and your sons with

you shall bear responsibility for your priesthood. [2]And your brethren, the tribe of Levi, the tribe of your father, you shall bring near with you *so that they may join with you and serve you.* But it is you and your sons with you who will be before the tent of the ʿēdût.

The Temple Scroll attempts to reconcile the disagreement between these texts by subtly rewriting Deut 18:6–7. Specifically, it reorders the words in v. 7 so that the Levites are portrayed not as *serving as priests* but rather *serving the priests,* as they do in Num 18. Temple Scroll (11Q19) 60:12–14 state:

> [12]Now if a Levite from one of your towns in all of Israel who [13]is sojourning there comes of his own desire to the place where I will choose to place [14]my name, *he, like all of his brothers, the Levites, shall serve the ones presiding there before me.*

In Deut 18:7, "the ones presiding there"—those officiating as priests—are Levites. They are further identified as the Levite's kinspeople, and they serve the name of Yahweh. Yet in 11Q19 60:14, "the ones presiding there"—the priests—are distinguished from the Levites, and the Levites are to serve them, the priests, rather than Yahweh.

By means of a creative syntactic rearrangement of Deut 18:7, placing the verb "they shall serve" between "the Levites" and "the ones presiding there," the Temple Scroll author redefined both the function and referent of "the ones presiding." What was an attributive adjective modifying "the Levites" in Deut 18:7 became a substantive to serve as the object of the verb "to serve." This alteration brought the line into accord with Num 18:2: "They may serve you (= the priests)."[39] With minimal intervention, then, the Temple Scroll author harmonized Deut 18 and Num 18 and, in so doing, championed the view of the latter over that of the former: the (non-Aaronid) Levites were made subordinate to the Aaronid priests.

A second example from the Temple Scroll highlights the manner in which its authors also sought a legal consistency within and among thematically related instructions in Deuteronomy.[40] Of course, from those authors' perspective, harmonizing instructions within the Deuteronomy scroll was no different from harmonizing laws found in different Pentateuch scrolls. This is because, as noted already, early Jewish interpreters perceived the Pentateuch as a single work. They did not recognize its combination of originally independent works; neither did the Pentateuch's division into multiple volumes affect its interpretation.[41]

11Q19 51:11–18 is an adaptation and expansion of the law concerning judges in Deut 16:18–20:

Deut 16:18–20 (MT)
[18]Judges and officials you shall appoint for yourself in all of your towns that Yahweh, your god, is giving you for your tribes. They shall judge the people with righteous judgment. [19]Do not pervert justice. Do not show favoritism, and do not take a bribe, for the bribe blinds the eyes of the wise and subverts the words of the righteous. [20]Rightness, rightness you shall pursue in order that you may live and possess the land that Yahweh, your god, is giving you.

11Q19 51:11–18
[11]Judges and officials you shall appoint for yourselves in all of your towns, and they shall judge the people [12]with righteous judgment. They shall not show partiality in judgment: they shall not take a bribe; [13]nor shall they subvert justice. For the bribe subverts justice, undermines righteous rulings, blinds [14]the eyes of the wise, produces great guilt, and thereby pollutes the temple with the transgression [15]of sin. Rightness, rightness shall you pursue, that you may live—that you may enter and possess [16]the land that I am giving you to possess for all time. Now the man [17]who does take a bribe and thereby subverts righteous justice shall be put to death. You shall not be afraid [18]to put him to death.

The Temple Scroll in this case reproduces nearly all of its parent text from Deuteronomy.[42] Its revisions and supplements focus on the extent of the effects of perverted justice (line 14) and the penalty for judicial misconduct (line 17). The unit also includes encouragement to enforce its rule (lines 17–18).

Significant for the present discussion is this Temple Scroll unit's combination of disparate Deuteronomic rules concerning the judiciary. This combination can be observed, paradoxically, in the text's introduction of the death penalty—a feature that is not present in any instructions concerning the judiciary in D but is arguably missing from Deut 16:18–20. That is, the question could easily be posed in response to the Deut 16 text, What is the punishment for a judge who accepts a bribe and thereby corrupts justice? The Deuteronomic law is silent on this question.

In his editio princeps of the Temple Scroll, Yigael Yadin treated this unit at length and argued that the scroll's association of the judges unit of Deut 16:18–20 with the judges unit of Deut 1:9–18 facilitated its introduction of the death penalty.[43] These two Deuteronomic texts, in addition to sharing the general topic of the judiciary, exhibit a significant amount of shared language. Yet one feature that they do not share is the line "Do not be afraid" (*l' tgwrw*), which appears in 11Q19 51:17. The Temple Scroll authors introduced this line in their Deut 16:18–20 base text, Yadin argued, on the basis of a third text, Deut 1:17:

> Do not show favoritism in judgment. You shall hear small and great alike. <u>Have no fear</u> (*l' tgwrw*) before a person, for justice belongs to God. But the matter that is too difficult for you you shall bring to me (Moses), and I will hear it.

In order to answer the question of what punishment befits judicial misconduct, the Temple Scroll authors associated the "do not fear" command in Deut 1:17 with the similar command in Deut 18:22:

> If the prophet speaks in the name of Yahweh and the word is not correct or does not come true, that is the word that Yahweh did not speak. The prophet spoke it presumptuously. <u>You need have no fear</u> (*l' tgwr*) of it.

This association was significant because the prophecy law also includes a stated penalty for false prophecy. Deut 18:20 states:

> But the prophet who presumes to speak a word in my name that I did not command him to speak or who speaks in the name of other gods—that prophet shall die.

Apart from Deut 1:17, Deut 18:22 is the only biblical text in which the "do not fear" (*l' tgwr[w]*) command appears. Given the otherwise loose connection between these texts, Moshe J. Bernstein and Shlomo Koyfman have suggested that association of these "do not fear" clauses is an early example of the later rabbinic hermeneutical practice of *gezera shawa*—interpretation by analogy on the basis of a linguistic similarity between two texts.[44]

Yet it appears that the Temple Scroll's authors drew more than the "do not fear" command from Deut 1:17. The rationale clause that immediately follows this command in Deut 1:17 provides an additional, thematic basis for associating the judiciary with the institution of prophecy. According to Deut 1:17, judges should not stand in fear of any litigant "because justice belongs to God." In other words, in their judicial decisions, D understood judges to be *mediating divine rulings*. Their work was thus very much akin to prophecy. The Temple Scroll authors concluded that perversion of divine mediation, whether prophetic or judicial, should merit the same penalty.[45]

Some scholars have argued that Deut 1:9–18 and 16:18–20 come from different hands and, as such, are at odds with each other.[46] Yet these two issues—compositional origin and content agreement—should be separated from each other. Regardless of whether these texts belong to the same compositional stratum, the plotline in which they are situated and the specific temporal details that attend them suggest that these two judicial appointments should be understood as complementary. The judges appointed after the departure from Horeb (Deut 1:9–18) served during the forty-year wilderness era, while the judges to be appointed according to Deut 16:18–20 were to serve "in all your towns that Yahweh, your god, is giving you," namely, after the Israelites' entry into the land. In other words, the story elements in D suggest that these are two different sets of judges. It is striking, then, that the Temple Scroll authors were so comfortable conflating the two units and, on that basis, drawing on a third text to supplement them further. In so doing, they paid little attention to the temporal distinctions (i.e., the story elements) that attend the pentateuchal instructions they rewrote and instead focused narrowly on the topical relations among these texts. In this way, their conflationary revisions of 11Q19 51:11–18 are quite similar to those already observed from 60:12–14.

4QMMT

A final, brief example can be observed in the Qumran text 4QMMT (4Q394–99), which is a compendium of halakhic rulings that interpret, conflate, and revise pentateuchal texts. Among this text's rulings is a treatment of the laws regarding the place of sacrifice in Lev 17 and Deut 12.[47] As discussed in Chapter 2, D relates Yahweh's insistence upon a single sacrificial site. Recall Deut 12:13–14 (cf. vv. 5, 11, 18, 21, 26):

> [13]Be careful lest you offer up your burnt offerings in any place that you see fit. [14]Rather, in the place that Yahweh will choose in one of your tribes— there you shall offer up your burnt offerings, and there you shall do all that I command you.

In Lev 17:3–4 and 8–9, Yahweh similarly requires sacrificial worship only at the single Israelite sanctuary:

> [3]Anyone from the House of Israel who slaughters an ox or a sheep or a goat in the camp or who slaughters (one of these animals) outside the camp [4]and does not bring it to the entrance of the Tent of Meeting to offer it as an

offering to Yahweh before Yahweh's dwelling, blood will be accorded to that person. He has shed blood, and that man will be cut off from the midst of his people.

[8]Now to them you shall say, "Anyone from the House of Israel or from among the sojourners in their midst who offers a burnt offering or well-being offering, [9]but does not bring it to the entrance of the Tent of Meeting to present it to Yahweh, that man will be cut off from his people."

Even as they agree that there should be a single location for Israelite sacrifice, these verses understand this location differently. This is because of the disparate chronological and geographical situations that these texts imagine for Israel's sacrifice. Situating sacrificial practice in the wilderness, Lev 17 identifies its locus as the Tent of Meeting that is within the Israelite camp. Deuteronomy 12, by contrast, refers to "the place that Yahweh (your god) will choose (from among all your tribes) to set his name," a locus that it imagines within the land of Canaan. Where the texts agree is in their designation of a single site and their lack of specificity regarding its location. In Deut 12, this is because, within D's fiction, the Israelites had not entered the land and thus did not yet know its geography. In the case of Lev 17, the camp and sanctuary are presented as mobile, moving through the wilderness as Israel journeys.

Recognizing their thematic ties, the authors of 4QMMT harmonized Deut 12 and Lev 17: they identified the single sacrificial site of each text as the same location. These authors also updated and specified the geographical claims of Deut 12 and Lev 17 in light of their contemporary context. 4QMMT B 27–30 and 60–61 state:[48]

[27]. . . Concerning what is written, "If a man slaughters in the camp [28]or slaughters outside of the camp an ox or sheep or goat," for . . . in the north of the camp. [29]Now we determine that the temple is the dwelling of the Tent of Meeting and Jerusalem [30]is the camp and outside of the camp is outside of Jerusalem.

[60]Jerusalem is the holy camp: it is the place [61]that he chose from all the tribes of Israel . . .

4QMMT B 27–28 is an approximate quotation from Lev 17:3,[49] and on its basis, B 29–30 equate the (Jerusalem) temple with the Tent of Meeting and Jerusalem with the camp in which the Leviticus text situates the Tent. For the sake of completeness, 4QMMT defines "outside of the camp" as "outside of Jerusalem." For the same reason, B 29 combines the two monikers for the sanctuary that appear in Lev 17:4—"the dwelling of Yahweh" and "the Tent of Meeting"—referring to "the dwelling of the Tent of Meeting." Then, in B 60–61, 4QMMT ties this language of the camp to the description of the sacrificial site in Deut 12: Jerusalem is both "the holy camp" (= Lev 17) and "the place that he chose from all the tribes of Israel" (= Deut 12). The preceding line, B 59, makes clear that the holy camp, Jerusalem, houses "the temple."

With these harmonizations, any potential discrepancies between the views of Deut 12 and Lev 17 concerning the proper cult site were effectively set aside. At the same time, these two texts were made directly relevant to the interpreter's contemporary context. It should be observed, moreover, that 4QMMT's authors read Deut 12 and Lev 17 as allegorical (Tent of Meeting = temple; camp = Jerusalem = "place" [*māqôm*]), and their assessment of the identity of the sanctuary and its site is consistent with that of many modern scholars who read these texts as allegories. The difference is that 4QMMT's authors were not attempting to reconstruct these texts' compositional contexts; they instead identified and defined the allegorical symbols in the texts in relation to their own context. That the symbolic intent of the texts' authors aligns with that identified by the 4QMMT authors can be judged coincidental. It is a feature of the geographical and religio-cultural heritage that these authors shared with the texts they were interpreting.

Conclusion

I began this chapter by highlighting the scholarly dispute concerning Deut 1:5 and its alleged characterization of Moses's speeches as commentary on the legislation that precedes them in the Pentateuch. The early reception of the Deuteronomy scroll also affords an opportunity to test this claim. As such, it serves as a fitting focus of this chapter's conclusion.

The various examples from the early history of D's reception considered here demonstrate that D's earliest interpreters were primarily concerned with its legal content and not its retelling of Israel's history. In this sense, the emphasis upon law in the commentary interpretation of Deut 1:5 is confirmed by the early history of interpretation. Yet the examples of pentateuchal reception above also show that, even as early readers of the Deuteronomy scroll focused especially on its laws, those readers did not subordinate Deuteronomic law to that found in the preceding pentateuchal scrolls. Nor did they privilege D's laws such that they were determinative for understanding other pentateuchal legislation. Early readers instead treated Deuteronomic rules as coequal with other pentateuchal laws.[50] That meant that Deuteronomic law was sometimes preferred in its harmonistic combination with other pentateuchal law; at other times, non-Deuteronomic legal perspectives were preferred. Yet in every case, *Deuteronomic law was treated as belonging to the same category as the other pentateuchal legislation with which it is combined.* The early reception of Deuteronomy thus represents a substantial challenge to the claim that Moses's Deuteronomic speeches are legal commentary and not full-fledged law.

The coequal rank of pentateuchal laws in their early reception is underscored by the basis claimed for their unity. The examples surveyed in this chapter show that pentateuchal law, read as part of the compiled Pentateuch, was assessed *topically* rather than *sequentially*, and when considered in this way, all pentateuchal legislation was judged of equivalent status. Put differently, early interpreters sought to harmonize topically related laws *on a single plane.*

It need not have been this way, of course. Early interpreters could have read pentateuchal laws sequentially, particularly as a feature of the pentateuchal fabula, as argued by Otto and others. Yet the Chronicler sought a Passover practice that included aspects both of the Deuteronomic prescription to boil the meat and of the Priestly prescription to roast it in fire (P), and the Temple Scroll authors integrated a firm distinction between priests and Levites—a Priestly view—into a D text that explicitly offered procedures for avoiding such a distinction.

Even though prioritization of one or another law may be observed in these examples (indeed, such prioritization is inevitable in instances of harmonization), the Priestly and Deuteronomic laws neither triumph nor fail—at least from the perspective of the ancient interpreters who engaged them. This is because the Priestly and Deuteronomic texts were considered parts of a single whole. Accordingly, in the face of the obvious differences he encountered, the Chronicler could characterize the harmonized Passover procedure he described as *"according to the (one) rule."*

Taken together, this evidence suggests that the earliest interpreters of pentateuchal law did not differentiate between *laws* in Exodus, Leviticus, and Numbers and *interpretive commentary* in Deuteronomy. In fact, it is precisely the temporality of this claim—the *secondness* of Deuteronomy in the commentary interpretation—that these interpreters rejected. In its place, they employed a hermeneutical principle much like that of later, rabbinic readers: "There is no chronology in the Torah."[51] This principle was driven by a conviction also well-known from later, rabbinic sources. When confronted with conflicting content, the rabbis averred, "Both of these are the words of the living God."[52] The prayer in Neh 9 demonstrates that early interpreters employed a similar approach to the pentateuchal storyline and, in so doing, found a way to combine disparate material.

Standing apart from this interpretive trajectory are the examples from Jeremiah and H presented in this chapter. Each of these texts attests interpretive reuse of D, but they are notable both for their engagement with D's distinctive storyline (in the case of Jeremiah) and for their nonharmonistic, exclusivist revisionary aims (in both cases). I have suggested that these differences can be accounted for in light of the material disposition of the text engaged. It appears that both Jeremiah and H interacted with the D work, not the Deuteronomy scroll. In this state, D's distinctive storyline could be appreciated by the Jeremian authors (or ignored, as in the case of H); D's laws could also be treated as a resource from which to draw rather than an authoritative perspective that was problematically challenged by other, equally authoritative perspectives in a Pentateuch. Though instances such as those discussed here from Jeremiah and H are relatively rare, they contribute an important first chapter in the long history of D's reception and, by virtue of their distinctiveness, underscore the dynamism of that history, particularly in its early period.

5 Dating Deuteronomic Composition

Among the pentateuchal sources, for which the paucity of contemporary historical references within or to these texts has made dating them notoriously difficult, D has been an outlier. Since the groundbreaking work of de Wette in the early nineteenth century, scholars have regularly claimed that (at least a core of) D is a late seventh-century BCE Josianic pseudepigraph. This dating has served as a touchstone for interpretations of D across the past two centuries. It has also been employed in pursuit of a number of other scholarly inquiries, including reconstructing the history of Israelite religion; identifying and situating a Deuteronomistic History; diagnosing influences across biblical prophetic, historiographic, and sapiential texts; investigating imperial influence in ancient Judah; and dating other pentateuchal materials.

More recent research, however, has demonstrated weaknesses in the so-called de Wette hypothesis, and several alternative methods for dating Deuteronomic texts have been suggested. These alternative methods have resulted in a number of proposed dates, some of which I have referenced already in the foregoing chapters. These dating proposals each draw upon a range of evidence and rely upon a set of critical evaluations of that data. Given the incompleteness of the evidentiary record, it is hardly surprising that scholars have offered significantly different judgments concerning the dating of D and its various parts.

After reviewing these proposals and the evidence upon which they are built, I turn to a new presentation and evaluation of the data. I show first that the evidence of literary interaction with datable texts—both D's reuse of existing texts and other texts' reuse of D—provides a time window for situating its composition, namely, in the last three quarters of the seventh century BCE. In order to elucidate the historical and political situation of Judah in this era, and with an eye toward narrowing the time window for D's composition, I then examine the material culture and other nonbiblical historical data for Judah and other parts of the southern Levant in the seventh century. Finally, I offer a tentative reconstruction of D's compositional context.

Taking the literary evidence for D's adaptation of Esarhaddon's Succession Treaty (EST), which dates to 672 BCE, as a starting point, I give extended attention to the circumstances of this reuse. Specifically, I consider the archaeological evidence of the EST tablet find spots, the practices of the Neo-Assyrian empire in relation to its provinces and client states (including Judah), and the connections and relations among Neo-Assyrian *adê* instruments that seek similar ends. All of this evidence has potential bearing on D's access to and reuse of EST and, when analyzed as a whole, recommends a date for D in the first half of the seventh century, that is, during Manasseh's reign in Judah. Some of the evidence even suggests that D was composed in the years immediately after the publication of the Esarhaddon *adê*.

Finally, I show that an early-seventh-century dating sheds significant interpretive light on individual D texts. With a focus on both the law of the king (Deut 17:14–20) and the Deuteronomic centralization law (Deut 12 and its reflexes in other D legislation), I suggest that D repeatedly responded to the actions and imperial ideology of the Neo-Assyrians, even as its project was first one of reconceiving a native literary work, the pentateuchal Elohistic source. In so doing, D formulated an etiology and allegory that constituted an ambitious—and ultimately unrealistic—religio-political claim for seventh-century Judeans.

The discussion below focuses on dating the main D composition, which I have suggested comprises most of the scroll of Deuteronomy. This is not to deny or otherwise minimize this text's subsequent additions, whether supplements to the independent D work or materials inserted into the Deuteronomy scroll. As I have argued in the foregoing chapters, there is strong evidence for such accretions. Yet in almost every instance, it is even more difficult to date these additions than to date the original D work. This is the case even in instances where the evidence for supplementation is relatively strong. To cite a brief example treated in Chapter 2, I argued on the basis of both literary and textual evidence that "this evil generation" in MT Deut 1:35 should be considered secondary. Though I am quite confident in this assessment, the evidence upon which it is built reveals little about when the addition was introduced. Accordingly, it cannot be dated with any specificity. The same is the case for larger sections of secondary material that can be identified in D (e.g., Deut 27*). This is because the basis for identifying these supplements, as discussed in Chapter 1, is usually literary, that is, related to the text's story world. Lacking reference to specific historical realities, secondary material can usually be situated only within relatively wide temporal windows (after an earlier work, before another work, after the compilation of the Pentateuch, etc.).

Before turning to this chapter's examination of the data, I should address one additional issue. It may seem curious that treatment of D's dating comes so late in this book. To be sure, in many studies of this kind, the text's historical situation is treated at the outset in order to provide a framework for addressing its other features. I have postponed this discussion because the evidence for dating D builds substantially on what can be gleaned from the issues discussed in the foregoing chapters. In a real sense, then, it is only after the presentation of the evidence and attendant arguments of those chapters that the strongest case for D's dating can be made.

Dating D: The Prevailing Options

The field of biblical studies has reckoned mostly with three datings for the Deuteronomic materials. The first two are more or less precise datings, each situating (a major portion of) D in the seventh century BCE; the third is a cluster of proposals that together stand as alternatives to the first two and represent a range of dates. These three options are (1) the accession/reign of Josiah, (2) the reign of Manasseh, and (3) the exilic and postexilic periods.[1] I have made reference to each in the foregoing chapters, but they have not been equally represented in the history of biblical studies. The dating to Josiah's reign has by far been the most prominent among scholars and continues to enjoy a significant amount of support. The dating to the time of Manasseh is less frequently endorsed, while datings to the exilic and postexilic periods have found more adherents over the past few decades.

Dating D to the Reign of Josiah

I have made occasional reference across this study to the de Wette hypothesis and its Josianic date for D. Yet it is worth reviewing this theory in more detail, including its origin, the evidence in support of it, and (especially owing to its popularity) its development and refinement over the past two centuries. In his 1805 dissertation, de Wette argued for the original independence of Deuteronomy from the rest of the Pentateuch, giving special attention to its distinctive and internally consistent content and style and clues within it that it knew (and thus was later than) much of the rest of the Pentateuch.[2] It was in the context of this argument—in fact, in a footnote—that de Wette made a passing reference to the likelihood that (at least part of) Deuteronomy could be linked to the Josianic book find account. In his subsequent *Beiträge zur Einleitung in das Alte Testament* (1806–1807), de Wette elaborated his argument, suggesting that 2 Kgs 22–23 contains a reliable historical kernel, namely, its description of a religious reform connected to a law book and enacted by Josiah, even as it misrepresents that law book, which he surmises was probably forged by Hilkiah (perhaps with the involvement of Shaphan and Huldah).[3] The seed of this elaboration is found already in de Wette's dissertation, in which he argued that D was likely penned by priests who sought to redress the faults of their contemporary context.[4]

A major contributor to the prominence and enduring influence of the de Wette hypothesis is the central role that it played for Julius Wellhausen in his reconstruction of Israelite religion in his *Prolegomena to the History of Ancient Israel*.[5] Wellhausen famously diagnosed a degenerative development in Israelite religion—one that moved from the lively, natural, spontaneous, and prophetic to the distorted, lifeless, disingenuous, and legalistic—and identified Deuteronomic law as the turning point from the first trajectory to the second.[6] In Wellhausen's view, D's centralization and purification of the cult were stifling and even alienating: they displaced true feeling and fervent religious practice, replacing them with dictated cultic observance and even hypocrisy. Within the pentateuchal materials, the initial turn to legalism in D was then fully realized in P's religion, which in turn led directly to rabbinic Judaism. Wellhausen concluded that this Judaism "has an entirely different physiognomy from that of Hebrew antiquity, so much so that it is hard even to catch a likeness."[7] Importantly, it can be contrasted with the repristinated, prophetic religion of Christianity:

> The Gospel develops hidden impulses of the Old Testament, but it is a protest against the ruling tendency of Judaism. . . . [Jesus's] monotheism is not to be satisfied with stipulated services, how many and great soever; it demands the whole man, it renders doubleness of heart and hypocrisy

impossible. Jesus casts ridicule on the works of the law, the washing of hands and vessels, the tithing of mint and cummin, the abstinence even from doing good on the Sabbath. Against unfruitful self-sanctification He sets up another principle of morality, that of the service of one's neighbour. . . . He contends for the weightier matters in the law, for the common morality which sees its aim in the furtherance of the well-being of others, and which commends itself at once to the heart of every one. Just this natural morality of self-surrender does He call the law of God; that supernatural morality which thinks to outbid this, He calls the commandment of men.[8]

Drawing on de Wette, Wellhausen identified the central legal corpus of D (chs. 12–26) as the law book "discovered" in the temple during the reign of Josiah and the impetus for cultic centralization and reform.[9] Moreover, though he viewed the relative dates of the pentateuchal sources differently than de Wette did (de Wette judged the Priestly texts early), Wellhausen was able to build upon key features of de Wette's analysis for his reconstruction of Israelite religion. Perhaps the detail from de Wette's dissertation that proved most influential for Wellhausen was de Wette's attribution of the Deuteronomic laws to the Jerusalem priesthood and identification of this legislation as an attempt by the priests to arrogate power to themselves. As would be the case for Wellhausen, this development entailed for de Wette a transition from *custom* to *law:* "That is to say, in part because customs and institutions based on those customs had, through the passage of time, fallen into disuse and forgetfulness, and in part because those customs and institutions no longer seemed to conform to reality, the priests, when they were about to introduce a new code of justice or ratify it by the authority of the laws, appear to have introduced our Deuteronomy."[10] De Wette elaborated further: "When the temple of Jerusalem was erected, and when cultic ritual and superstition significantly increased, the authority, as well as the power, of the priests increased also. That power they desired to confirm and establish by legislation concerning both the unique status of the holy place and the Levites."[11]

Though his reconstruction was not identical to de Wette's, it is clear that the major elements of Wellhausen's schema, including the progression in Israelite religion from custom to law, the association of this development with an ambitious, self-interested priesthood, and its historical grounding in Josianic cultic reform, were carried over directly from de Wette.[12] Eckart Otto's frank conclusion is thus apt: "Without W. M. L. de Wette, there is no Wellhausen."[13]

Yet even as de Wette and Wellhausen each touted a Josianic dating for Deuteronomic law, it is worth noting that this chronological anchor contributed little to their overall theses. As discussed already, these scholars' ideas pushed primarily in different directions, and their conclusions would have been substantially unaffected if the date of D were shifted. The Josiah account in 2 Kings simply provided a convenient mooring for these scholars' historical reconstructions. There is no reason to doubt, of course, that de Wette and Wellhausen made their arguments for the Josianic dating of Deuteronomic law because they believed it was true. Yet in judging the prominence of this theory, it is useful to observe its impact in its context. Josianic dating lent credibility to the larger claims that de Wette and Wellhausen were making at a moment when many were quite optimistic about the historical reliability of biblical narratives. Moreover, even if these scholars' larger claims were rejected, the association of Deuteronomy with Josiah's reform could still be accepted.[14]

The obvious weakness of the de Wette hypothesis is precisely this optimism toward the biblical accounts of Josiah.[15] What evidence *external* to the biblical texts really exists to support the claim of Josianic religious reform? And even if there was such a reform, what evidence exists to connect a D composition to it? Moreover, if the nonbiblical evidence is assessed apart from the biblical material, what does it suggest? It should be noted that de Wette himself recognized the problem of accepting the historical reliability of the biblical accounts. He thus largely discounted the Chronicler's account of Josiah, and he took it as his responsibility to justify his acceptance of certain elements from the Kings account.[16]

A number of scholars have attempted to address such issues further and, in several cases, have settled on a modified form of the de Wette hypothesis. For example, in his recent reassessment of the literary and archaeological evidence, Christoph Uehlinger has made the case for what he terms "a well-grounded minimum," that is, a middle way between extreme skepticism toward and wholesale endorsement of the biblical accounts of Josianic reform. In service of this goal, Uehlinger provides an evaluation and synthesis of existing research that prioritizes archaeological evidence over literary evidence (without discounting the latter entirely) and materialist and sociopolitical explanations of data over narrowly ideological ones.

Uehlinger's study begins with an important acknowledgment: "'Josiah's reform,' regardless of whether exposed by 'maximalists' or 'minimalists,' is essentially a scholarly construct built upon the biblical tradition; without that tradition no one would look out for a 'cult reform' when studying the archaeology of Judah of the late Iron Age II C."[17] What Uehlinger does find in the archaeological record, however, is some evidence for cultic changes akin to those described in the biblical accounts of Josiah in the second half of the seventh century BCE. For example, he observes a shift from the use of anthropomorphic and theriomorphic iconography on Judean seals in the eighth and seventh centuries to a general avoidance of such imagery in the sixth century. He also discerns in the seventh century (and especially its second half) a resistance to Egyptian motifs and a notable paucity of Egyptian objects in Jerusalem in comparison with their prevalence in the southern Levant at this time, especially to the south of Jerusalem and along the Mediterranean coast.[18] Yet Uehlinger rightly observes that while these and other comparable features of the archaeological record could relate to an alleged purge of specific religious ideas and practices, they do not provide direct support for a centralization of the Judean Yahweh cult in the Jerusalem temple.[19]

Drawing especially on the work of Hermann Spieckermann,[20] Uehlinger also concludes that certain elements of the so-called *Reformbericht* ("reform report") in 2 Kgs 23:4–20 are historically reliable. These features include references to Josiah's removal of *kmr*-priests (2 Kgs 23:5), an Asherah image (v. 6), horses and chariots dedicated to the sun god (v. 11), and roof altars (v. 12). Each of these details can be correlated with known features of contemporary Aramean and Assyrian astral and other religious practices in the eighth and seventh centuries.[21] Uehlinger concludes that it is likely that Josiah enacted some religious changes that are described in the biblical accounts. Yet he also observes that these details do not necessarily add up to a *reform*, let alone the cult centralization foregrounded by D; they may be understood instead as part of a larger set of sociopolitical changes in the wake of diminished Assyrian influence and increased Egyptian presence in the southern Levant in the second half of the seventh century.[22]

Those who have identified a direct, literary relationship between EST and D (especially Deut 13 and 28) have typically identified the seventh century as the most likely moment for Deuteronomic reuse of this Assyrian text. (The Neo-Assyrian empire would not survive the end of the century, raising questions about access to EST afterwards.) It is not surprising, then, that some scholars have also identified D's relationship with EST as a new foundation for the de Wette hypothesis. Otto, for example, rejects as circular the argument for the seventh-century dating of D on the basis of the biblical account of Josiah. Nonetheless, he embraces a Josianic date for (an early version of) D in light of the evidence of its dependence upon EST.[23] As discussed in Chapter 3, this reconstruction often includes an evaluation of D's reuse of EST as subversive: in the waning moments of the empire, Judean authors gave voice to their protest against Assyrian sovereignty by turning a paradigmatic royal demand for loyalty against the empire. Finally, for Otto, D's revision of EST also serves as a starting point and historical grounding for delineating strata in Deuteronomy.[24]

Hans Ulrich Steymans offers a somewhat complex theory for D's composition and dating, part of which can be characterized as a modified version of the de Wette hypothesis. As Otto does, Steymans takes explicit account of the Esarhaddon *adê*. He proposes that the original D materials were a "pamphlet" focused on centralization—a portion of what is now Deut 12—and dating to the reign of Hezekiah. During the reign of Manasseh, this early text was supplemented with materials based on EST. Yet this augmented work, comprising portions of Deut 12, 13, 28, and perhaps some other material, was not publicized and fell into obscurity. Steymans argues that this work was the text subsequently found in the Jerusalem temple during the reign of Josiah and that it became the basis for Josiah's reform. Unlike for de Wette, then, for Steymans the Josianic book find is not a fabrication; in his view, an old book was actually discovered.[25]

Dating D to the Reign of Manasseh

Though it is hardly as common as the Josianic dating, a number of scholars in recent decades have assigned D and/or its fundamental ideas to the first half of the seventh century and in particular to the reign of Manasseh (r. 697–643 BCE).[26] Two main arguments have been offered in support of this view. The first concerns the influence of the Esarhaddon *adê* text upon D, which can be put in service of dating D to the first half of the seventh century as readily (or, as I argue below, even more readily) as it can for dating D to that century's second half. Indeed, this identified textual dependence suggests that D's composition could have occurred as early as ca. 670 BCE. The second main argument relates to specific Deuteronomic content that is consistent with the limited details known of Manasseh's reign.

There are very few written sources (biblical or nonbiblical) that describe Manasseh. As I discuss further below, there is also very little extant archaeological evidence from this period. Even so, the evidence that does exist can be correlated, mostly inversely, with perspectives found in D. For example, the few references to Manasseh from contemporary Assyrian sources depict the Judean monarch as a dutiful subject of the Neo-Assyrian empire. Such sworn allegiance to Assyria and its patron deity, Assur, as expressly required by EST, is at direct odds with the singular fidelity that D insists that Israel pledge to Yahweh (Deut 6:4–5).[27] Similarly, D's strong condemnations of (what it presents as) heterodox religious practices find a ready target in the cultic practices attributed to Manasseh in the biblical accounts (2 Kgs 21:2–9 // 2 Chr 33:2–9).

The portrayal of Manasseh as a loyal Assyrian subject in the nonbiblical sources is consistent with the biblical depiction of his lengthy reign (2 Kgs 21:1 // 2 Chr 33:1). Taken together, these details suggest that Manasseh was a successful vassal ruler who secured his own status by carefully manag-ing Judah's relationship with its Assyrian imperial overlord. If his biblical depiction is to be trusted, Manasseh's cosmopolitan religious attitudes may also have contributed to his strong diplomatic relations with Assyria.

The second major line of evidence brought in support of dating D to the reign of Manasseh is the so-called law of the king in Deut 17:14–20. This brief text is notable for a number of reasons, including the fact that it is the only pentateuchal text that addresses Israelite kingship. As noted in Chapter 1, for this reason some view it as an important instance of both etiology and allegory in D. In view of such assessments, it is unsurprising that this text's dating is highly contested.

One analysis of Deut 17:14–20 situates this text in the context of—and as a response to—Manasseh's reign. Scholars such as Gary Knoppers and Bernard M. Levinson have observed the inconsistency between the depic-tion of kingship in the narratives of Samuel and Kings on the one hand and the dictates of Deut 17:14–20 on the other. The characterizations of Israelite and Judean kings in the Former Prophets are much more consis-tent with what is known of stereotypical royal custom in the ancient Near East in the first millennium BCE than are the restrictive prescriptions in Deut 17:14–20.[28] This inconsistency casts doubt upon a straightforward theory of a Deuteronomistic History that stretches from Deuteronomy through Kings. D's restrictions upon the monarchy also call into question Josiah's supposed endorsement of a work that included them.[29]

Responding to these problems, Levinson has suggested that D's law of the king might be better situated in the time of Manasseh. Dating D in this way resituates its text in relation to the monarchy: rather than receiving the monarchy's endorsement or even emerging from it, D can be viewed as a statement of opposition. In this reconstruction, D can be understood as a response to "Manasseh's pragmatic foreign policies," which is to say, his cooperation with Assyrian imperial power.[30] In other words, it is Manasseh specifically who is the target of D's restrictions on kingship.

Building on suggestions made by Ernest Nicholson,[31] Nili Wazana has recently made a different argument for dating the base layer of D's law of the king to "the late eighth and early seventh centuries BCE."[32] Acknowledging the same distinctive elements in D's presentation of kingship that Knoppers and Levinson do, she suggests that D's law is not aimed at Manasseh or any other Judean ruler. Instead, its restrictions are directed at the Assyrian emperor himself—and in relation to a specific scenario. The Neo-Assyrian empire sometimes converted conquered regions into Assyrian provinces. This was the case for Samaria after its defeat in 722 BCE. If Judah were to experience the same fate, it would fall under direct Assyrian rule, making the Assyrian emperor its king.

It is this scenario that D's law seeks to avoid. Wazana points out that D's criteria for kingship each counter central features of Assyrian imperial rulership. According to Deut 17:15, Israel's king must be chosen by Yahweh and be a native Israelite. Moreover, he must refrain from amassing horses, wives who would lead him astray, and excessive wealth (vv. 16–17). The Assyrian king was understood to be selected by the god Assur and was, of course, not an Israelite. Moreover, imperial ambitions of the first millennium BCE required horses for cavalry forces,[33] diplomatic marriages, and substantial accumulation of wealth to support both regular operations and expansion. Wazana also notes that the framing of D's law of the king in relation to popular demand (vv. 14–15) may be more than biblical stereotype (cf. Judg 8:22–23; 9; 1 Sam 8; 10:18–19; 12). She suggests that it may be directed against support within Judah for Judah's establishment as an Assyrian province.[34]

Dating D to the Exilic/Postexilic Period

As observed in Chapter 1, attempts to date D to the exilic or postexilic period have been especially closely correlated with and even inspired by the interpretation of D as allegory.[35] This is particularly the case for D's fictive, Mosaic frame, which scholars have often sought to separate from (portions of) D's legislative core. The result is a staged development for D and, with it, a series of dates for its incremental growth.

Especially important for many scholars who locate this work (or a new version of it) in the exilic period are the themes of exile and return contained within it (e.g., Deut 30:1–10). They have noted, moreover, the correspondence of these themes with apparently late material elsewhere in the Deuteronomistic History (e.g., 1 Kgs 8). This social and theological profile is then identified in the basic contours of D's story (imminent entry into the land) and, because of Moses's prominent role in that story, to content that foregrounds Moses, his mediation (e.g., the Exodus, the Decalogue), and his life experiences that might be particularly meaningful to an exilic/postexilic audience (e.g., Moses's death outside of the land).[36] D's centralization focus has even been correlated with exile. With some caution, Reinhard Kratz has suggested that the fall of Jerusalem prompted the early D work, which was an attempt to stave off the decentralizing effects of exile.[37]

Juha Pakkala has recently renewed and extended earlier arguments in favor of dating most or all of D no earlier than the destruction of Jerusalem in the early sixth century. He argues that the de Wette hypothesis and its reliance upon the historicity of the Josianic reform described in 2 Kgs 22–23 has problematically made a seventh-century date for D the default scholarly position—even for those who would critique the Josianic thesis. Pakkala also rejects the value of EST for dating D, suggesting that even if such a direct connection between these texts could be established, it would not rule out adaption long after the publication of the Assyrian *adê*. Thus even as he endorses a strongly redaction-critical approach, he breaks with many who would date at least an early edition of D (*Urdeuteronomium*) to the seventh century.

Pakkala presents ten specific arguments in favor of this position. They focus on the lack of historical references in D (e.g., no direct references to Jerusalem, Judah, temple, or king), D's future-oriented perspective, the impracticality of several of its laws, theological perspectives in D that are well-situated in the exilic period (e.g., D's so-called name theology), and D's apparent lack of influence in Yahwistic religious practice (evidenced especially by the Jerusalemite support for an Elephantine temple to Yahweh). These details suggest to Pakkala that D does not reflect the real situation of Judean political autonomy in the seventh century and thus should not be assigned a preexilic date.[38]

Assessing the Evidence Anew

Even as permutations of the de Wette hypothesis continue to enjoy significant influence in the field, the dating proposals reviewed above—and the strengths and weaknesses that can be perceived in them—suggest that a reevaluation is in order. In what follows, my intent is to offer a proposal that takes account of as much evidence as possible, even as any conclusions must remain tentative owing to the limited nature of the data.

Relative and Absolute Dating: Literary Revision in D

The evidence for D's reuse and revision of extant textual material, as discussed in Chapters 2 and 3, is strong. Especially clear is D's utilization of the Covenant Code and the larger Elohistic source of which it is a part; evidence for D's more limited reuse of portions of the J source is likewise compelling. By themselves, these instances of literary revision permit only a relative dating of texts in relation to each other: J and E are, by necessity, antecedent to D. Yet even without the ability to date J and/or E more specifically, their historical priority over D, when combined with other reconstructable details, proves significant. As I argue below, especially in the case of the E source's altar law and D's reorientation of it, it is possible to coordinate biblical text, archaeological data, and known historical events to propose a plausible sociohistorical context for D.

Adding considerable weight to this reconstruction is D's likely dependence upon the Esarhaddon *adê* text of 672 BCE. As noted already, the precise dating of this text, coupled with the demise of the Neo-Assyrian empire at the century's end, invites investigation of the seventh century as a plausible context for D's composition. This, of course, includes the half century before Josiah, coinciding with the period of Manasseh's and Amon's reigns. For the present argument, EST serves as a *terminus post quem* for D, yet in this role it also serves as a reference point for establishing more specific dates for the other works from which D borrows.

A similar approach can be used to approximate a lower limit for D's composition. As argued in Chapter 4, texts such as the Holiness (H) stratum of the pentateuchal Priestly source and the prophetic book of Jeremiah are early examples of texts that knew and responded to D. If dates can be established for them, these dates can also serve as a *terminus ante quem* for D.

Scholars continue to debate the dates of (the various parts of) Jeremiah and H. One small but suggestive piece of evidence for dating H is its use of the locution *nś' ḥēṭ'* ("to bear sin") to denote liability for punishment (Lev 19:17, 20:20, 22:9, 24:15; Num 9:13; Num 18:22, 32).[39] H uses this expression alongside the equivalent *nś' 'āwôn* with no apparent semantic distinction (Lev 17:16; 19:8; 20:17, 19; 22:16; Num 18:1, 23). In a few instances, both expressions appear within a single line or in adjacent lines, in each case carrying the same meaning (Lev 20:19–20, Num 18:22–23). In the earlier P work that H supplemented, while *nś' 'āwôn* appears repeatedly (Exod 28:38, 43; Lev 5:1, 17; 7:18; 10:17; 16:22; Num 14:34, 30:16), *nś' ḥēṭ'* never does. Outside of H, *nś' ḥēṭ'* appears only twice in the Hebrew Bible—in Ezek 23:49 and Isa 53:12.[40]

The distribution of *nś' ḥēṭ'* in the Hebrew Bible is striking in light of this clause's similarity to the Neo-Babylonian legal idiom *ḫiṭu ša šarri šadādu/zabālu*, "to bear responsibility for the king's punishment." The latter clause is a technical expression of conditional legal responsibility for fault that appears exclusively in Late Babylonian documents.[41] Two examples of this *ḫiṭu* clause even appear in the cache of approximately two hundred cuneiform documents that record Judean presence and activity in Mesopotamia in the sixth and fifth centuries BCE.[42] One of these two examples was written in *Āl-Yaḫūdu* (that is, Judahtown—apparently a special Judean-populated locality in Babylonia) in the tenth year of Darius (ca. 513 BCE); the other was written in Babylon in the third year of Xerxes (ca. 484 BCE).[43]

The Ezekiel and Second Isaiah texts that attest the *nś' ḥēṭ'* clause are readily dated to the exilic/early postexilic period. At the same time, the regular use of the *ḫiṭu* clause in contemporary Babylonian texts, combined with the well-established existence of a semantic equivalent in Hebrew (*nś' 'āwôn*), suggests that the infrequent use of *nś' ḥēṭ'* in these biblical texts is due to language contact during the Babylonian exile. If this judgment is correct, the attestations of *nś' ḥēṭ'* in H provide a basis for its dating to the sixth century BCE and probably to the exilic period more specifically. Other details in H seem to support this dating, including this text's threats of divine abandonment in Lev 26:30–33, which align with other exilic and postexilic texts but stand at odds with the earlier texts, including P.[44]

All of these details combine to add further support for a seventh-century dating for D. Yet given the wide parameters that they chart—the greater part of a century—they also recommend a more detailed investigation of the historical and archaeological data from the southern Levant in the late eighth to the early sixth centuries BCE—the period that has been termed "the long seventh century."[45] Specifically, what is needed is further consideration of how these data might be correlated with and shed light upon the content of D and its literary relatives and how those literary relationships might be illuminated though historical contextualization.

Archaeology and the History of Judah in the Seventh Century BCE

Most of the seventh century found Judah in the grasp of adjacent regional powers, most notably, the Neo-Assyrian empire. Yet because of Neo-Assyrian imperial policy, this subjugation did not result in pervasive decline. Following the incursion by Sennacherib's army in 701 BCE that crushed the regional resistance led by Hezekiah, the southern Levant enjoyed an extended period of stability. This so-called *Pax Assyriaca* was designed by the Assyrians to extract resources from the territory by affording subject polities both substantial autonomy and protection from other aggressors (though without the benefit of imperial investment in local economic development).[46] Moreover, the material culture evidence suggests that the extent of Sennacherib's destruction was more localized and thus less devastating than the more bombastic claims of his royal campaign account suggest.

The archaeological evidence of late-eighth-century destruction across surveyed and excavated Judean sites, combined with settlement pattern data from the late eighth and early seventh centuries, indicate that Sennacherib's army focused its attack on the Shephelah region (the lowlands to the west and south of Jerusalem, adjacent to the Philistine coastal region). This was for good reason, both political and economic. The Shephelah was a major population center and economic driver in late-eighth-century Judah.[47] Focusing its attack there was an effective way for the Assyrian army to damage the Judean polity and thereby subdue it. Presumably to ensure that Judah could not regain its strength and to penalize the kingdom for its resistance, the Assyrians facilitated the annexation of the Shephelah region by the Philistine city-states (according to the Sennacherib account, by Ashdod, Ekron, and Gaza) after their attack.[48] In addition, the Lachish reliefs in Nineveh make clear that Sennacherib used his incursion in the Shephelah as a warning to other would-be rebels.

The Assyrians' focus on the Shephelah region of Judah also coincided with their concern to secure the coastal highway and the political and economic opportunities it afforded—opportunities that had been exploited during the reign of Sargon II (d. 705 BCE) but were interrupted by the southern Levantine revolt.[49] The route that Sennacherib followed down the Mediterranean coast highlights this aim, and at its southern end, of course, lay Egypt, a much more significant prize than the southern Levantine states (and one that Esarhaddon would eventually conquer in 671 BCE).[50] According to Sennacherib's Third Campaign account, the southern Levantine rebels even appealed to Egypt for military assistance, but the Assyrian army defeated the Egyptians and Ethiopians at Eltekeh.

In contrast to the coastal regions, the Judean highlands, including the Judean capital of Jerusalem, held little or no strategic significance for the Assyrians.[51] Sennacherib's so-called siege of Jerusalem was more likely a blockade—not a full-fledged siege—which accords with its outcome, namely, the confirmation of Hezekiah's compliance, not the destruction of the city.[52] An equally important goal of Sennacherib's advance on Jerusalem, as reflected in the Assyrian campaign account, was the liberation of the loyal Assyrian vassal ruler in Ekron, Padi. Having resisted the southern Levantine anti-Assyrian coalition, Padi was taken captive and held in Jerusalem. Sennacherib freed Padi and reinstated him in his city-state.[53]

As for Judah itself, what could be achieved through destruction was accomplished already in the Shephelah. By keeping the Judean ruler, royal city, and state infrastructure in place, the Assyrians were more likely to extract valuable resources from the region, beginning with a punitive tribute payment in response to Hezekiah's rebellion. As many have noted, the laconic "A Account" in Kings (2 Kgs 18:13–16) is consistent with this reconstruction and even corroborates specific details of the Assyrian account's tribute claim.[54]

Sennacherib's description of Hezekiah in his Third Campaign further underscores Jerusalem's insignificance to Assyria. The image of Hezekiah's confinement—"like a bird in a cage in Jerusalem, his royal city" (*kīma iṣṣūr quppi qereb Ursalimmu āli šarrūtīšu*)—is undeniably vivid and rhetorically forceful. Yet it depicts the Judean king's humiliation and subjugation precisely by highlighting that he was *not* deposed.[55] Hezekiah instead retained his position in a thoroughly weakened condition, almost certainly because the threat he posed to the empire was insufficient to warrant his replacement. As noted already, from the Neo-Assyrian perspective, this was the preferred outcome. Yet the very fact that Hezekiah was spared creates a contrast between him and those Levantine rulers who were deposed and replaced (e.g., Luli in Sidon and Sidqa in Ashkelon). This contrast adds to the evidence that Judah and its ruler were of little consequence to the Assyrian empire and its pursuit of its goals in the southern Levant.[56]

The archaeological, epigraphic, and other historical evidence of Judah during the first half of the seventh century is meager. As noted already, there are a few references to Manasseh in Assyrian texts, each portraying the Judean king as a loyal subject,[57] but there is no clearly datable evidence in the Judean archaeological record.[58] The biblical accounts of Manasseh are quite sparse and carry a strong ideological inflection.[59] The epigraphic record from the Neo-Assyrian empire during this period reveals that there was significant political intrigue both in the Assyrian heartland and in several of the empire's peripheral areas,[60] yet there is no evidence that Judah attempted to extricate itself from its position as an Assyrian vassal.

The second half of the seventh century saw the decline and eventual demise of the Neo-Assyrian empire. Assyria experienced significant political upheaval in various parts of the empire, but especially in Babylonia. In the southern Levant, Egypt was able to assert regional control in the last third of the century, dominating the region during most of the reign of Josiah.[61] Between 615 and 612 BCE, the Medes and Babylonians successfully attacked individually and then in tandem the major Assyrian cities of Arrapha, Nineveh, Kalhu, and Assur. In 609 BCE, the last Assyrian king, Assur-uballit II, was killed at Harran, and with their defeat of the Egyptians at Carchemish in 605 BCE, the Babylonians became the new imperial power in the southern Levant. Yet because there was no significant destruction within the southern Levant itself during this period, very few material culture remains can be dated confidently to this period.

A Tentative Reconstruction of D's Compositional Context

Paul E. Dion has suggested that "the closer to 672 BC one places the composition of Deuteronomy 13, the easier to understand are its precise contacts with the vassal treaties of Esarhaddon."[62] In the reconstruction offered here, I suggest that taken together, several lines of evidence recommend dating the entirety of the main D composition, not just Deut 13, to the reign of Manasseh. The case is in part circumstantial, but the weight of the evidence proves greater for this dating than for any other option.

A first set of evidence that recommends dating D to the first half of the seventh century relates to this text's reuse of EST and the historical contextualization of that reuse. As discussed in Chapter 3, some scholars have sought to explain D's borrowings from EST as contributors to a subversive response to Assyrian hegemony. Alternatively, I have argued that this reuse needs first to be contextualized within D's larger literary project. In that project, D's major concern is reimagining and regrounding the religious ideas of the pentateuchal E source, not polemicizing against or otherwise attempting to undermine the Assyrian empire. In this reconstruction, the prominence of EST and its correspondence with the covenantal Zeitgeist in which D's authors wrote explain their recourse to the Assyrian text.[63] At the same time, the Deuteronomic authors' limited investment in EST also helps to explain their piecemeal engagement with its contents (mainly, though probably not exclusively, in Deut 13 and 28).

Though these arguments for understanding the nature of D's reuse of EST differ from each other, they each require D's authors to have accessed the Assyrian text and to have attended to its specific content details. To assess when and how such a scenario could take place requires comparison with what is known of other exemplars of EST and *adê* texts more generally. Very little information is preserved concerning the deposition and use of *adê* texts, whether in the Assyrian heartland or the empire's peripheries.[64] Examining the limited data available, Jacob Lauinger has cautiously suggested that the use of Assyrian *adê* tablets, including EST, may have extended over long periods of time. Building on the arguments of Andrew R. George and others,[65] Lauinger highlights especially the status of the *adê* tablet (*ṭuppi adê*) as a "Tablet of Destinies," as known from myths such as Enuma Elish and Anzu and as apparently employed in ritual contexts, including the annual *akītu* ceremony. He also notes that the Nimrud tablets survived for more than half of a century, perhaps because of their ritual use.[66]

Yet other evidence calls into question the perdurance of at least some kinds of *adê* oaths/impositions and, in particular, those addressing royal succession. For example, Sennacherib issued a succession *adê* on behalf of Esarhaddon (SAA 2 3), but Esarhaddon subsequently imposed his own loyalty oath upon his subjects (SAA 2 4). On the basis of its contents, Simo Parpola and Kazuko Watanabe characterize the latter text as an "Accession Treaty."[67] Similarly, after Assurbanipal successfully assumed the throne (669 BCE), the dowager queen Zakutu, Esarhaddon's mother, imposed another loyalty oath, different from EST, upon Assurbanipal's older brothers, the rest of the royal family, and the whole empire in support of Assurbanipal's rulership (SAA 2 8).[68] Apparently in neither case was the succession treaty document reused with, and its oath reimposed upon, the new king's subjects.

It is also clear that the language of *adê* texts was crafted to fit contemporary circumstances. In her new *adê*, and in line with his change in status from the time when EST was issued, Zakutu refers to Assurbanipal not as "the great crown prince designate" (DUMU MAN GAL *šá É. UŠ-ti*), as he is regularly described in EST, but as "the king of Assyria" (MAN KUR *aš-šur*). Though significant portions of Esarhaddon's Accession Treaty are broken, it is clear that the expected titular change appears there, too: Esarhaddon is referred to as "lord" (EN = *bēlu*, SAA 2 4:7′, 9′), a title regularly employed in the *adê* texts in conjunction with "king" (MAN = *šarru;* cf. also line 17′, which includes a [stereotyped] reference to the king [LUGAL]).[69]

In the cases of both Esarhaddon and Assurbanipal, the details surrounding the enactment of a new *adê*, with content functionally equivalent to that of its predecessor, after (or right as) the king assumed the throne, are not entirely clear.[70] Notwithstanding the adjurations against future revocation or rebellion in the succession *adê*s (e.g., SAA 2 6:377–93), it is possible that in the Realpolitik of the empire, once the retiring king who imposed the oath was gone, the oath's power was effectively undermined.[71] This is the impression given by the Zakutu *adê*, which, before adjuring the royal family, political appointees, court officials, and "Assyrians high and low," specifically names Assurbanipal's two older brothers—those most motivated to challenge Assurbanipal's right to the throne—as the first two subjects of its oath (SAA 2 8:3–8). As Parpola has suggested, it is likely that in imposing this *adê*, the dowager queen was attempting to exert social and political pressure upon any who might aspire to unseat Assurbanipal during the transition of power. On this logic, Parpola even conjectures that the Zakutu *adê* should be dated specifically to the month between Esarhaddon's death and Assurbanipal's formal accession ceremony and that it was likely implemented at the coronation.[72] Probably influencing Zakutu's action was the fact that her husband, Sennacherib, had been assassinated by the sons whom he had passed over when he selected Esarhaddon as his successor. Esarhaddon, too, had experienced repeated internal challenges to his reign.[73] As Hayim Tadmor in particular has emphasized, the relationship between the king and his subjects could exist without a written *adê*. This detail suggests that special circumstances influenced the repeated and targeted use of *adê* instruments of the early seventh century.[74]

It is also possible that, notwithstanding their grandiose, mythic frameworks and their occasional references to multiple generations of subjects,[75] the narrow focus on power transition in succession *adê*s logically rendered their contents time-bound.[76] Assurbanipal assumed the Assyrian throne in 669 BCE, and he remained there until his death in 631 BCE. An *adê* imposed by the king's father and characterizing the king as the crown prince hardly matched the realities of such a lengthy reign. This ill fit is rendered even more glaring given that it was possible to issue new *adê*s with updated details.[77] At a minimum, the existence and contents of Esarhaddon's Accession Treaty and the Zakutu Treaty suggest that some Assyrian *adê* documents and in particular those trained specifically on succession had relatively short lives.

As noted above, Lauinger's arguments for the perdurance of the *adê* focus especially on its tablet as a ritual object. Bearing the seal of the "Tablet of Destinies"—and thereby participating in the divine realm—the *ṭuppi adê* probably became an object of veneration. In support of this conclusion, Lauinger has noted that the Tayinat *adê* was found among an assemblage that included tablets of *iqqur īpuš* whose amulet shape suggests that they served as votives.[78] Moreover, both the Tayinat *adê* tablet and the *iqqur īpuš* tablets exhibit physical features that suggest their function as display copies. In the case of one *iqqur īpuš* tablet (T-1701 + 1923), there is even evidence that its text was not meant to be read, for it omitted content that made it impossible to consult.[79] Watanabe has also highlighted evidence for tablet veneration in earlier periods of Assyrian history, including visual representations of deified tablets.[80]

Paired with the evidence that an *adê*'s charge may have been short-lived (either by design or simply in particular instances), these observations recommend distinguishing between the treatment of the *ṭuppi adê* as an object of veneration and the deployment of its contents.[81] As a ritual object, the *ṭuppi adê* may have been retained and even esteemed long after its specific content details were superseded. Given that the visual markings on the tablet (especially the seal impressions) denoted its divine status, it could be argued that relativizing its content was particularly easy, especially in the farther reaches of the empire where cuneiform literacy was especially meagre.[82]

More recently, Lauinger has offered an additional argument for continued use of the *adê* text—or at least a part of it—with specific reference to
EST. Taking his cues especially from the Nimrud tablets' find spot (in the
Ezida temple's throne room, which was part of that section of the temple
where the *akītu* ceremony was performed) and the status of the *adê* tablet
as a "Tablet of Destinies," Lauinger has suggested that the verbatim oath in
EST (lines 494–512) that was to be sworn by the *adê*'s subjects would have
been employed annually in *akītu* ceremonies performed in Nabu temples
across the empire. In this usage, the *adê* oath would reinscribe annually the
destiny of the Assyrian subjects.[83]

Lauinger's suggestion for such continued use is intriguing, and he offers it with appropriate caution. Yet his proposal also prompts a number
of questions, especially in light of the evidence discussed above. As noted
there, if EST was to continue to function annually, especially after Assurbanipal's accession, it is difficult to explain the Zakutu *adê*'s address to all Assyrians and its equivalent requirements to those in EST (i.e., loyal support
of Assurbanipal). Such equivalence would amount to redundancy and as
such would call into question the absolute authority of EST. Esarhaddon's
Accession Treaty poses the same difficulty in relation to the succession *adê*
of Sennacherib. The inconsistent inclusion of a verbatim oath in *adê* texts
also raises questions regarding the standardization of an *akītu* practice like
the one that Lauinger proposes. As Parpola and Watanabe observe, vows
akin to the one in EST also appear in two other known *adê* texts (SAA 2
4 and 9) but, even accounting for textual damage, not in at least three others.[84] Among the *adê*s that omit the subject-voiced oath is the Zakutu text.
Under Lauinger's theory, one might posit that a succession *adê*'s oath was
sometimes replaced by an updated one for annual *akītu* affirmations (e.g., in
the case of Esarhaddon's Accession Treaty) but was retained in other cases.

This replacement proposal could also address the above-noted issue of
using the appropriate title for the emperor once he ascended to the throne.
Of course, it is also possible that, notwithstanding its presentation as a verbatim vow, a succession treaty's oath could have been updated in an ad hoc
fashion to reflect the once–crown prince's change in royal status. Yet this
suggestion, like the others entertained here, requires speculation significantly beyond the available data. Until additional evidence emerges—and
in light of the evidence adduced here that recommends against it—it seems
better not to make strong claims about the perdurance of the contents of
succession *adê*s, including their oaths, in Assyrian imperial practice.[85]

Even though they allow only a partial view, the details of *adê* use examined here have implications for reconstructing the historical context of D's reuse of EST. The apparently short life of succession *adê* content, combined with D's detailed interest in that content in the case of EST, suggests that a date closer to the publication of EST is more plausible for D's composition than one further removed from it. That is, given that a succession *adê*'s contents were meaningful and prominent in the immediate wake of its imposition, it is more likely that D's authors would have had access to EST in that moment than in a different one. For the same reasons, D's detailed attention to EST's content also fits this time frame better than a later one.

The evidence does not permit a single reconstruction of the deposition of EST tablets, but each of the plausible interpretations is consistent with Judean scribal access to this text in the first half of the seventh century BCE. One possibility is that D's authors accessed EST only outside of Judah. In considering the different find spots for the known EST exemplars, Steymans has suggested that the Nimrud exemplars were deposited in the location where the Medes, their named subjects, paid their tribute. In his view, because these subjects were seminomadic, housing the tablets in Nimrud assured their safety.[86] Karen Radner and Lauinger have developed this theory, the latter with specific reference to the Tayinat exemplar. They have argued that tablet deposition can be correlated with location of tribute payment not only in the case of the Medes named in the Nimrud tablets but generally. That is, the *adê* tablet by which each Assyrian subject swore loyalty may have been deposited in the location where that subject paid tribute.[87] As Lauinger has observed for Tayinat, after its subjugation by Tiglath-pileser III in 738 BCE, the city (which was known locally as Kinalia/Kunulua and which served as the capital of the state known as Patina/Unqi) was made the capital of an Assyrian province.[88] Given the city's status as a provincial capital and thus a site for regional tribute collection and other administrative oversight, it is reasonable that the *ṭuppi adê* by which the local governor of Kunulua and other regional officials swore allegiance should be deposited there and not in the Assyrian center.[89]

If this deposition theory is correct, it has implications for understanding the circumstances of Judean interactions with EST. Given that Judah was never made a province, even though it was an Assyrian vassal, this theory would rule out the existence of an EST tablet in its capital, Jerusalem.[90] At the same time, D's detailed reuse of EST suggests that its scribe(s) interacted with an actual copy of the text. If Jerusalem housed no such tablet,

Judean scribes would have had to travel elsewhere to access one. The provincial capital of Samaria (Samerina) was nearby and easily accessible;[91] it is also clear that diplomatic delegations traveled from the Assyrian empire's peripheries to its center.[92] If Judean scribes encountered an EST tablet only away from Judah and Jerusalem, it is more likely that they would have done so during that time when its contents had contemporary relevance and thus greater prominence, namely, in the period immediately after its publication.

Another possibility is that an EST tablet was in fact deposited in Jerusalem.[93] Frederick Mario Fales has emphasized that the EST text includes an order for tablet display that implores its subjects, "Guard like your god" (*kî ilīkunu lā tanaṣṣarāni*) the *ṭuppi adê* that "has been set up before you" (*ina maḫrīkunu šakinūni*) (SAA 2 6:408–9). This adjuration requires a ritual display much like the one attested at Tayinat in its Building XVI temple and one that could be replicated by all Assyrian subjects in their locales, regardless of their status as tribute collection sites. Fales speculates that the deposition of the Nimrud exemplars of EST in Nimrud rather than Media may indicate that the Median city-lords named in them were not present at the ceremony in which the oath was imposed and thus did not collect the tablets assigned to them.[94]

Steymans has also argued in favor of a Jerusalem deposition of EST. On the basis of the Tayinat tablet's invocation of the goddess Šarrat-Ekron (vi 47 = 466), Steymans has suggested that an EST tablet must have been installed at Ekron, which was, like Judah, an Assyrian vassal and not a province. He concludes, "It is inconceivable that a vassal state like Ekron had a copy of EST, while the neighboring vassal state Judah did not."[95]

If the instructions of EST lines 408–9 are prioritized and combined with an explanation for the Nimrud tablets like Fales's and a conclusion concerning the Šarrat-Ekron curse like Steymans's, it is possible to suggest that an EST tablet was deposited in Jerusalem and potentially even installed in its temple. In this scenario, the situation in Jerusalem would resemble very closely that found in the Tayinat province, with the Assyrian client state (Judah) enacting the words of the *ṭuppi adê*, including the *adê*'s adjuration to venerate the tablet itself, in its locale. Though the extant evidence does not allow final confirmation of this theory, it is consistent with the apparent production of EST tablets for all imperial provincial rulers and clients and with Manasseh's known vassal status.[96]

A second set of evidence for dating D to the first half of the seventh century BCE relates to how this dating fits with and otherwise illuminates other Deuteronomic content. As noted above, some scholars have attempted to connect the law on kingship in Deut 17:14–20 with Assyrian influence in Judah or even identify it as an indictment of Manasseh himself. While the latter proposal struggles to explain the law's details, including its insistence upon the Israelite king being native-born, the former seems likely. As Wazana has argued, the law's particulars correspond with known imperial ruling practices and, in so doing, target the Assyrian emperor and the possibility of direct Assyrian control in Judah.

If this analysis is correct, the law of the king is one of the more transparent instances of allegory in D and a rare, focused response to specific Assyrian imperial practices.[97] It also suggests that D sometimes used different approaches when it addressed its Assyrian imperial context. As discussed in Chapter 3, D's revision of EST contains no specific, reactionary features that mark that literary interaction as polemical or subversive. This is not because D's authors would have endorsed EST's demands. Though the Assyrians likely never attempted to impose a full-blown Assur cult in Judah (or other client states),[98] all indicators suggest that D's authors would have objected to the *adê*'s requirement to swear an oath in the name of Assur and various other gods, to acknowledge Assur as their deity, and to treat the *adê* tablet like a deity (SAA 2 6:25–40, 393, 408–9).[99] The argument here, however, recognizes that D's covenant framework and exclusivist religio-political vision derive from its main literary patrimony, the pentateuchal E source, and that D reuses and adjusts EST within that framework. With D's adaptation of EST so situated, it is difficult to identify within it arguments that could be construed as specifically anti-Assyrian that D did not already include and endorse on the basis of E.[100] As I have suggested already, EST provides content by which D filled out and updated its Elohistic patrimony.

This discussion highlights an important difference between D's law of the king and its adaptation of EST and one with implications for understanding D's resistance to Assyrian domination. Like its reuse of EST, D's law of the king is situated within the larger framework of its revision of E. Yet it does not replicate content or perspectives already found there; indeed, legal treatment of the Israelite monarchy is a well-observed lacuna in the Covenant Code.[101] The law of the king thus stands apart from D's Elohistic inheritance; its anti-Assyrian stance constitutes its distinctive contribution in D and helps to explain its inclusion in the D project.

Notwithstanding the differences just observed, the law of the king does align well with D's reuse of EST in at least two respects. The first relates to its audience and aim. I have argued that D's focus in its revision of EST, and thus its audience for this reuse, was an internal, Judean one. The law of the king can be understood similarly. As analyzed by Wazana, this law makes its case to an internal, Judean audience, even as it considers an external reality—the Assyrian ruler. The law of the king and D's reuse of EST also align with regard to dating. If this law indeed targets direct Assyrian rule in a potential province, a date in the first half of the seventh century is more plausible. In the second half of the century, the Neo-Assyrian empire turned substantially away from the southern Levant and soon after experienced significant decline (and eventual collapse). It follows, then, that Assyria became a less pressing concern for Judeans at that time.

While some scholars continue to correlate a Josianic dating for D with resistance to Assyrian imperial power and/or other Assyrian cultural influence, including the influence of EST,[102] the details of treaty use described above and the decline of Assyria across the seventh century recommend against such a reconstruction. Significant Assyrian influence in the southern Levant is both unlikely in the second half of the century and demonstrable in the first half. Some scholars have sought to account for this state of affairs by arguing that it was precisely in the face of Assyrian decline that Judeans were able to reassert their cultural and political independence.[103] This possibility cannot be ruled out, but it encounters a significant challenge in the evidence of the short-lived use and impact of Assyrian *adê* texts. Given the state of the evidence, then, to maintain a date for D in the late seventh century (or later) almost requires disavowing Assyrian influence in the work.

Dating D to the first half of the seventh century also plausibly situates its major legal innovation, the centralization of the cult (Deut 12), in relation to real historical events and the E law that its centralization legislation revises. As Martin Rose and Elizabeth Bloch-Smith have argued, the preservation of Jerusalem after Sennacherib's devastation of Judah's major centers, viewed from a particular perspective, lent significant prestige to the city and its temple.[104] It is likely that D's centralization legislation reflects a theological interpretation of Jerusalem's survival in the face of the Neo-Assyrian onslaught. That interpretation is similar to the one found in the "B Accounts" of Sennacherib's assault in 2 Kgs 18–19: Jerusalem was spared because it was Yahweh's chosen cult site.[105] D operationalized this interpretation legislatively and, situating its law within its story of Israel's past, integrated it into its etiology and allegory.

This interpretation of history also accounts for D's complete reversal of a major tenet of E's religious program. The Neo-Assyrian military campaigns in the southern Levant, culminating in Sennacherib's attack in 701 BCE, could be understood as a repudiation of Exod 20:24 and its claim that Yahweh endorsed a proliferation of local altars: "You shall make for me an earthen altar, and you shall sacrifice upon it your burnt offerings and your well-being offerings, your sheep and your cattle. *In every place where you call on my name, I will come to you and bless you.*" From the perspective of D's authors, history had proved that Yahweh preferred a single worship site in Jerusalem, and they adjusted E's legislation—and Israel's history—accordingly. The extent to which centralization became a guiding legislative principle in D underscores its importance and, by extension, the significant and recurrent challenge that E's altar law posed. Understanding the Assyrian devastation of Judah as a prompt for D's revisionary project helps to explain the strength and far-reaching nature of this work's centralization claim.

Conclusion

Though it has included a variety of proposals, the debate over D's dating has been dominated by this text's association with Josianic reform, a position that was argued by the prominent biblical scholars who bookended the nineteenth century, de Wette and Wellhausen. I have suggested here that this seventh-century BCE dating is substantially correct, though not because of any claimed connection with Josiah or the book find story. Instead, the literary, epigraphic, archaeological, and other historical evidence combine to recommend a date for the D work in the first half of the seventh century and perhaps even toward the end of its first third. This dating best accords with the circumstances necessary for D's interaction with EST. It also offers the most plausible context for understanding several individual D texts, including its centralization law and its law of the king. To be sure, a long reception history for D has ensued, especially after its integration into the Deuteronomy scroll. Yet it is from the seventh century BCE that this influential piece of literature likely originates and, so situated, its details can be explained most persuasively.

Conclusion: Literature in History and the Scriptural Pentateuch

As promised at its outset, this book has not attempted to treat every detail in Deuteronomy. Though its chapters have offered any number of interpretations of individual texts, these analyses have primarily been exemplary, modeling and advancing the volume's distinctive approach to reading Deuteronomy. The lead concern of this approach has been to theorize the Deuteronomic text as literature and to highlight the significance of this theorization for its interpretation. As I have argued in these pages, such a theorization has implications for understanding virtually all aspects of Deuteronomy, including its compositional analysis, its revisionary reuse of source materials, its historical contextualization, and its early reception history. Positioned amidst a robust scholarly conversation, this historically situated, literary analysis has sought a firm distinction from the scriptural approaches that have long dominated Deuteronomy's interpretation. This insistence upon distinguishing between literature and Scripture and their attendant fictive versus real discourses, I have suggested, counters interpretive trends not only beyond the academy but also within it.

Emerging from this theorization of the Deuteronomic texts is a new appreciation for the extent to which the D work, as a piece of literature, is thoroughly guided by its internal field of reference. Where this internal field of reference breaks down—primarily in cases of narration and characterization—is precisely where compositional complexity can be (and regularly has been) observed. Appreciation of D's literariness also sheds light on the particular ways that this text sought relevance in its compositional context. For example, it helps to explain how D's authors could appropriate their literary forebears and introduce the significant changes to them that they did. D's authors were bound neither by a real world beyond their work nor by other works that told similar stories with familiar characters. Recognition of D's literary quality also contributes to understanding the contemporaneity its authors sought for their work. This is most evident in D's etiology and allegory, which seek to explain a past that would yield the present that D envisioned. In its allegory, D even contains specific, symbolic reference to its compositional context.

D's concern to appeal to its present likely also stands behind its reuse of EST. Rather than offering a subversive response to Neo-Assyrian imperial ideology and practice, D's selective appropriation of EST's content put this *adê* text in service of its central aim, namely, to recast the story of Israel's wilderness journey and Moses's Horeb lawgiving that it inherited from the pentateuchal E source. In this effort, D's authors drew upon the prominent political discourse of their moment.

With respect to this issue of D's historical contextualization, the foregoing chapters clarify the extent to which this imaginative, literary work can be understood as self-consciously situated "between the tragedies"—one experienced and the other anticipated. Like other Judean authors, D's authors interpreted the Assyrian onslaught of 701 BCE and its aftermath in religio-political terms. Yet unlike other works that took account of Sennacherib's invasion, D's focus was not the miraculous preservation of Jerusalem. The Deuteronomic authors instead understood this event as an indictment that brought with it an important theological clarification: the worship at multiple cult sites that was championed by E and evidenced in real historical practice amounted to "each one doing whatever was right in his own eyes," a scenario that Yahweh had explicitly denounced (Deut 12:8).

The catastrophe of 701 presented an opportunity for change. For D's authors, Sennacherib's incursion even demanded it. These authors thus reimagined Israel's foundations in light of their newfound theological insights, and they did so ruefully. Drawing upon the explicit threats of their Assyrian overlord, they imagined Yahweh's behavior in imperial terms. Perhaps most importantly, this meant that having spared Judah once, Yahweh would not do so again. Future disloyalty would result not only in catastrophe but in destruction and deportation (Deut 28:20–44). What Yahweh required—again, like Judah's Assyrian overlord—was total devotion expressed in action: "You shall love Yahweh, your god, with all your heart, with all your self, and with all your strength" (Deut 6:5; cf. SAA 2 6:266–68).

The high-stakes political world in which Judah found itself provides a ready explanation for both D's theological anxiety and the stridency of its demands. The Assyrian emperors dealt in ultimate terms and had shown their willingness to act on their threats. For D's authors, Yahweh was no less severe—and even more powerful. There could be only a single path for Judah, and no deviation would be tolerated (Deut 28:14). D wrote these details into the story world that it imagined so vividly, creating from them a past whose resonances with the present were both urgent and incisive.

These observations, especially in relation to D's curse section, shed further light on the contribution that EST made to D. They apply as well to D's creative adaptation of EST material in Deut 13. Assyrian hegemony helped define and articulate a circumstance that would justify a prophet's death as collateral damage in a divine loyalty test (Deut 13:2–6). It also created conditions in which family members and close companions could be expected to betray their close bonds to inform on each other (Deut 13:7–12).

It should be noted that social configurations such as these could also be expressed positively, and D's authors wrote their history accordingly. Specifically, they promoted the kinship of the Israelite community—a band of siblings who all looked to their divine father, Yahweh. Suggesting that this arrangement was instituted already before their ancestors were established in their land, D's story suggested that careful maintenance of this design would preserve the seventh-century Judeans there.

This book has engaged only the earliest period of D's (and Deuteronomy's) reception. Yet even this limited consideration has made clear that interpretation of D quickly ranged far from its origins in the late Neo-Assyrian period and the social and theological politics of that era. The examples of the early reception of D examined here have also demonstrated that an important contributor—perhaps the *most* important contributor—to its interpretative transformation was its incorporation into the compiled Pentateuch. So situated, D's narrative of Horeb revelation and Moab recitation was transformed into a book of laws, interpretation of which was dominated by attempts to harmonize its legal content with that found elsewhere in the Pentateuch. This early pentateuchal interpretation set a course for the future scriptural reception of Deuteronomy, a reception characterized by both creativity and vibrancy. Substantially lost, however, was D's distinctive literary contribution and, in particular, its plotline. Recovery of this work, as argued here, promises new insight into Judean history and thought in the seventh century BCE. It is equally valuable as a point of departure for analyzing the history of Deuteronomic reception.

Notes

Introduction

1. For the classic formulation of the theory of a Deuteronomistic History, see Noth, *Deuteronomistic History.* For an overview and assessment of more recent formulations of the Deuteronomistic History theory, see esp. Römer, *Deuteronomistic History.*

2. On the (alleged) influence of Deuteronomic thought and language across the biblical corpus, see esp. Weinfeld, *Deuteronomic School;* see also the essays in Schearing and McKenzie, *Those Elusive Deuteronomists.*

3. On the impact of Wellhausen's *Prolegomena,* see esp. Smend, "Julius Wellhausen and His *Prolegomena*" (see also the other essays in this special volume of *Semeia,* titled *Julius Wellhausen and His* Prolegomena to the History of Israel); Smend, "Wellhausen in Greifswald"; Barton, "Wellhausen's *Prolegomena*"; Stackert, *Prophet Like Moses.*

4. Judging by the number of scrolls of Deuteronomy attested among the Dead Sea Scrolls compared with the number of scrolls attested for other biblical books, Deuteronomy occupied a central place already in (at least some) early Jewish circles. See, e.g., Tov, *Textual Criticism,* 96–98; Schorch, "Which Kind of Authority?," 1–2. Deuteronomy is also one of the Hebrew Bible texts most often cited in the New Testament (alongside Psalms and Isaiah). For recent discussion of the impact of Deuteronomy in Second Temple Judaism and early Christianity, see the essays in Menken and Moyise, *Deuteronomy in the New Testament.*

5. For an overview of this approach, see Baden, "Re-Emergence of Source Criticism"; Stackert, *Prophet Like Moses,* 19–26. For a fuller discussion, see Schwartz, "Torah," and Baden, *Composition.*

6. Deut 1:9–18 is a clear example of the reuse of the E material from Num 11* with no reference to the J material with which it is interwoven in this chapter. For discussion of this phenomenon and its implications, see Dillmann, *Numeri, Deuteronomium und Josua,* 609–11, 677–79; Baden, "Deuteronomic Evidence."

7. The blood plague may be divided as follows: J: vv. 14–18, 20 beginning from "he raised up," 21a, 23–25; P: vv. 19–20 (through "just as Yahweh commanded"), 21b, 22. See Greenberg, "Plague Narrative," 248.

8. For a detailed discussion of the source division of the blood plague and a reconstruction of its compilation, see Schwartz, "Torah," 187–91.

9. As demonstrated by Baruch J. Schwartz, this text can be divided as follows: P: v. 1 and the first words of v. 2 ("These are the generations of Jacob"); E: vv. 2 (except the first three words), 11b–18, 21–22, 24, the first words of 25 ("They sat down to eat"), 28aα, 29–30, 36; J: vv. 3–11a, 19–20, 23, 25 (except the first words), 26–27, 28aβ–b, 31–35 (Schwartz, "Joseph's Descent"; Schwartz, "How the Compiler").

10. Schwartz notes that "Hebron" in v. 14 should likely be attributed to the compiler (replacing what was originally a different geographical designation). The compiler apparently introduced it here to harmonize E's account with the location of Jacob's settlement preserved from P in Gen 35:27 ("How the Compiler," 266–67 n. 10).

11. Translations here and throughout, unless otherwise noted, are my own.

12. This source division of vv. 26–28 also facilitates an explanation for v. 36 (E), where the Midianites, having transported Joseph to Egypt, sell him to Potiphar: "The Midianites sold him into Egypt, to Potiphar, Pharaoh's official, the chief steward."

13. For further discussion of this example, see Stackert, "Pentateuchal Coherence," 260–62. A comparable example of reassigning an action from one party to another is found in Exod 24:11bβ, where the subject of the eating and drinking verbs has been reassigned in the compiled text from the whole Israelite people (24:8) to the ascent party in vv. 9–11bα (Moses, Aaron, Nadav, Avihu, and the seventy elders). For discussion, see esp. Chavel, "Kingdom of Priests," 190–92.

14. Many (even most) interpreters, including modern readers, have treated the Deuteronomy scroll primarily as Scripture. On early Jewish and Christian interpretation generally, see, e.g., the various essays in Sæbø, *Hebrew Bible, Old Testament;* Mulder and Sysling, *Mikra;* and Paget and Schaper, *New Cambridge History of the Bible.* For special attention to the impact of readers' assumptions on their interpretations, to be discussed below, see Kugel, *Traditions of the Bible.*

15. For the notion of Scripture as related first to its role within a reading community (and thus its reading practices), see W. Smith, *What Is Scripture?,* 17–20; Graham, "Scripture"; Watts, "Using Ezra's Time," 492–93.

16. For treatments of the category of Scripture itself, see, e.g., Levering, *Rethinking Scripture;* Wimbush, *Theorizing Scriptures;* W. Smith, *What Is Scripture?;* Kort, *"Take, Read."* For a recent attempt to apply the theorization of Scripture specifically to the Pentateuch, see Watts, *Understanding the Pentateuch.*

17. Watts has identified the Persian period as the likely origin of scriptural reading practices and has pointed, in particular, to the narrative of Neh 8 as an example ("Using Ezra's Time"). With due caution concerning Neh 8, as I show in Chapter 4, the history of interpretation bears out this general dating.

18. Kugel, *Traditions of the Bible,* 1–41 (esp. 14–19). It should be noted that the roots of these principles are likely older than their early Jewish and Christian mani-

festations. For example, William Schniedewind has traced the paradigm of divinely revealed text to the Neo-Assyrian period and argued for its relevance for the scripturalization of Judean texts ("Scripturalization in Ancient Judah").

19. For discussion of such features as markers of unity, see Stackert, "Before and after Scripture."

20. See esp. John Barton's discussion of the early, two-part structure of the biblical canon ("the law and the prophets") and the way that this division conceptualized as prophetic many texts that, on their face, are not prophetic (*Oracles of God*, 35–95).

21. Compare the similar perspective in the biblical book of Daniel (e.g., Dan 9:20–27, 12:9), which is not far removed temporally from the Habakkuk commentary. For discussion of secrecy and inspired interpretation in Daniel, see Jassen, *Mediating the Divine*, 214–21.

22. On the Qumran Habakkuk commentary and its importance for understanding notions of prophecy and biblical interpretation in late Second Temple Judaism, see, e.g., Jassen, "Prophets and Prophecy," 324–26. For recent treatments of *pesher* generally as a category of biblical interpretation, see Machiela, "Qumran Pesharim as Biblical Commentaries"; Jassen, "Pesharim and the Rise of Commentary."

23. B. Smith, *On the Margins*, 25.

24. B. Smith, *On the Margins*, 28.

25. Harshav, *Explorations in Poetics*, 1–31.

26. In this sense, my interest is in exploring and applying a definition of literature itself, a task that B. Smith explicitly disavows in her discussion of fictive discourse (*On the Margins*, 85). Nonetheless, note that Smith acknowledges precisely this fictive framework as the distinction between literary and nonliterary works: "A history of the Civil War may be conceived, in some very peculiar sense, as having the Civil War as its compliance-class, but in that sense no war at all is the compliance-class of the *Iliad* or, indeed, of *War and Peace*. A reader who fails to comprehend the nature of fictions may be as likely to look for Prince Andrey's grave as for Napoleon's Tomb, but the fact that we can locate the latter and not the former does not make one part of Tolstoy's novel any less fictional than another" (ibid., 11).

27. One might call to mind the categorization pronounced in some Christian contexts as part of liturgical readings of the Bible: "The word of God for the people of God."

28. B. Smith, *On the Margins*, 55–75.

29. B. Smith, *On the Margins*, 58–60.

30. Bell, *Ritual Theory, Ritual Practice*, 109–10. On strategic misrecognition in ritual practice more generally, see pp. 98–110.

31. Watts, "Using Ezra's Time," 492–504; Watts, *Understanding the Pentateuch*, 3–6. Watts rightly notes that among the scriptural ritual foci he identifies—semantic

meaning, oral performance, and iconic veneration—the evidence from the earliest attested period is strongest for semantic interpretation ("Using Ezra's Time," 501).

32. B. Smith, *On the Margins*, 44–50.
33. White, "Value of Narrativity."
34. White, "Value of Narrativity," 15.
35. White, "Value of Narrativity," 24.

Chapter 1. What Is Deuteronomy?

1. For a recent, helpful overview of the question of genre in Deuteronomy and the various scholarly assessments, see Strawn, "Moses at Moab," 156–69.
2. This is not to discount the smaller textual issues that do appear in Deuteronomy. In a few instances in the coming chapters, I treat specific text-critical issues and consider how they affect the interpretation of Deuteronomic texts. The largest number of textual differences among the ancient witnesses to Deuteronomy appear in the Samaritan Pentateuch and related manuscripts, though LXX manuscripts also regularly attest small harmonizations. For discussion, see, e.g., Schorch, "Samaritan Version of Deuteronomy"; Tov, "Textual Harmonizations"; Hobson, *Transforming Literature*, 128–31.
3. For theorization of the abstract "work" and its attestation in a particular manuscript (i.e., its textual attestation), see esp. Tanselle, *Rationale*. For discussion of this distinction in the context of biblical studies, see Hendel, "What Is a Biblical Book?" For the purposes of pentateuchal studies, an additional level of analysis can be identified. A literary work can be distinguished from a scroll, and a scroll's conventional content can be distinguished from any particular manuscript, which attests textual peculiarities.
4. On the meaning of the Greek τεῦχος as "scroll case" as well as "roll of writing material," see Dogniez, "Greek Translation," 112. For discussion, see Carr, "Rethinking the Materiality," 608–9 passim.
5. Haran, "Book-Scrolls"; Haran, "Size of Books in the Bible"; Haran, "Book-Size and the Device of Catch-Lines"; Haran, "Book-Size and the Thematic Cycles." See now also Carr, "Rethinking the Materiality," which builds especially upon Haran's insights and emphasizes the issue of conventional use. Note also the earlier observations of Abraham Kuenen, who noted that pentateuchal content corresponds with its scroll divisions and argued that these divisions were the work of the pentateuchal redactor (*Historico-Critical Inquiry*, 341–42). In relation to the Enneateuch and from a different perspective, see Schmid, "Buchtechnische"; Levin, "Cohesion and Separation."

Scholars have debated the issue of scroll technology and its limits. Drawing on later, rabbinic evidence (*b. B. Bat.* 13b; *Sop.* 3.4) and the lack of a firm disconfirmation, Emanuel Tov has suggested that a complete Torah scroll might have been possible at Qumran. Yet Tov also admits that such a scroll would have likely measured 25 to 30 meters ("Copying of a Biblical Scroll," 125). Undermining the plausibility of this claim is the fact that the largest biblical scroll from Qumran, the Great Isaiah Scroll (1QIsaᵃ), measures only 7.34 meters (24.1 feet; fifty-four columns and nearly complete; see Digital Dead Sea Scrolls at http://dss.collections.imj.org.il/isaiah; on the variable size of columns within a single scroll and between scrolls of the same work, see Tov, "Copying of a Biblical Scroll," 110–12; for detailed discussion of the difficulty of estimating the lengths of damaged scrolls, see Ratzon and Dershowitz, "Length of a Scroll"). Joseph Blenkinsopp has suggested that a full Torah scroll would have measured 33 meters, a length that, if possible, would have been unwieldy and thus avoided (*Pentateuch*, 46). Carr estimates a full Torah scroll at 33.2 to 36 meters and similarly argues that, while possible, its unwieldiness makes its production and use unlikely ("Rethinking the Materiality," 614).

6. There has sometimes been confusion between or conflation of the D composition and the book (i.e., scroll) of Deuteronomy in the history of modern scholarship. For example, in his recent construal of points of consensus and debate in penta- teuchal studies, Reinhard Kratz stated, "A further consensus is the assumption that we can distinguish and isolate two distinct literary strata within the Pentateuch: *the book of Deuteronomy*, whose original independence has been recognized since Wilhelm Martin Leberecht de Wette, and the so-called Priestly Writing (P)— including the Holiness Code (H)—in Genesis–Numbers, whose literary extent was established by Theodor Nöldeke" ("Pentateuch in Current Research," 34, em- phasis added). Similarly, Eckart Otto regularly employs designations such as "the pre-exilic (deuteronomic) book of Deuteronomy," "the deuteronomistic book of Deuteronomy," and "the post-Deuteronomistic book of Deuteronomy" as short- hand to describe stages in the development of a D composition (see, e.g., Otto, "History of the Legal-Religious Hermeneutics"). I will employ the term "Deutero- nomic" in this book to refer to materials belonging to the D work that I describe.

7. The discussion below of D's compositional history and literariness treat these issues in detail.

8. See, e.g., Ruth. For discussion of Ruth as a single-authored composition (and one that draws extensively upon pentateuchal material), see esp. Chavel, *Oracu- lar Law*, 250–56; J. Schipper, *Ruth*, 18–19. For arguments in favor of inconsis- tency as endemic to ancient Near Eastern composition, see Greenstein, "The- ory and Argument," 83–84; Berman, *Inconsistency in the Torah*. Note also that the early readers of the Pentateuch perceived inconsistencies in the Pentateuch and actively sought to resolve them. A parade example in the Bible is the har- monization in 2 Chr 35:13 of the rules for preparing the Passover in Deut 16:7 and Exod 12:9. I return to this issue in Chapter 4.

9. Haran, "Book-Size and the Thematic Cycles," 176. Note the synchronically ori- ented comments of Jean-Pierre Sonnet on this point (*Book within the Book*, 24).

10. On the meaning of this claim and its relation to Deut 34:10a, see Stackert, *Prophet Like Moses,* 122–23, 136–44.

11. See Baden, *Composition,* 146–48. For corresponding non-Documentary reconstruction of literary connections in the pre-Deuteronomic source materials, see, e.g., Kratz's discussion of the tie between Num 25:1a and Deut 34:5–6 (*Composition,* 125–26).

12. This approach also aligns with the compiler's principles of maximal preservation and minimal intervention. Under a different set of principles for combining texts, the compiler could have omitted certain framing details from his sources; he could also have made changes to these details.

13. See, e.g., Driver, *Deuteronomy,* 7.

14. For discussion of the source division of Deut 34, see esp. Baden, *Composition,* 147–48. For an overview of options suggested for this chapter's compositional history, see, e.g., Römer and Brettler, "Deuteronomy 34."

15. Regarding the D composition and the question of ancient media, Haran argued that D's use of "this scroll" to refer to itself suggests that it stands at the transition point between the use of papyrus and skin for scrolls ("Book-Scrolls," 116–18).

16. See, e.g., Pakkala, "Textual Developments."

17. Resistance to the combination of genres in pentateuchal works can be traced back to the nineteenth century. For example, Wellhausen famously objected to the combination of narrative and law in P, proclaiming it poorly executed and unnatural:

> This combination of Deuteronomy with the Jehovist was the beginning of the combination of narrative and law; and the fact that this precedent was before the author of the Priestly Code explains how, though his concern was with the Torah alone, he yet went to work from the very outset and comprised in his work the history of creation, as if it also belonged to the Torah. This manner of setting forth the Torah in the form of a history-book is not in the least involved in the nature of the case; on the contrary, it introduces the greatest amount of awkwardness. How it came about can only be explained in the way above described; an antecedent process of the same nature in literary history led the way and made the suggestion. (*Prolegomena,* 345)

> Wellhausen elsewhere refers to the "monstrous growths of legislative matter" that attend P's historical narrative as "certainly intolerable" ("in der That unerträglich," *Prolegomena,* 342; this comment does not appear in the 1878 edition).

18. For summary of the various arguments, see Driver, *Deuteronomy,* lxvii–lxxii (with Driver's own doubts concerning the identification of different hands in the two sections).

19. Milstein, *Tracking the Master Scribe.*

20. Noth, *Deuteronomistic History,* 13–16.

21. Wellhausen, *Composition*, 193; Haran, *Biblical Collection*, 2: 54–58; for elaboration of his theory, see pp. 253–74; contrast Haran, "Book-Scrolls," 117 n. 10.

22. Baden, *Composition*, 130–36.

23. See, e.g., Veijola, *Deuteronomium*, 122–23. For the reverse argument, namely, the addition of 4:44ff. (in stages) on the basis of 1:1–5, see Kratz, "Headings," 37–41.

24. Chavel, "Literary Development of Deuteronomy 12." Chavel's analysis builds upon and counters several others, most notably, Levinson, *Deuteronomy and the Hermeneutics*, 23–52. For an early example of the sort of supplementary model (*Ergänzungshypothese*) that Chavel proposes, see Hölscher, "Komposition und Ursprung," 179–83. For a helpful overview of compositional analyses of Deut 12, see Otto, *Deuteronomium 12–34*, 1: 1147–50. Though it is tantalizing to imagine possibilities, it is not evident how one might connect the different laws that Chavel identifies with a theory of multiple, originally distinct D compositions.

25. See, e.g., Bertholet, *Deuteronomium*, 31; Rofé, "Strata of the Law." In line with observations like Chavel's, some scholars have even identified in Deut 12 the original core of the D composition. See, e.g., Steymans, "Deuteronomy 28," 12. For an attempt to reconstruct a three-stage development of the Deuteronomistic History (spanning from the Neo-Assyrian period to the Persian period) in relation to the layers in Deut 12, see Römer, *Deuteronomistic History*, 56–65.

26. Driver, *Deuteronomy*, 316. For recent arguments that the reference to the scroll in 28:58 is exophoric, i.e., self-referential and not part of the text's story world, see Lester, "Deuteronomy 28:58"; Arnold, "Deuteronomy's Book." For astute arguments against self-reference in D, see Sonnet, "Fifth Book," 202 n. 12.

27. See Deut 4:13; Stackert, *Prophet Like Moses*, 131–34.

28. Stackert, *Prophet Like Moses*, 77–80. See also the discussion in Chapter 2.

29. Crouch, *Making of Israel*, 204.

30. On the brotherhood ethic in D and its introduction alongside of D's literary inheritance, see, e.g., Otto, *Deuteronomium: Politische Theologie*, 274–314.

31. Lohfink, "Distribution of the Functions of Power," 339. See also Lohfink, "Zum deuteronomischen Zentralisationsformel"; Kratz, *Composition*, 117–18.

32. Lohfink, "Distribution of the Functions of Power," 343–44; Braulik, "Sequence of the Laws." For critique of these claims, see, e.g., Otto, "Von der Gerichtsordnung zum Verfassungsentwurf"; Levinson, *Deuteronomy and the Hermeneutics*, 8–10.

33. For early examples of *Numeruswechsel* as a basis for compositional analysis in D, see Steuernagel, *Deuteronomium und Josua*, and Hölscher, "Komposition und Ursprung." For recent examples, see Kratz, *Composition*, 117–18 (Kratz combines number variation with reliance upon the Covenant Code and the primacy of cult centralization as the bases for reconstructing *Urdeuteronomium*); Arnold, "Number Switching." For critique of this approach, see, e.g., McCarthy, *Treaty and Covenant*, 188–89 n. 1; Weinfeld, *Deuteronomy 1–11*, 15–16; Römer, *Deuteronomistic History*, 73–74.

34. Robert Polzin identified fifty-six verses in Deuteronomy that belong to the third-person narrator (*Moses and the Deuteronomist*, 29). However, this count is for the Deuteronomy scroll, not the D composition.

35. Fox, "Frame-Narrative and Composition" (for Deuteronomy and other ancient Near Eastern examples, see pp. 92–94).

36. Genette offers an extended examination of the literary preface. See his *Paratexts*, 161–293.

37. Genette, *Paratexts*, 197.

38. Contrast the analysis of Polzin, who assigns vv. 1–5 to the narrator (*Moses and the Deuteronomist*, 30). The argument here is closer to that of Sonnet, who refers to "the staging of Moses as orator" in 1:1 (*Book within the Book*, 27).

39. The distinction between preface and narrative need not indicate the presence of different hands in the composition (though neither does it exclude it). In the case of 1:1–2, 4 and 1:5, that 32:45–47 apparently combine elements from 1:1 and 5 suggests that preface and narrative may belong to the same stratum. For example, the omniscient narrator in 32:45 refers to "all of these words," which recalls "These are the words" from 1:1. Likewise, "the words of this teaching" in 32:46 combines "the words" of 1:1 with "this teaching" of 1:5. In the comparable introduction at the end of Deut 4, vv. 45–49 correspond functionally with 1:1–2, 4, and 5:1 is the equivalent to 1:5, i.e., the beginning of the storytelling.

40. With specific reference to classical texts, see the discussion of Schmitz, *Modern Literary Theory*, 6–10. With reference to biblical texts and narrative texts in particular, see Alter, "How Convention Helps Us Read," esp. 116–18.

41. A recent assertion of this nature that does at least attempt a minimal definition is found in Bloch, "Aramaic Influence and Inner Diachronic Development." Bloch states, "The fact that the books of the Hebrew Bible constitute literature—that is, writings intended to be read, studied and copied on repeated occasions, without being confined to a specific situation of social or economic life—can be taken for granted" (85).

42. To take a very prominent example, see Alter, *Art of Biblical Narrative*. For helpful critique of Alter on the issue of literary criticism vs. historical criticism and the importance of their combination, see Geller, "Some Pitfalls." In defining biblical (and other) texts as literature, Alter has emphasized the complex discourse of literary texts that affects their meaning/interpretation and, in particular, the aesthetic pleasure that factors in their communication. See Alter, *Pleasures of Reading*, 28–29. For his part, Meir Sternberg has argued that literary analysis must pay attention to various historical details. Yet he also reduces approaches to "source-oriented versus discourse-oriented inquiry," advocating the latter (*Poetics*, 14).

43. Harshav, *Explorations in Poetics*, 19–21.

44. Harshav, *Explorations in Poetics*, 1, emphasis added.

45. Harshav, *Explorations in Poetics*, 7.

46. Harshav, *Explorations in Poetics*, 14–15.

47. In this sense, the external field of reference serves as a model for the internal field of reference. Yet it is also drawn into the story world and made subordinate to or even part of its internal field. See Harshav, *Explorations in Poetics*, 28–30.

48. Harshav, *Explorations in Poetics*, 17, 20.

49. Harshav, *Explorations in Poetics*, 3.

50. Harshav, *Explorations in Poetics*, 15.

51. Harshav, *Explorations in Poetics*, 27.

52. The field of biblical studies has rarely engaged directly Harshav's literary theorization (and then usually in relation to poetry rather than prose; see esp. Dobbs-Allsopp, *On Biblical Poetry*, 95–177). For Harshav's direct commentary on biblical narrative, see, e.g., *Explorations in Poetics*, 265–68. As a founder of what has been termed "the Tel Aviv School of Poetics and Semiotics," Harshav worked closely alongside Meir Sternberg, whose analysis of biblical narrative has had a significant impact on biblical studies. Moreover, though Sternberg did not interact closely with Harshav's theorization in his work on biblical narrative, he worked with a similar basic stance, stating that "the internal premises established by the discourse . . . alone determine reliability in interpretation" (*Poetics*, 51). For an overview of the Tel Aviv School, see Mintz, "On the Tel Aviv School"; McHale and Segal, "Small World"; see also Harshav's brief description (*Explorations in Poetics*, 252–57).

53. Harshav, *Explorations in Poetics*, 8.

54. As Sternberg has observed, biblical narrators exhibit a baseline reliability: "The Bible always tells the truth in that its narrator is absolutely reliable. Historians may quarrel with his facts and others call them fiction; but in context his remain accounts of the truth communicated on the highest authority" (*Poetics*, 51).

55. Seth L. Sanders points to this issue when he labels the compiled Pentateuch, with its interwoven sources, "a sort of metaliterary collection" ("What If There Aren't Any Empirical Models?," 300–301).

56. As discussed in the Introduction, scholars have rarely addressed the question of what the "literature" of "biblical literature" entails, much less as (potentially) distinguished from the category of Scripture. James W. Watts is a rare exception, yet he works with an imprecise and largely assumed definition of literature, taking as his starting point that biblical texts simply are literature. Thus, even as he acknowledges the difficulties in the compiled Pentateuch that defy literary norms, he describes it as simultaneously literature (with "poor literary form") and Scripture (*Understanding the Pentateuch*, 20–23).

57. For a social scientific perspective on such reading practices, see Stackert, "Pentateuchal Coherence."

58. See esp. Long, *Problem of Etiological Narrative*. For consideration beyond the form-critical, see, e.g., van Dyk, "So-Called Etiological Elements" (with special focus on rhetorical and folkloristic elements).

59. Harshav observes that in biblical stories, the internal field of reference can be "anchored" in an "accepted" external field: "The author's newly introduced fictional referents, then, are presented as extensions of referents known outside the fiction; together, they constitute one new internally coherent Field" (*Explorations in Poetics*, 25). Within pentateuchal studies of the last century, this "accepted" external field substantially overlaps with notions of tradition history.

60. B. Smith, *On the Margins*, 55–57.

61. This process is sometimes understood as iterative and thus functional beyond the initial compositional context in its various receptions. See the discussion below.

62. For further discussion of the pentateuchal compositions as political allegories, see Stackert, *Prophet Like Moses*, 28–31; Stackert, "Political Allegory." The discussion here draws especially on the latter article, applying its arguments concerning the Priestly source to the Deuteronomic source.

63. Fletcher, *Allegory*, 2–3.

64. Frye, *Anatomy of Criticism*, 90–91. Note that Frye also considers examples of allegory that step outside the conventions of literature.

65. Rosenberg, *King and Kin*, 12.

66. Some scholars have argued for a more thoroughgoing allegory in pentateuchal material that seeks to find an external referent for virtually every element within the text. See, e.g., Miller, "J as Constitutionalist"; Oswald, "Defeating Amalek."

67. See White, *Metahistory*, 5–11.

68. Pakkala, "Date of the Oldest Edition," 392–93. For critique of this view, see, e.g., Otto, "History of the Legal-Religious Hermeneutics," 226.

69. "Die Exilsgeneration setzt sich in Dtn 5, 3 von ihren Vätern vor der Katastrophe ab. Die Überlebenden der Katastrophe sind die Adressaten des Deuteronomiums und mit ihnen sei der Bund geschlossen" (Otto, *Deuteronomium 1–11*, 2: 680–81). For Otto, identification of the Deuteronomic allegory is a key component in his compositional analysis. In his view, a preexilic composition that included a revision of the Covenant Code laws (which, Otto claims, had no Mosaic or covenant framework when accessed by the preexilic Deuteronomic author) and materials that respond to Neo-Assyrian hegemony was supplemented with the Mosaic frame and wilderness setting in the exilic period. For a summary of Otto's compositional analysis and its successive stages, see his "History of the Legal-Religious Hermeneutics."

70. Mayes, *Deuteronomy*, 147.

71. Römer, *Deuteronomistic History*, 124. For extension of allegory in Deuteronomy to the Persian period, see, e.g., Otto, "Anti-Achaemenid Propaganda."

72. Notwithstanding the popularity of this theory, even scholars whose work otherwise aligns closely with that of its adherents have occasionally raised important questions about its cogency. See, e.g., Pakkala, "Date of the Oldest Edition," 396; Albertz, "Possible *Terminus Ad Quem*," 276. Albertz asks plainly,

"Was there ever a Deuteronomic legal corpus that was not styled as a speech of Moses just before the occupation of the land?" A number of scholars from the late nineteenth and early twentieth centuries endorsed the connection between D's laws and its Mosaic framework. For discussion, see Driver, *Deuteronomy,* lxv–lxvii.

73. See, e.g., Otto, "History of the Legal-Religious Hermeneutics," 212–25. For a more circumspect assessment, see Römer, *Deuteronomistic History,* 49–56.

74. See, e.g., Clements, "Jerusalem Cult Tradition"; Levinson, *Deuteronomy and the Hermeneutics,* 4, 23 n. 1. See also 1 Kgs 8:16//2 Chr 6:5–6. For the suggestion that D's "place" was originally Gerizim and, with it, that D originated in the North, see Schorch, "Samaritan Version of Deuteronomy." Schorch also discusses ancient interpretation of the central sanctuary as an allegorical symbol for Jerusalem. See further discussion of this phenomenon in Chapter 4.

75. See, e.g., Driver, *Deuteronomy,* xxxii, xlvi–lxii.

76. See, e.g., Nelson, *Deuteronomy,* 244; Nielsen, *Deuteronomium,* 185. Arguing that most of Deut 17:16 (everything following "Only he shall not multiply horses for himself") is a later insertion that introduces the allegory in this unit, Albertz suggests a date at the beginning of the sixth century BCE ("Possible *Terminus Ad Quem,*" 281–90). For further discussion, see Chapter 5.

77. See, e.g., Nathan MacDonald's recent discussion of the dating of Deuteronomy, where he emphasized that the ambition and literary inventiveness of the Deuteronomic authors significantly complicate the identification and interpretation of the text's allegory, which then complicates the attempt to date the text through its allegorical references ("Dating of Deuteronomy," 431–32; cf. also Crouch, *Making of Israel,* 177–78).

78. Frye, *Anatomy of Criticism,* 90; cf. Fletcher, *Allegory,* 325–26.

79. Quilligan, *Language of Allegory,* 225–27; Rosenberg, *King and Kin,* 13–15.

80. Sonnet, *Book within the Book,* 4–5. Note that Sonnet understands Deuteronomy (not D) as a consistent work. See esp. Sonnet, "Fifth Book."

81. See Frye, *Anatomy of Criticism,* 89–92. Fletcher notes the optimistic intent of allegorical writing: "The correspondences of allegory are open to any who have a decoder's skill" (*Allegory,* 325).

82. Quilligan, *Language of Allegory,* 227.

83. Harshav, *Explorations in Poetics,* 172–73.

84. Rosenberg, *King and Kin,* 46.

85. For discussion of D's laws as nonlegal, see, e.g., Chavel, "Legal Literature"; Stackert, *Rewriting the Torah;* Wright, *Inventing God's Law.* For comparison with cuneiform documents of real legal practice, see esp. Wells, "Law or Religion?"; Milstein, "Making a Case."

86. See, e.g., Wells, "What Is Biblical Law?"

87. Gilmer, *If-You Form;* Sternberg, "If-Plots in Deuteronomy"; Sonnet, "Fifth Book," 220–26; Gilmer, "If-Plots in Deuteronomy."

88. For discussion of the underspecification of both second- and first-person address, see, e.g., Beneviste, *Problèmes de linguistique générale*, 1: 251–54.

89. Note also that sometimes the issue of *Numeruswechsel* and distinguishing the addressee of the second-person formulation in D have been combined, with the suggestion that the switch from singular to plural could indicate direct address of the text's audience (Albertz, "Possible *Terminus Ad Quem*," 281).

90. De Wette, "Dissertatio Critica."

91. For further discussion, see Chapter 5.

92. Wellhausen, *Composition*, 186–93; Wellhausen, *Prolegomena*, 33, 280. Many scholars have followed this view, often in a modified form. For example, Norbert Lohfink has argued for a non-Mosaic Deuteronomic law on the basis of 2 Kgs 22–23 and Deut 6:17 and 28:45 ("Die Bundesurkunde des Königs Josias"; Lohfink, "Deuteronomium"). Richard Elliott Friedman has also identified Deut 12–26 as the earliest layer in D ("Three Major Redactors"). For further discussion of a non-Mosaic D, see below.

93. For the distinction between fictive speech and real speech, see the discussion of Scripture vs. literature in the Introduction.

94. The concept of "privilege law" originates in Max Weber's sociological analysis. It refers to a phenomenon observable in the early development of law in which membership groups created for themselves special requirements and opportunities enforceable within the group. For the application of this concept to biblical law and the covenant relationship between Yahweh and Israel (thus "divine" privilege law), see esp. Horst, *Privilegrecht Yahves*.

95. Otto, "History of the Legal-Religious Hermeneutics," 212–16; Otto, *Deuteronomium 12–34*, 1: 1093–99, 1108–12. A number of scholars have argued for a version of this thesis, in many cases with Deut 6:4 (and its second-person address) as the opening of the putative early D work. See, e.g., Preuss, *Deuteronomium*, 100–101; Lohfink, "Deuteronomium," 390–91; Veijola, *Deuteronomium*, 175; Kratz, *Composition*, 124–25, 131; Kratz, "Headings," 45–46; Steymans, "Deuteronomy 13," 108.

96. It is possible that the Temple Scroll from Qumran also features such direct address of the reader by the deity. This cannot be determined with certainty, however, because the beginning of the work, with whatever framing it contained, has been lost. For a brief overview of this text and its major issues, see Crawford, *Rewriting Scripture*, 84–104.

97. For general characterizations of biblical historical texts, see Brettler, *Creation of History*. On the Josianic reform accounts, see the discussion in Chapter 5. See also Römer, *Deuteronomistic History*, 49–56; Ben-Dov, "Writing as Oracle."

98. Putative evidence that is advanced in support of this claim is easily dismissed. For example, Lohfink has suggested that the relative clause *'ăšer ṣiwwāk* (pausal, with divine subject) in Deut 6:17 and 28:45, which he argues characterizes D's laws as promulgated by the deity and not by Moses, is out of place

in the Mosaically framed D ("Deuteronomium," 390–91). Lohfink's objection ultimately concerns a perceived inconsistency in Deuteronomic formulation. If Moses regularly appears as the subject of the verb in *ʾăšer ṣwh* clauses in D, can the deity serve as the subject in Deut 6:17 and 28:45? Nothing about these examples contradicts the story of Moses's mediation of law in D. There is thus no reason to posit on their basis an alternative framework for D's laws. For earlier critique of attempts to redefine the speaker in D, see, e.g., Kratz: "The supposition that Deuteronomy was originally a divine speech is pure speculation" (*Composition*, 124).

99. Römer, *Deuteronomistic History*, 124.

100. Strawn, "Slaves and Rebels," 188. For earlier treatment, see already von Rad, *Problem of the Hexateuch*, 28–29. For more nuanced views, see Markl, "Deuteronomy's Frameworks"; Markl, *Gottes Volk im Deuteronomium*, 70–79; Sanders, *Invention of Hebrew*, 137–38, 163. Sanders in particular points to the social and political significance of D's prominent direct address to the Israelite people in the midst of its story world.

101. Strawn, "Slaves and Rebels," 166–67, 189.

102. On the concept of "breaking the fourth wall" in literature (a form of metalepsis), see, e.g., Genette, *Narrative Discourse*, 235–37, 243–51; Kukkonen and Klimek, *Metalepsis in Popular Culture*. Markl rightly identifies "until this day" in 2:22 and 3:14 as the third-person narrator's use of "today" ("Deuteronomy's Frameworks," 277; he also includes 34:6, but I am leaving this example aside because, in my view, it does not belong to D; it is possible also to include 10:8 alongside 2:22 and 3:14, though it is difficult to determine whether this line is voiced by the narrator or by Moses). For discussion of "frame breaks" in D and the way that they reinforce differentiation between Moses's fictive audience and the work's narratee/implied reader, see Polzin, *Moses and the Deuteronomist*, 31–32. Sonnet argues that the frame breaks work together with Mosaic character speech to bolster the reliability of the work overall ("Fifth Book," 200).

103. A rare instance of the breakdown of D's fictive world appears in Deut 11:8–15, where the first-person speech that begins in Moses's voice switches without explanation to the deity's voice. Verses 13–15 contain this shift: "[13]If you indeed heed my commands that I am commanding you today, to love Yahweh your god and to serve him with all your will and self, [14]then I will give rain to your land in its season, the early rain and the later rain. You will gather your grain, wine, and new oil, [15]and I will provide grass in your field for your animals, and you will eat and be satisfied." Noteworthy in this instance is the reference to "my commandments" in v. 13, which, apart from an overtly divinely voiced instance in the Decalogue (5:10), is the only instance in D where the first-person possessive pronominal suffix is used in relation to commandments. More common is Moses's reference to Yahweh's commandments with the third-person singular possessive suffix ("his commandments," Deut 4:40; 6:2; 7:9; 8:2, 11; 11:1;

13:5, 19; 26:17, 18; 27:10; 28:1, 15, 45; 30:8, 10, 16). Deut 29:4–5 contains another such instance. For discussion, including of the versional evidence, see Sonnet, *Book within the Book*, 39.

104. The claim, I would argue, requires moving beyond the phenomenon of "aesthetic illusion," namely, the reader's feeling of immersion in a text's story world. As Werner Wolf notes, aesthetic illusion is accompanied by a persistent recognition of the difference between the story world and the real world ("Illusion [Aesthetic]," 276; for this notion in relation to D's readers, see Sonnet, "Fifth Book," 201). What Römer, Strawn, and others who have argued similarly imagine is something more akin to "psychological participation"—being "caught up in the story" through, among other things, identifications with characters in a manner that produces significant emotional and other responses (Walton, *Mimesis as Make Believe*, 240–89). I would suggest that psychological participation often features in scriptural reading practices, from their identification of the text as divine to their ritual use of the biblical text and their insistence upon its fundamental relevance for readers in all times and places.

105. The repeated adjurations in D to "remember" are similarly all addressed to the Israelite characters in the text, not to the reader. See Deut 5:15; 7:18; 8:2, 18; 9:7; 15:15; 16:3, 12; 24:9, 18, 22; 25:17. An instance such as 16:3, appearing as part of a ritual that is presumably to be performed repeatedly in the future, is one that may suggest an allegorical use of the second person in D. Yet even in this instance, there seems to be no reason to understand the second-person address to include anyone but the Israelite characters being addressed by Moses, namely, those who actually experienced the Exodus from Egypt.

106. Note the similar, general conclusion of Sonnet ("Fifth Book," 200): "As in any other biblical work, the book's (rhetorical) thrust is primarily meant for the reader, who will learn countless lessons from Moses' address, but never as the direct addressee of the prophet."

107. Levinson, *Deuteronomy and the Hermeneutics*, 152. For other examples, see von Rad, *Problem of the Hexateuch*, 28–29; Arnold, "Reexamining," 18–19; Strawn, "Slaves and Rebels," 164–67, 184–91; cf. also the more nuanced evaluation in Markl, "Deuteronomy's Frameworks," 278.

108. *B. Shavuot* 39a; *Tanh. Nitz.* 8, each citing Deut 29:13–14; cf. *Exod. Rab.* 28:6, which extends the interpretation to Deut 5:22, understanding this verse's "he did not continue" (*yāsap*) as "he did not cease" (*yāsûp*).

109. Von Rad's argument in favor of a transhistorical reading leaves open the possibility of the exact rejoinder offered here. Of the supposed confusion of generations in Deut 5:3, he states, "In a literary presentation of the matter it would be meaningless so to discount the passage of time; such a procedure could carry no conviction with a post-Mosaic generation." He thus introduces what he identifies as assumptions of cultic observance for understanding this text, assumptions by which, he contends, "past, present, and future acts of God co-

alesce in the one tremendous actuality of the faith" (*Problem of the Hexateuch*, 29). Yet if no such generational confusion exists in Deut 5:3, presumably von Rad would admit of the literary fitness of the text and withdraw his argument.

110. See, e.g., Strawn, "Slaves and Rebels," 165–67, 173–74. Strawn proposes a process of "literary inscription" in which the text's audience is written into it. Recognizing the difficulties that generation change creates in D, Strawn creatively suggests considering not just the first and second generations but also a generation "1.5." A similar struggle to make sense of the text within its story world prompts the identification of allegory in the case of Moses's exclusion from the land (Deut 1:37, 3:26, 4:21; cf. Mayes, *Deuteronomy*, 147).

111. Quilligan's description of allegoresis (allegorical interpretation) has strongly religious overtones: "As members of an elite sect of initiates, allegorical critics already know how to read, and when they engage in reading a text they find something they already know is hidden within it" (*Language of Allegory*, 227). This characterization closely matches the scriptural reading practices of early Judaism and Christianity discussed in the Introduction. Strawn's discussion draws especially upon Jon D. Levenson's explanations of biblical texts as scriptural ("Slaves and Rebels," 184–91, citing the discussion of the concept of "the literary simultaneity of Scripture" in Levenson, *Hebrew Bible*, 62–81).

Chapter 2. Literary Revision in Deuteronomic Composition

1. Already in his 1805 dissertation, de Wette observed the thoroughly learned character of Deuteronomic composition in relation to other pentateuchal material, even suggesting that the Deuteronomic author had committed the earlier material to memory (though note that de Wette understood D to be dependent on portions of both the non-Priestly and the Priestly material in Exodus–Numbers). See Harvey, Jr., and Halpern, "'*Dissertatio Critica*,'" 79, 84). For more recent discussion of the learned nature of D's composition, see, e.g., Levinson, *Deuteronomy and the Hermeneutics*; Stackert, *Rewriting the Torah*.

2. In this sense, the usage of *tôrâ* in 17:18 is equivalent to its usage in verses such as 1:5; 4:8, 44. See Driver, *Deuteronomy*, 212.

3. Compare the characterizations of the contents of the other pentateuchal scrolls in the names assigned to them in the LXX (*Genesis*, denoting creation/origins; *Exodos*, referencing Israel's departure from Egypt; *Levitikon*, referring to issues of relevance to the Levitical priesthood; and *Arithmoi*, referencing census taking in the desert). For discussion of these titles, see Dogniez, "Greek Translation."

4. Scholars have made several detailed proposals for additional source materials that D may have employed. See, e.g., Rofé, *Deuteronomy*, 103–19 (arguing for earlier collections of judicial laws subsequently incorporated into D); Otto, *Deuteronomium: Politische Theologie*, 203–17 (arguing for the influence of the

Middle Assyrian laws upon D); and Milstein, "Making a Case" (arguing for the use of fictive legal cases on analogy to the existence of such texts in Mesopotamia). On the question of the sequence of the laws in D, see esp. Rofé's essay "The Arrangement of the Laws in Deuteronomy" (*Deuteronomy,* 55–77).

5. See esp. Levinson, *Deuteronomy and the Hermeneutics,* passim; Otto, *Deuteronomium: Politische Theologie,* 217–364.

6. See, e.g., Blenkinsopp, *Pentateuch,* 210; Najman, *Seconding Sinai,* 24; Stackert, *Rewriting the Torah,* 211–24.

7. For an extensive treatment of literary revision in the Hebrew Bible, see Fishbane, *Biblical Interpretation.*

8. On the distributive sense of *běkol hammāqôm* ("in every place"), see esp. Chavel, "Kingdom of Priests," 175–77 n. 15. On the reading of *tazkîr* ("you call") for the MT's *ʾazkîr* ("I call"), see Tigay, "Presence of God," 203–4; Chavel, "Kingdom of Priests," 177 n. 16.

9. For detailed discussion of D's centralization law and its reliance upon the Covenant Code's altar law, see Levinson, *Deuteronomy and the Hermeneutics,* 23–52.

10. For the nuance of the verb *rʿy* as "to choose, select for oneself," see *HALOT* 2: 1159 (with examples).

11. See esp. the festival laws in Deut 16:1–17, where the Israelites are commanded to appear before Yahweh three times each year. A single sanctuary makes possible sustained divine presence. Though E's deity does not reside in earthly sanctuaries, there is no reason to conclude with Benjamin D. Sommer (*Bodies of God,* 38–57) that E employs a "fluidity model" of divine presence, with the deity physically present in multiple locations simultaneously.

12. For a full discussion of this case, see Stackert, *Rewriting the Torah,* 129–41.

13. A comparable meaning is attested for this root in the Akkadian of the Neo-Assyrian period. For discussion, see Stackert, *Rewriting the Torah,* 132–33.

14. Given the pragmatic orientation of this law, it is likely that the seven-year count applies to fields individually rather than to the entirety of a farmer's land. Such a rotational model would then afford the landowner an annual crop, even as it would provide the poor annual access to charity.

15. Stackert, "Why Does Deuteronomy?"

16. For review and analysis of the references to the exodus tradition in D, see Childs, "Deuteronomic Formulae"; Kreuzer, "Exodustradition."

17. Some scholars have argued that Deut 24:8 relies upon Priestly traditions (see, e.g., Milgrom, *Leviticus 23–27,* 2256). Yet even as skin disease is well-known from Priestly texts (esp. Lev 13–14), it is unclear that D here has any specific knowledge of them.

18. Note not only the lexical similarity but also the morphosyntactic accord between Exod 3:21 and Deut 15:13. For discussion, see Stackert, *Rewriting the Torah,* 160. Some scholars have argued for the opposite direction of dependence (see, e.g., Daube, *Studies in Biblical Law,* 49–50).

19. For extensive treatment of this text, see Stackert, *Prophet Like Moses,* 128–35.

20. For alternative compositional analyses and assignments for Exod 17:8–16, see recently Tanner, *Amalek;* MacDonald, "Anticipations of Horeb" (note, however, that the linguistic and thematic parallels that MacDonald observes [14–16] all link this unit to other E texts); Berner, "Wasserwunder"; Oswald, "Defeating Amalek."

21. Exod 17:16 contains a well-known textual corruption that is not easily explained. The suggestion here is that the word division in *ks yh mlḥmh* in the first half of the verse is incorrect and that the *kāp* is a mistaken substitute for an original *nûn* due to graphic similarity. This emendation yields in v. 16a: *ky yd 'l nsy hmlḥmh lyhwh b'mlq.* For discussion of the problems and options, see Houtman, *Exodus,* 2: 388–91. For the *kāp/nûn* interchange, see esp. Childs, *Book of Exodus,* 311–12.

22. Driver, *Deuteronomy,* 288.

23. See, e.g., Tigay, *Deuteronomy,* 236.

24. See the Elohistic references to the "fear of God" in Gen 20:11; 42:18; Exod 1:17, 21; 18:21. For discussion of the fear of God in E and D, see esp. Weinfeld, *Deuteronomic School,* 274–76; Jindo, "Fear of God."

25. See Weinfeld, *Deuteronomic School,* 274–75. Rather than seeing D's Amalek narrative as responding to the chronology of the event as described in E, Weinfeld suggests that D may have had a different tradition upon which it relied in its reformulation of the E Amalek episode.

26. The discussion here draws from Stackert, "Wilderness Period."

27. The J account in Num 13–14 comprises 13:17b–20, 22–24, 26*–31, 33; 14:1b, 11–25, 39–45. The P account comprises 13:1–16, 17a, 21, 25–26*, 32; 14:1a, 2–10, 26–38. For this source division, see Baden, *J, E, and the Redaction,* 114–17. For treatments of posited complexity within these source divisions, see Kugler, "Threat of Annihilation"; Kislev, "Priestly Spies Story."

28. For contrasting treatments of D's spies account, see, e.g., Otto, *Deuteronomium im Pentateuch und Hexateuch,* 12–109, and Baden, *J, E, and the Redaction,* 118–30. For a recent reevaluation of the relationship between the spies accounts in Num 13–14 and Deut 1:19–46 and reassertion of D's dependence upon the non-Priestly spies account in Num 13–14*, see Kugler, *When God Wanted,* 87–92.

29. For the source division of Exod 16 and discussion of it, see Baden, "Original Place"; Stackert, "How the Priestly Sabbaths Work," 102–4.

30. The LXX does not attest the reference to the forty years in v. 2. However, it does reference the forty years in v. 4, suggesting that the variant in v. 2 is not significant for the present discussion. On the syntax of *zh* + (numeral +) unit of time, see, e.g., Gen 31:38; Deut 2:7; 1 Sam 29:3; Zech 1:12, 7:5; see also Holmstedt, "Analyzing זה Grammar." Scholars have debated the composition of Deut 8, sometimes identifying multiple strata within this text. For discussion of scholarly views and a new proposal, see Veijola, "'Mensch lebt nicht vom Brot allein.'"

Veijola identifies vv. 2–6 as the latest stratum in this text (154–58). As argued here, however, these verses are well integrated into and play an important role in the larger argument of D. Removing them creates significant problems for understanding earlier posited forms of the work, which then casts doubt on the claim that they are late.

31. D telescopes the J manna account, never actually telling what the instructions were that Israel had to obey in order to get the manna successfully and learn thereby that one lives by every word that issues from Yahweh's mouth. It thus appears that D assumes here the content of J without fully rehearsing it. This instance differs from some others, such as D's reference to Baal Peor in 4:3 or to Miriam in 24:9, where D arguably assumes knowledge of an event that D does not narrate. In the latter cases, the references to prior events function adequately in their context to support the point that D seeks to make, even if the details of the tradition referenced are not accessible to D's audience. In the case of the manna in 8:3, by contrast, without the instruction that the Israelites should gather only enough for each day and none for the Sabbath (Exod 16:26), the lesson of living by the command of the deity makes little sense.

32. See esp. McKay, "Man's Love for God," 432. It has long been observed that D employs the wilderness sins of the Israelites as illustrations meant to persuade its audience to turn away from faithlessness. Shemaryahu Talmon argues against the "nomadic ideal" view of the wilderness in the Pentateuch, observing that it is consistently portrayed in these texts as a period of disobedience and punishment ("'Desert Motif'"). Yet as shown here, it is important to delineate a third characterization for the wilderness: idyll, punishment, and *training ground*.

33. See *HALOT*, 1: 702; *BDB*, 650; for the meaning "to give an experience," see esp. Greenberg, "נסה in Exodus 20:20."

34. On the basic contours of the Hebrew *lb/lbb*, including its function as the "voluntative center" of the human, see Fabry, "לב; לבב." See also Carasik, *Theologies of the Mind*; Krüger, "'Herz'"; Avrahami, *Senses of Scripture*, 22–31. For the variety of references to the mind in D, see Weinfeld, *Deuteronomic School*, 304.

35. As Greenberg observed, Judg 3:1–2 similarly combines the verbs *nsy* and *yd* (and *lmd*) to convey the sense of training ("נסה in Exod 20:20," 276). On the corruption of this text and possible explanations for it, see Moore, *Judges*, 76–77. Note, too, as does Moore, that LXX Σ translates *nsy* in Judg 3:1 with ἀσκῆσαι ("to form, train").

36. The sense of *nsy* here corresponds closely with its prominent use in the Elohistic Horeb revelation (Exod 20:20) that D rewrites (Deut 5). For extensive discussion of this text and D's creative revision of it, see Stackert, *Prophet Like Moses*, 75–82, 128–35. See also Weinfeld, *Deuteronomic School*, 317.

37. On the meaning of *môṣā' pî yhwh* and the different scholarly proposals for understanding it, see esp. Perlitt, "Wovon der Mensch lebt." On the connection

between D's manna lesson and its focus on the Israelites' senses in their observance of Yahweh's commands, see Weitzman, "Sensory Reform," 133.

38. As Avrahami notes, biblical authors likewise acknowledge the destructive effects
of divine words. See, e.g., Jer 5:14 and Hos 6:5 (*Senses of Scripture*, 146).

39. MacDonald, *Not Bread Alone*, 84–85.

40. Compare the similar claim in Deut 9:24.

41. *Pace* Driver (*Deuteronomy*, 108) and Weinfeld (*Deuteronomic School*, 172), who
each emphasize the rhetorical/nonliteral sense of D's insistence upon the du-
rability of the Israelites' garments. As demonstrated here, these elements are
an integral part of D's claim of divine preservation of the Exodus generation
across the forty years of wilderness sojourn. Note, too, that exceptional health is
apparently a response to the tradition of Israelite death in the wilderness.

42. Dillmann, *Numeri, Deuteronomium und Josua*, 239. Dillmann further observed
that the absence of an equivalent for "before your eyes" in the LXX rendering of 1:30 may be an attempt by its translator to address the issue of generation change in this text and to harmonize it with the J and P accounts in
Num 13–14.

43. Weinfeld, *Deuteronomy 1–11*, 238. Weinfeld ultimately concludes that in D, "Israel throughout its generations" is addressed as a single "corporate personality."

44. Mayes, *Deuteronomy*, 165, 212. For discussion, see now also Kugler, "Moses
Died," 202.

45. See, e.g., Driver, *Deuteronomy*, lxviii–lxix, 83 ("The fact that the greater part of
those who stood at Horeb, 40 years before, had passed away, is disregarded");
Mayes, *Deuteronomy*, 165 ("This means that strictly speaking there is a contradiction of chs. 1–3 with respect to the assertion that there the generation which
had entered into covenant with Yahweh at Horeb died while wandering in
the wilderness [cf. 2:14ff.]"); Weinfeld, *Deuteronomy 1–11*, 237–38 ("According to
Deuteronomy, the people addressed by Moses on the plains of Moab and sworn
there to keep the covenant [26:16–19, 29:9–14] must also keep loyalty to the
Sinaitic covenant [the Decalogue, ch. 5], in spite of the fact that the new generation addressed by Moses on the plains of Moab was not present at Horeb");
and with an eye toward the text's allegory, Otto, *Deuteronomium 1–11*, 2: 680–81.
In several instances, biblical scholars have taken the claims of Deut 1:35, 39 and
2:14–16 (largely) at face value. For recent examples, see Levinson, *Deuteronomy
and the Hermeneutics*, 151–52; Taschner, "Bedeutung des Generationswechsels";
Biberger, *Unsere Väter und Wir*, 332–61; Arnold, "Reexamining." Yet as I discuss
below, there is evidence of late interpolations in these verses that introduce the
claim of generation change to a text that lacked it.

46. Some scholars, of course, have accepted the plain sense of this text. For example,
Arnold B. Ehrlich states, "Die hier ausgesprochene Behauptung setzt voraus,
dass Moses die Generation anredet, welche die Offenbarung am Horeb er-
lebt hatten, nicht die ihr folgenden Generation" (*Randglossen zur hebräischen*

Bibel, 2: 267). Note also Alfred Bertholet's observation that, notwithstanding the claim that the Israelites enjoyed miraculous health during the wilderness period, Deut 5:3 does not mean that no Israelites died in the desert. It means instead that mature adults survived the forty years (*Deuteronomium,* 21).

Apart from the possible identification of the *'abôt* here as the Exodus generation, scholars have debated whether they are the patriarchs or simply earlier generations of Israelites. In several instances in D, *'abôt* are explicitly identified as the patriarchs (e.g., Deut 1:8, 6:10, 9:5, 29:12, 30:20). Other instances are more easily understood as general references to previous generations (e.g., Deut 8:16; 13:7; 28:36, 64; 31:16). At least one example is a combination (Deut 10:22). Given that 5:3 is focused on covenant making, it is tempting to see the contrast as one between the patriarchs and the present generation (see, e.g., Haran, *Biblical Collection,* 2: 165). In the end, however, it may not be possible to decide between previous generations and the patriarchs in this instance.

For arguments against the identification of the fathers as the patriarchs in D, see Van Seters, "Confessional Reformulation"; Römer, *Israels Väter,* 266–71. For a rebuttal to Römer, see Lohfink, *Väter Israels im Deuteronomium.* For summary of the debate, see Schmid, *Genesis and the Moses Story,* 67–69; Arnold, "Reexamining."

47. The similar text in Deut 29:13–14, which likewise states that it is not only with Moses's hearers that the covenant is struck, is fully consonant with this argument. As 29:15–16 make clear, Moses's audience is the Exodus generation. Thus, those "not here" in v. 14 are best understood to be future generations, that is, the descendants of the characters that Moses addresses in the story world. See, e.g., Driver, *Deuteronomy,* 323; Markl, "Deuteronomy's Frameworks," 278.

48. For discussion of the combination of elements from the different pentateuchal sources as a marker of postcompilational interpolation, see Bar-On (Gesundheit), "Festival Calendars."

49. Dillmann, *Numeri, Deuteronomium und Josua,* 239; Steuernagel, *Deuteronomium und Josua,* 6; Driver, *Deuteronomy,* 25–26; Biberger, *Unsere Väter und Wir,* 86; Germany, *Exodus-Conquest Narrative,* 217 (note that Germany also views vv. 36–38 and the beginning of v. 39 as secondary). For opposing arguments, see the comments of Wevers, who notes the basic ambiguity in the text concerning which men are referenced, the superiority of the LXX reading here, and the presence of a harmonizing gloss in the Hexapla (*Greek Text of Deuteronomy,* 21). Otto likewise argues for the originality of MT 1:35 (*Deuteronomium im Pentateuch und Hexateuch,* 17–18; Otto, *Deuteronomium 1–11,* 1: 373).

50. For discussion and additional bibliography on Num 32:7–15 as a late interpolation, see Marquis (Feldman), "Numbers 32," 429–31.

51. D claims that the spies initially returned a positive report (Deut 1:25). However, it is clear from the Israelites' response to the spies that their report also included discouraging elements (1:27–28) that Yahweh deemed faithless.

52. Compare the similar tradition in Num 14:36–38 (P). Note, however, that in P, the faithless spies die in a plague while the adult population is to die off slowly during the forty-year wilderness sojourn. If the main part of Deut 2:14 is authentically D, D claims that the faithless spies will die off slowly during the desert trek while the rest of the Israelites survive. At the same time, 2:15 could be understood as consistent with a divinely ordained plague. The alternative analysis is to see much of Deut 1–3 as post-P and influenced by it. Though attractive in certain respects, such an analysis does not explain well the versional evidence for textual growth that seeks to align elements in Deut 1–3 with the P account in Num 13*–14*.

53. If this analysis is correct, "the warriors" (ʾanšê hammilḥāmâ) in Deut 2:14 and 16 refers to the spies and not to the entire adult male population. It would thus connote something like "the men (searching out the possibility) of war." Neither P nor J employs this moniker in its spies account. It appears elsewhere in the Torah only in Num 31:28 and 49. See also Josh 5:4, 6 (MT); 6:3; 10:24. The MT Josh 5 examples suffer from a similar ambiguity as the Deut 2 examples, and it is possible to explain "until the death of the entire nation, the warriors" of Josh 5:6 in a similar way as Deut 2:14. For discussion of the shorter text in LXX Josh 5, see Nelson, *Joshua*, 72–77.

54. See Wevers's comments on the variants in the Greek witnesses (*Greek Text of Deuteronomy*, 35–36).

55. Compare the harmonizing disambiguation in Targum Neofiti, which reads *kl dr' ʿm' ʿbdy qrbh*, "the entire generation, the people, the warriors."

56. See the similar views of Dillmann (*Numeri, Deuteronomium und Josua*, 244) and Steuernagel (*Deuteronomium und Josua*, 9). Bertholet objects to Dillmann's analysis as circular reasoning, pointing to Dillmann's attempt to retain a single author in relation to texts such as 5:3 and 11:2–7 (*Deuteronomium*, 9).

57. See esp. Lohfink, "Canonical Signals."

58. The LXX does not include an equivalent for the MT's *ʾšr ʾmrtm lbz yhyh wbnkm* and reads "every young child" (καὶ πᾶν παιδίον νέον) instead of "your children" (*wṭpkm*). SamP does not include *ʾšr lʾ ydʿw hywm ṭwb wrʿ*. There is no immediate scribal explanation for these variants. For detailed discussion, see Lohfink, "Canonical Signals."

59. See already Kuenen, "Bijdragen to de critiek van Pentateuch en Jozua"; Dillmann, *Numeri, Deuteronomium und Josua*, 240; Driver, *Deuteronomy*, 28; Addis, *Documents*, 2: 38; Lohfink, "Canonical Signals"; Baden, *J, E, and the Redaction*, 121 n. 65. *Pace* Wevers, who explains the LXX as an attempted improvement upon the MT (*Notes on the Greek Text of Deuteronomy*, 23).

60. See Lohfink, "Canonical Signals," 37–40. Lohfink extends his canonical argument by advocating a connection between Deut 1:39 and Gen 2–3 in light of the former's use of the clause *ʾšr lʾ ydʿw hywm ṭwb wrʿ* (cf. Gen 3:5, 22).

61. See Stackert, *Prophet Like Moses*, 130–33.

62. For discussion of these issues, see Haran, "B'aberît 'Covenant,'" 212); Haran, *Biblical Collection*, 2: 128–30; Stackert, *Prophet Like Moses*, 77–82.

63. For the claim that the Decalogue is consciously shaped with the laws of the Covenant Code in view, see, e.g., Kratz, "Dekalog im Exodusbuch." The argument here, relocated to the Deuteronomic context, is similar in certain respects.

64. It does appear, however, that D understands the rules of the Decalogue to remain in effect even after Israel receives the laws of the second covenant. It is thus explicable, for example, that D does not repeat a Sabbath law in its second covenant (for recognition of this lacuna, see, e.g., Hossfeld, "Dekalog," 57). Neither does this second covenant legislation include a basic law against homicide. This lacuna is significant in the case of D's revision of E's asylum law (Exod 21:12–14), which focuses only on the asylum places (Deut 19:1–13) and adjudication of homicide cases but does not include an equivalent to the basic law against homicide (Exod 21:12) that heads the E treatment that D revises. For the laws revealed to Moses at Horeb as supplementary to the Decalogue, see already *Mek. Nez.* 1; Ibn Ezra, Rashi. For early Jewish and Christian sources that view the Decalogue as a précis or epitome of the rest of the pentateuchal laws, see Kugel, *Traditions of the Bible*, 639–40, 679–80. For discussion of the relationship of the Decalogue to the other Deuteronomic laws in modern scholarship, see esp. Braulik, "Sequence of the Laws."

65. These two life stages are conceived within the parent-child metaphor as overlapping rather than sequential (as one might expect). Yahweh carries the "infant" Israel throughout its wilderness journey, even as he also trains the Israelites to obey his laws.

66. Proverbs repeatedly concludes that the one who accepts discipline is wise (Prov 8:33, 13:1, 19:20). For comparison with the parent/child imagery in wisdom texts, see McKay, "Man's Love for God." For comparison between D and wisdom thought more generally, see esp. Weinfeld, *Deuteronomic School*, 244–319. Weinfeld highlights D's focus on parental instruction and its similarity to that found in wisdom texts (303). He also notes the correspondence between D's parental imagery for Yahweh and that in Hosea (368–69).

67. See Fishbane, *Biblical Interpretation*, 327. The specific nuance of the verb *'ny* (D) in Deut 8:3, where it is paired with the verb *r'b* (H) and contrasted with the verb *'kl* (H), is likely deprivation. It is comparable to the verb's use in the formulation *'ny npš* (debasement/deprivation of the body/gullet) in texts such as Lev 16:29, 31; 23:27, 29, 32; Num 29:7; Isa 58:3, 5; and Ps 35:13, which describe fasting rites. In this usage, *'ny npš* is profitably coordinated with *'wy npš* (desire of the body/gullet), which may carry connotations of the will; see Chavel, *Oracular Law*, 73 n. 188. On fasting rites, see esp. Lambert, "Fasting as a Penitential Rite," 483–85, 504–9. In P's manna account, in contrast to D's, the Israelites first complain of their hunger (Exod 16:2–3), and Yahweh responds to their complaint by provisioning them with food (v. 12). It is unclear in J whether the

deity imposes the Israelites' hunger or not. The opening of the J account may not be extant, and its test—the schedule and extent of the Israelites' manna gathering—is consistent with either divine imposition of hunger or its natural occurrence.

68. On the new covenant in Jeremiah and its context, see, e.g., Weinfeld, "Jeremiah and the Spiritual Metamorphosis," 26–35; Couroyer, "Tablette du Coeur"; Carasik, *Theologies of the Mind,* 24, 72, 106, 110; Finsterbusch, "'Ich habe meine Tora'"; Mastnjak, *Deuteronomy and the Emergence,* 200–206. Having concluded that Judah is unteachable, the deity introduces the writing on the mind in Jer 31:33 in order to obviate the need for the Israelite remembrance that D repeatedly adjures: "A Torah that is written on the heart marries the permanence of writing to the awareness of the mind" (Carasik, *Theologies of the Mind,* 72).

69. As Carasik notes, the goal in D is for Israel to so love (= express loyalty toward) the deity with the entire mind (Deut 6:5; cf. 29:18) that there is no room for "self-generated thought" that might lead to an alternative to Deuteronomically defined obedience (*Theologies of the Mind,* 209–13).

70. See already König, *Stilistik, Rhetorik, Poetik,* 54–55. See also Talmon, "'Desert Motif,'" 220. For a brief history of scholarship on the span of forty years in the Hebrew Bible, see Araújo, *Theologie der Wüste,* 30–34.

71. This issue is noticeable only when different traditions of the Israelites' wilderness sojourn are compared. When read in isolation, D's forty years are sufficiently cohesive, even if not specifically rationalized.

72. Strawn, "Moses at Moab," 173.

73. I have addressed this issue, in relation both to D and to other pentateuchal legislation, elsewhere. See Stackert, *Rewriting the Torah,* 209–25; "Holiness Legislation"; and "Relationship of the Pentateuchal Codes." The argument here builds upon these discussions.

74. Already de Wette, for example, argued that D's legislation was "a new set of laws" that "supplemented, corrected, or abrogated, the ancient laws" (Harvey, Jr., and Halpern, "'Dissertatio Critica,'" 84).

75. Levinson, *Deuteronomy and the Hermeneutics,* 20–21. I have argued previously in favor of this view. See Stackert, *Rewriting the Torah,* 209–25 (esp. 219–20). For the most extensive attempt to theorize literary subversion in relation to D, see Crouch, *Israel and the Assyrians,* esp. 15–45.

76. See esp. Stackert, "Before and After Scripture."

77. See Baden, "Literary Allusions."

78. This view has a long, distinguished pedigree in biblical studies. For example, when addressing the possibility that pentateuchal legislation may not reflect actual judicial practice, Wellhausen stated, "It is, moreover, rarely the case with laws that they are theory and nothing more: the possibility that a thing may be mere theory is not to be asserted generally, but only in particular cases" (*Prolegomena,* 355).

79. Levinson's words quoted above exemplify this view, as do additional statements from Levinson. The following is illustrative: "In the case of ancient Israel, the concepts of textual stability, prestige, and authority necessitated subsequent adaptation, interpolation, reinterpretation, and transformation" (*Deuteronomy and the Hermeneutics*, 15).

80. See Baden, "Literary Allusions," 127 n. 30. Baden suggests that prestige is ultimately a subspecies of authority.

81. Otto states, "Deut. 19:2–13* read alone without its counterpart was deficient in a legal collection with a law of cult-centralization as a *Hauptgebot* (principal regulation), because in the book of Deuteronomy no hint was given at the asylum-function of this central sanctuary or that there should no longer be an asylum-function connected with this sanctuary" ("History of the Legal-Religious Hermeneutics," 218).

82. Otto, "History of the Legal-Religious Hermeneutics," 217–18.

83. Otto, *Kontinuum und Proprium*, 116.

84. Otto, "Mose, der erste Schriftgelehrte"; Otto, "History of the Legal-Religious Hermeneutics," 237–38.

85. Mattison, *Rewriting and Revision*, 13 (see also pp. 14–18). Strawn also employs the term "amendment" to characterize Deuteronomic revision ("Moses at Moab").

86. Mattison acknowledges that his view is very similar to Otto's (*Rewriting and Revision*, 14). Where Mattison disagrees with Otto is regarding the existence of a non-Mosaically framed D composition and the relationship between D and the pentateuchal Priestly Holiness legislation. Otto views the Holiness laws as a further, agglutinative supplement to D's laws ("History of the Legal-Religious Hermeneutics," 237) while Mattison views them as incompatible with D and thus undermined in the compiled Pentateuch (*Rewriting and Revision*, 16).

87. Najman, *Seconding Sinai*, 19–29.

88. Berman, *Inconsistency in the Torah*, 116. See the larger discussions on pp. 107–36, 171–98.

89. Berman, *Inconsistency in the Torah*, 179.

90. Otto, "History of the Legal-Religious Hermeneutics," 237; Berman, *Inconsistency in the Torah*, 188.

91. Berman, *Inconsistency in the Torah*, 113–16.

92. Strawn has suggested that a replacement model works better on the central legal section of Deuteronomy but less so on its revisionary presentation of Israel's past ("Moses at Moab," 174). The argument here is precisely the reverse: it is in D's narrative framework that its internal field of reference and literary autonomy are established. For additional discussion, see Stackert, "Holiness Legislation."

93. See, e.g., Stackert, *Prophet Like Moses*, 129; cf. Baden, "Literary Allusions," 116–28. As noted above, D interacts with J in only a very limited manner. D's revi-

sionary intent is thus much more obviously directed at E. Its reuse of J material appears to be in service of this main project.

94. For discussion, see, e.g., Baden, *Composition*, 126–28, 139–46; Stackert, *Prophet Like Moses*, 70–167.

Chapter 3. Ancient Near Eastern Influence in Deuteronomic Composition

1. An influential, early dissent was Perlitt, *Bundestheologie im Alten Testament*. Perlitt argued against virtually any ancient Near Eastern treaty influence in D and claimed that the notion of covenant was a Deuteronomic invention in Israelite thought. Perlitt's argument struggles to explain biblical covenant texts that appear to be pre-Deuteronomic (as discussed in Chapter 2). It also fails to account for the significant parallels between Deuteronomic material and ancient Near Eastern (especially Neo-Assyrian) treaty texts. For further development of Perlitt's arguments that takes the ancient Near Eastern material into greater account, see esp. the work of Christoph Koch, discussed below.

2. See, e.g., Rollston, "Inscriptional Evidence"; Sanders, *Invention of Hebrew*.

3. Mendenhall, "Covenant Forms." For extended discussion and evaluation, see McCarthy, *Treaty and Covenant*, 37–85.

4. Korošec, *Hethitische Staatsverträge*, 11–14. It should be noted that Mendenhall did not think that this treaty form originated in Hatti but that it was borrowed from Mesopotamia ("Covenant Forms," 53–54).

5. Mendenhall took much of biblical narrative as historically accurate, at least in broad strokes, and criticized scholars who would raise questions about its historicity ("Covenant Forms," 64–65). In a ranging and mildly polemical reconsideration of his thesis, Mendenhall largely restated his historical reconstruction, including his emphasis upon the Decalogue, and then teased out its implications for the present (Mendenhall, "Suzerainty Treaty Structure"). It is perhaps no surprise that Mendenhall's work has been endorsed especially by scholars who reject some or all critical method. See discussion below.

6. Mendenhall, "Covenant Forms," 61–67.

7. Mendenhall's argument concerning Deuteronomy is sometimes difficult to follow and even appears inconsistent. Though he argued for "the basic nature of the old amphictyonic covenant" ("Covenant Forms," 73) in Deuteronomy (i.e., the covenant form that shared the Hittite form), he also stated: "It is well known that biblical traditions preserve for us a number of references to covenants of different sorts. There are only two traditions, however, that fall into the form described above [i.e., the Hittite treaty form]" (61–62). Moreover, in his 1990 article, Mendenhall offered a strong summary characterization regarding the suzerainty treaty form in Deuteronomy: "The unknown writers of Deuteronomy had nothing to do with creating *ex nihilo* that old treaty structure:

they returned to the remote past for traditions that had been contemptuously ignored for centuries" ("Suzerainty Treaty Structure," 96).

8. Mendenhall, "Covenant Forms," 75. Though he broke with Wellhausen over the antiquity of law in Israelite religion, Mendenhall reproduced various other features of Wellhausen's devolutionary schema. See Levinson, "Revisiting the 'and' in Law and Covenant," 28–31. For a broader treatment of Wellhausen's views on law and religion, see Stackert, *Prophet Like Moses,* esp. 2–19, 195–99.

9. Mendenhall, "Covenant Forms," 66.

10. Mendenhall, "Covenant Forms," 60, 66.

11. Kline, *Treaty,* 28.

12. Craigie, *Book of Deuteronomy,* 24. Note, however, that Craigie also made allowance for all of the Deuteronomy scroll in his analysis.

13. Weinfeld, *Deuteronomic School,* 59–66.

14. McCarthy, *Treaty and Covenant,* 157–87.

15. Mendenhall, "Covenant Forms," 53–54.

16. Berman, "Histories Twice Told," 250. See the similar statement in Berman, "CTH 133," 44. For additional discussion, see Levinson and Stackert, "Between the Covenant Code," 133–36. Notably, Berman has repeatedly appealed to Harry A. Hoffner's arguments in favor of Hittite influence upon biblical texts (e.g., "Histories Twice Told," 250; "CTH 133," 44), yet Hoffner's studies on the subject have been shown to be highly problematic methodologically. For critique, see esp. Malul, *Comparative Method,* 60–62, 100–101.

17. For extended discussion of these methodological issues, see Malul, *Comparative Method,* esp. 93–112. Berman has attempted to marshal Malul's arguments in support of his claims (see esp. Berman, "Historicism and Its Limits"). However, Berman misrepresents and/or misconstrues Malul's approach. For detailed rebuttal, see Levinson and Stackert, "Limitations"; Quick, *Deuteronomy 28,* 41–56.

18. Malul, *Comparative Method,* 97.

19. Sandmel, "Parallelomania."

20. Koller, "Deuteronomy and Hittite Treaties." Though Koller left him out of his discussion of the Hittite treaties and Deuteronomy, it is really with Malul that he has the most serious methodological disagreements.

21. For incisive critique of claims of direct influence in the case of the Sumerian city laments and Lamentations, see Malul, *Comparative Method,* 111–12.

22. See esp. Malul, *Comparative Method,* 134–44; Samuel L. Boyd, "Exodus 21:35." As Boyd notes, it is possible (and even likely) that the particular text that the author of Exod 21:35 used did not look exactly like the extant copies of Eshnunna. This is mainly due to the rendering of the second phoneme of the Akkadian root *nkp* as /g/ (represented with Hebrew *gimel, ngp*). Intervocalic /k/ in Neo-Assyrian is rendered in Hebrew as /g/, but this is not the case for Babylonian intervocalic /k/, which Hebrew renders as /k/. Yet the Eshnunna law as attested

has doubled *k* (*ikkim-ma*), which should not render in Hebrew as /g/. This detail suggests that the Akkadian *Vorlage* employed in Exod 21 may have differed from that in the known Eshnunna tablets. See Samuel L. Boyd, "Exod 21:35," 18–20. For a linguistic perspective on the relative value of types of evidence for identifying ancient language contact, see Thomason, "Determining Language Contact."

23. See, e.g., Westbrook, "Law Codes," 257; Malul, *Comparative Method*, 147–48; Wright, *Inventing God's Law*, 218–20. It should be noted, however, that the issue of transmission is not entirely conjectural in this case. Though there is no specific evidence for the Eshnunna laws' transmission, there is significant evidence of Israelite and Judean cultural contact with Mesopotamia. See esp. Chapter 5 for discussion of such contact. No equivalent evidence exists for the Israelites/Judeans and the Hittites.

24. It is important to recognize, however, that this methodologically rigorous approach does not leave general similarities unexplained. As scholars have long noted, similarities between Hittite and Israelite/Judean culture can be observed. The question is how they are to be explained. At present, there is insufficient evidence to warrant a claim for direct Hittite influence in Israel/Judah or its texts. For discussion, see Levinson and Stackert, "Limitations of 'Resonance.'"

25. If an attempt is made to account for D's compositional issues alongside the claim for Hittite influence, the employment of the treaty form must be delayed until the end of the compositional process, thereby increasing the temporal distance between Hittite texts and their alleged Deuteronomic inheritor.

26. Kline, *Treaty*, 21; Craigie, *Book of Deuteronomy*, 22. Mendenhall's historical positivism and negative characterization of "mere literary analysis" ("Suzerainty Treaty Structure," 93) strike a similar tone.

27. Kline and Craigie both affirmed the unity of Deuteronomy and suggested a Mosaic dating for it (Kline, *Treaty*, 27–44; Craigie, *Book of Deuteronomy*, 21–29). Berman has likewise advocated "a Late Bronze Age Hittite background" for Deuteronomic texts ("CTH 133," 43).

28. Mendenhall, "Covenant Forms," 74.

29. "We have no sympathy for von Rad's failure to recognize the historicity of the covenant renewal presented in Deuteronomy as a particular ceremony conducted by Moses in Moab" (Kline, *Treaty*, 29–30).

30. Kline, *Treaty*, 29–30, 48. See also Berman, "Histories Twice Told," 248. As discussed in Chapter 2, D does not actually endorse generation change, which presents another problem for an argument such as this one.

31. In many instances, Moses's speeches even entail recollections of speeches he claims to have delivered previously. They are thus *representations of representations*. See Sonnet, *Book within the Book*, 258–59.

32. For the argument that native covenant traditions from ancient Israel cannot be traced directly to the ancient Near Eastern treaty tradition, see, e.g.,

Brekelmans, "Wisdom Influence in Deuteronomy." See further discussion of Brekelmans below.

33. For recent discussion of the genre of EST, including the basic meaning of *adê*, see esp. Lauinger, "Neo-Assyrian *adê*"; Radner, "Neo-Assyrian Treaties as a Source," 310–12.

34. Perhaps most notable is the similarity between EST's adjuration to "love" the crown prince, Assurbanipal, "like yourselves" (*ki-i nap-šá-te-ku-nu la tar-'a-ma-a-ni*, SAA 2 6:68) and the famous command to love Yahweh in Deut 6:5. See Moran, "Ancient Near Eastern Background," 80.

35. Wiseman, *Vassal-Treaties of Esarhaddon*, 26. See the more recent editions of this text in Watanabe, *Die adê-Vereidigung*; Parpola and Watanabe, *Neo-Assyrian Treaties and Loyalty Oaths*.

36. Borger, "Asarhaddon-Verträgen"; Moran, "Ancient Near Eastern Background."

37. Weinfeld, "Traces of Assyrian Treaty Formulae"; Weinfeld, *Deuteronomic School*, 116–29; Frankena, "Vassal-Treaties."

38. Allen, "Rearranging the Gods." On the arrangement of the curses in relation to the arrangement of gods in Neo-Assyrian texts, see now also Sanders, *From Adapa to Enoch*, 172–73; W. Morrow, "Have Attempts?," 149–54.

39. Allen, "Rearranging the Gods," 11. Allen is, of course, careful to note that D may rely upon another text that, like EST, presented the distinctive Sin/Shamash curse sequence or may have even developed this sequence independently (11 n. 20).

40. Koch, *Vertrag, Treueid und Bund*, 230–31. More recently, and in light of the discovery of the Tayinat tablet of EST, Koch has argued for the increased likelihood of EST as the specific medium of contact for D and its curse formulation ("Bundestheologie und autoritativer Text," 43–44). For earlier claims that a common ancient Near Eastern curse tradition may account for Deuteronomy's curses, see, e.g., Tigay, *Deuteronomy*, 497.

41. Steymans, "Eine assyrische Vorlage"; Steymans, *Deuteronomium 28*, esp. 143–49; Steymans, "Neuassyrische Vertragsrhetorik."

42. Polk, "Deuteronomy and Treaty Texts," 137–205. Polk's critique of Steymans highlights in several instances the overidentification of D's reuse of EST. Similar overidentification can be observed in Steymans, "Deuteronomy 13." For additional critique, from the perspective of translation theory, see Crouch and Hutton, *Translating Empire*, 229–55.

43. Steymans, "Eine assyrische Vorlage."

44. Otto, *Deuteronomium: Politische Theologie*, 68; see also Otto, "Ursprünge der Bundestheologie," 37. More recently, Otto has tempered this characterization. See, e.g., *Deuteronomium 12–34*, 1: 1239: "Dtn 13, 2–12 ist in der deuteronomischen Fassung der spätvorexilischen Zeit eine Verbindung von Sprache und Motive originär israelitisch-judäischen und gleichzeitig neuassyrischen Ursprungs." See also Otto, *Deuteronomium 12–34*, 2: 1994–99, where Otto consistently refers to the "Rezeption" of EST in Deut 28.

45. See esp. Dion, "Deuteronomy 13," 204–5; Levinson, "'But You Shall Surely Kill Him!'"; Levinson, "Recovering"; Levinson, "Textual Criticism"; Levinson, "Neo-Assyrian Origins"; Levinson, "Esarhaddon's Succession Treaty."

46. W. Morrow, "Have Attempts?," 144.

47. See, e.g., Dion, "Deuteronomy 13," 153; W. Morrow, "Have Attempts?," 144 (with additional bibliography).

48. See, e.g., Rütersworden, "Dtn 13," 198–99; Koch, *Vertrag, Treueid und Bund,* 156; W. Morrow, "Have Attempts?," 145. Drawing on Dion ("Deuteronomy 13," 200), Morrow even suggests that EST's three-part list (prophet, ecstatic, inquirer) has been rendered into Hebrew as a two-part list, making it a case of (loose) translation. For further discussion of the possibility of translation of EST in D, see below.

49. Nissinen, *References to Prophecy,* 161.

50. For detailed discussion, see Stackert, *Prophet Like Moses,* 153–57.

51. Levinson, "Neo-Assyrian Origins," 25–27; cf. Otto, *Deuteronomium 12–34,* 1: 1226, 1234–35.

52. Levinson, "Esarhaddon's Succession Treaty," 343; Levinson, "Neo-Assyrian Origins," 30–32. For the practice of inverted citation, see Seidel, "Parallels"; Beentjes, "Inverted Quotations."

53. Steymans, "Deuteronomy 13," 119. For Berman's argument, see his "CTH 133," 31–35.

54. Brekelmans, "Wisdom Influence in Deuteronomy," 34.

55. See, e.g., Sanders, *From Adapa to Enoch,* 157.

56. Quick, *Deuteronomy 28,* 182–83; see the similar argument of Ramos, "Northwest Semitic Curse Formula." For the claim that transmission of Assyrian ideas was primarily oral, see already W. Morrow, "Tribute from Judah"; see also Sanders, *From Adapa to Enoch,* 173–77. In his recent reassessment, Morrow follows Quick ("Have Attempts?," 153). With specific reference to Deut 13, see also Steymans, "Deuteronomy 13," 104.

57. Levinson, "Neo-Assyrian Origins," 30. For a similar assessment, see Otto, *Deuteronomium: Politische Theologie,* 86; Otto, "Political Theology."

58. Crouch, *Israel and the Assyrians,* 15–45.

59. Crouch, *Israel and the Assyrians,* 92. For similar critique, see Quick, *Deuteronomy 28,* 24.

60. More recently, Morrow has argued against the subversion thesis on other, less secure grounds. He has posited that the reuse of EST in Deut 13 and 28 stems from an earlier, pre-D oath intended to secure loyalty to Manasseh. By the time this text was taken up and incorporated into D, it no longer featured subversive intent toward Assyria. It is on this basis, then, that Morrow rejects the subversion thesis ("Have Attempts?," 156–58).

61. W. S. Morrow, "Cuneiform Literacy"; Crouch, *Israel and the Assyrians,* 154–55; Quick, *Deuteronomy 28,* 54–63.

62. Quick, *Deuteronomy 28,* 63. In positing an Aramaic translation, Quick follows esp. Steymans, *Deuteronomy 28,* 284–312. See more recently Steymans's argument for direct Akkadian reuse ("Deuteronomy 28," 2, 11; and "Deuteronomy 13," 104).

63. The account of Sennacherib's barricade of Jerusalem in 2 Kgs 18–19 famously suggests that most Judeans were not fluent Aramaic speakers, to say nothing of their reading and writing abilities (2 Kgs 18:26). For discussion of Judean literacy more generally, see, e.g., Rollston, *Writing and Literacy,* esp. 127–35. Rollston argues against any significant literacy among the nonelite Judeans. William M. Schniedewind has argued for widespread Judean literacy beginning in the seventh century BCE (*How the Bible Became a Book,* 91–117).

64. Quick overlooks this evidence and partially mischaracterizes the arguments of Morrow when she cites him in support of her claim that "an Aramaic translation of Esarhaddon's Succession Treaties is a necessary hypothesis for any positive assessment of the connections between the Succession Treaties and Deuteronomy 28" (*Deuteronomy 28,* 63 and n. 102). Morrow explicitly allows for limited cuneiform knowledge among the Judean elite ("Cuneiform Literacy," 208–9). More recently, Morrow has speculated that Judean knowledge of Akkadian was oral only and did not extend to reading ("Have Attempts?," 139).

65. Samuel L. Boyd, "Exodus 21:35"; Machinist, "Assyria and Its Image"; Aster, "Image of Assyria." Note that, taken together, the examples that these scholars have adduced, as well as the others discussed here, suggest a stronger Akkadian facility than Morrow acknowledges.

66. Machinist, "Assyria and Its Image," 728–29 (quotation from 729).

67. For the observed parallel between the Hebrew and Akkadian texts, see, e.g., Heidel, *Gilgamesh Epic,* 265–67; Speiser, *Genesis,* 52; Cohen, *Biblical Hapax Legomena,* 33–34, 53–54 n. 8; Malul, *Comparative Method,* 95–96. For the Akkadian usage of *kapāru* and *kupru,* see *CAD* K, 178–80, 553–55.

68. The noun *kupru* appears repeatedly in the known Mesopotamian Flood traditions, but it is not accompanied by the verb *kapāru.* See, e.g., Gilgamesh X:263; XI:55, 66.

69. Samuel Lanham Boyd, "Contact and Context," 268–74. See also Samuel L. Boyd, "The Flood."

70. Quick, *Deuteronomy 28,* 61–62.

71. For discussion of the full corpus of cuneiform finds from Canaan, see now Horowitz, Oshima, and Sanders, *Cuneiform in Canaan.* As Horowitz, Oshima, and Sanders note, only two small fragments exist from Jerusalem, both of which likely date to the Late Bronze Age. From the Neo-Assyrian period, eighteen texts have been found in the southern Levant (ibid., 18–22, 99–100).

72. See esp. Tadmor, "Aramaization of Assyria"; Folmer, "Aramaic as *Lingua Franca*"; Schniedewind, *Social History of Hebrew,* 79–88; Sanders, *From Adapa to Enoch,* 167–69.

73. As discussed below, there is evidence of Aramaic from elsewhere in the southern Levant; see esp. Bloch, who offers a regional assessment of the use of Aramaic in the Iron Age Levant ("Aramaic Influence," 90–94). Note, too, the general observation of Alan R. Millard: apart from a handful of royal inscriptions, "the quantity of extant texts in Aramaic, written earlier than 600 B.C.E. is remarkably small, taking into account the number of kingdoms and the wide area they covered" ("Assyria, Aramaeans and Aramaic," 207–8). Millard ascribes this paucity to "the widespread use of perishable writing materials" (210). For convincing critique of the claim that Aramaic writing proliferated in the Neo-Assyrian empire on perishable materials, see F. Mario Fales, "Use and Function," 123–24; Samuel L. Boyd, *Language Contact*, 160–64. Moreover, as Boyd emphasizes, the earliest attested administrative example of epigraphic Aramaic from Judah is the early Persian period Aḥiab seal (*Language Contact*, 83, 101, 368–69). Quick acknowledges the absence of Aramaic epigraphic evidence but ascribes it to the perishability of the media while also emphasizing the possibility of oral transmission (*Deuteronomy 28*, 181).

74. See, e.g., Folmer, "Aramaic as *Lingua Franca*," 377; Frederick M. Fales, "Aramaic Epigraphy"; Samuel L. Boyd, *Language Contact*, 114–228 (and esp. 105 n. 166; 121).

75. Zilberg, "Assyrian Provinces," 77.

76. See Frederick M. Fales, "Multilingualism," 99–102; Frederick M. Fales, "Aramaic Epigraphy," 5–7; Folmer, "Aramaic as *Lingua Franca*," 379–81; Sanders, *From Adapa to Enoch*, 181–83.

77. Some scholars have raised questions about the possibility of an Aramaic translation of EST. Crouch has argued that this text's use of Akkadian is an expression of imperial power and thus likely not to be rendered in a different language. She has also suggested that a translation was impractical and unnecessary (*Israel and the Assyrians*, 157–58). Steymans has suggested that a translation would have damaged the Akkadian style/rhetoric of EST ("Deuteronomy 13," 104). On the genre-specific use of Aramaic, see esp. Samuel L. Boyd, *Language Contact*, 164–73.

78. Watanabe, "Study of Assyrian Cultural Policy"; Samuel L. Boyd, *Language Contact*, 152–55. Because of these Neo-Assyrian practices, Watanabe identifies a certain realism in the biblical account of the Assyrian *rab šaqê*'s address of the Judeans blockaded in Jerusalem in Hebrew ("Judean") ("Study of Assyrian Cultural Policy," 487).

79. For discussion of the local orientation and scribal practice of Aramaic treaty texts, see Crouch, *Israel and the Assyrians*, 163–64, and esp. Samuel L. Boyd, *Language Contact*, 144–55. For a helpful discussion of "imperial imitation" in Iron Age Levantine vernacular compositions more generally, see Sanders, *Invention of Hebrew*, 120–22.

80. Barr, *Comparative Philology*, 123. Regarding Akkadian proficiency, see the similar claims of Morrow, albeit with a modern rather than ancient comparison:

"We need not imagine a degree of cuneiform literacy in 8th–7th century Judah much different from the rudimentary knowledge acquired by many modern students" ("Cuneiform Literacy," 209).

81. For similar questions concerning the regular translation of Akkadian texts into Aramaic for the purpose of Judean reception, see Crouch, *Israel and the Assyrians*, 149 n. 6.

82. See also the comments of Crouch, *Israel and the Assyrians*, 158–60.

83. For critique of this view, see, e.g., Rüterswörden, "Dtn 13," 42; Levinson, "Neo-Assyrian Origins," 29; Crouch, *Deuteronomy and the Assyrians*, 47–92; Crouch and Hutton, *Translating Empire*, 229–31.

84. See Crouch and Hutton, *Translating Empire*, 231–55.

85. Malul, *Comparative Method*, 124–25.

86. Crouch, *Israel and the Assyrians*, 93.

Chapter 4. Deuteronomic Reception and the Compiled Pentateuch

1. Mayes, *Deuteronomy*, 116; Ska, "Structure du Pentateuque"; Otto, "Mose, der erste Schriftgelehrte"; Veijola, *Moses Erben*, 216; Nihan, "Holiness Code between D and P," 106–7. For rebuttals of this view, see Braulik and Lohfink, "Deuteronomium 1,5"; Schaper, "'Publication' of Legal Texts."

2. Otto, "History of the Legal-Religious Hermeneutics," 237–38.

3. With respect to the literary intent assigned to each stage, a statement like Otto's above similarly works to harmonize D's composition and its compilation. Yet to claim that the significant differences that persist in the compiled Pentateuch somehow cohere—and that these differences always have—only restates and extends the confusion that prompted the modern critical study of these texts. See the helpful discussion of harmonization's limits in Zahn, *Rethinking Rewritten Scripture*, 147–48; see also Stackert, *Rewriting the Torah*, 215–18.

4. For discussions of the relationship between D and Jeremiah, see, e.g., Thiel, *Jeremia 1–25*; Thiel, *Jeremia 26–45*; Gross, *Jeremia*; Sharp, *Prophecy and Ideology*; Mastnjak, *Deuteronomy and the Emergence*.

5. See esp. Mastnjak, *Deuteronomy and the Emergence*, 31–35.

6. As Mastnjak notes, these are the only two occurrences of the expression "fully in the way that I/Yahweh your god commanded" in the entire Hebrew Bible. Moreover, the context imagined is identical, namely, Yahweh's commands to Israel in the wilderness, with the Jeremian text citing the precise scenario recounted in D (*Deuteronomy and the Emergence*, 42–44; see also now Fabrikant-Burke, "Tradition as Innovation," 19–20).

7. On its face, this claim could be understood as consistent with D's view of future prophecy (Deut 18:15–22). The real problem in the case of Jeremiah is the series of speeches in the collection of prophetic oracles ascribed to him. These oracles go far beyond what is envisioned in Deut 18:15–22. For detailed discussion

of the latter text and its expectation for post-Mosaic prophecy, see Stackert, *Prophet Like Moses*, 135–44.

8. Mastnjak, *Deuteronomy and the Emergence*, 45–46.

9. For discussion of Moses's single appearance in Jeremiah and the question of Jeremiah as "a prophet like Moses," see esp. Holladay, "Jeremiah's Self-Understanding"; Holladay, "Jeremiah and Moses"; Mastnjak, *Deuteronomy and the Emergence*, 40–42.

10. See, e.g., Milgrom, "Concerning Jeremiah's Repudiation." Milgrom unsuccessfully attempts to show that Jer 7:22 aligns with pentateuchal Priestly thought. See also Barton, "Prophets and the Cult." Barton suggests that in Jeremiah's telling, sacrifice "crept in" after the wilderness period in some unspecified manner (120).

11. Weinfeld, "Jeremiah and the Spiritual Metamorphosis," 53–54. Weinfeld observed that Radak already made a similar argument. Several scholars have attempted to connect the Jeremian perspective with the exilic period (e.g., Thiel, *Jeremia 1–25*, 127–28; Eidevall, "Prophetic Cult-Criticism," 163–64).

12. The implication of D, then, is precisely what is also reflected in texts such as Amos 5:25: "Did you present sacrifices or offerings to me during the forty years in the wilderness, O House of Israel?" For discussion, see, e.g., Wolff, *Joel and Amos*, 264–65; Eidevall, *Amos*, 170–71. Eidevall argues that Amos 5:25 does not anticipate a negative answer to its question. However, it is more likely that this text, like Jer 7:22, views the wilderness lawgiving as D does.

13. As some commentators have noted, the transition from Moses's recollection of Yahweh's speech at Horeb in v. 31 back to his own speech to the Israelites in Moab in v. 32 is abrupt (see, e.g., Weinfeld, *Deuteronomy 1–11*, 326; Nelson, *Deuteronomy*, 85). Some have also struggled over the *qātal* (perfective) verbal form ṣiwwâ, arguing that it is disruptive and thus secondary given the fact that in D, Moses has not yet relayed the laws to the Israelites (e.g., Mayes, *Deuteronomy*, 174; Rofé, *Deuteronomy*, 31–32). Others have suggested that careful attention to the story world and its depiction of Moses as offering a retrospective makes vv. 32–33 unobjectionable (see, e.g., Weinfeld, *Deuteronomy 1–11*, 326; Mastnjak, *Deuteronomy and the Emergence*, 44). No matter the origin of Deut 5:32–33, it seems clear that these verses belonged to the version of D that was employed by the author of Jer 7:22–23.

14. See Stackert, "Holiness Code and Writings." For alternative arguments that identify H as a/the pentateuchal redactor, see, e.g., Otto, "Heiligkeitsgesetz Leviticus 17–26"; Knohl, *Sanctuary of Silence*, 101–3; Nihan, *From Priestly Torah*, 548–59.

15. See, e.g., Cholewiński, *Heiligkeitsgesetz und Deuteronomium*; Otto, "Innerbiblische Exegese"; Nihan, "Holiness Code between D and P"; Stackert, *Rewriting the Torah*.

16. On the identification of Num 18 as H, see esp. Knohl, *Sanctuary of Silence*, 53–54, 72–73; Stackert, *Rewriting the Torah*, 191–98.

17. This discussion draws especially on Stackert, *Rewriting the Torah*, 165–208. For other recent treatments of the relationship of the tithe laws in Deut 14 and Num 18, see Nihan, "Priestly Laws of Numbers," 120–32; Fuad, "Pentateuchal Tithe Laws."

18. Stackert, "Holiness Legislation," 196.

19. For broader treatments of pentateuchal interpretation in Chronicles, see, e.g., Shaver, *Torah and the Chronicler's History Work;* Maskow, *Tora in der Chronik.*

20. For treatment of the Chronicler's account of Josiah's Passover, see Japhet, *I & II Chronicles*, 1044–55.

21. This is a well-known example. In addition to the commentaries, see esp. Fishbane, *Biblical Interpretation*, 134–38; Ben Zvi, "Revisiting."

22. On the verb *bšl* and its specific meaning "to boil" (and not "to cook"), see Fishbane, *Biblical Interpretation*, 135–36; Ben Zvi, "Revisiting," 240–41.

23. Beyond the direct language correspondences marked here, the inverse correspondence between "not in water" in Exod 12:9 and "in fire" in 2 Chr 35:13 is likely significant and part of the consonance that the Chronicler sought to draw with the pentateuchal law. See the extended discussion in Ben Zvi, "Revisiting," 241–45 (but note that Ben Zvi reaches the unlikely conclusion that "boiling in fire" means roasting).

24. Without accompanying qualification, *kammišpāṭ* is a Priestly formulation in pentateuchal legislation. Similar formulations appear in E in Exod 21:9, 31.

25. For discussion of the Chronicler's historiographical method, see Brettler, *Creation of History*, 20–47.

26. See Welch, "Nehemiah IX"; Myers, *Ezra-Nehemiah*, 168. Myers attempts a full listing of the possible intertextual references in Neh 9:6–37 (167–69).

27. For cautions against simplistic characterization of the prayer as Deuteronomi(sti)c, see esp. Williamson, "Structure and Historiography," 127–28; Newman, *Praying by the Book*, 64–65, 68–69.

28. See, e.g., Welch, "Nehemiah IX," 133; Myers, *Ezra-Nehemiah*, 168.

29. It is noteworthy, however, that Neh 9:21 also paraphrases in part its Deuteronomic source material. Its use of the verb *kwl* is not reflected in D, though it does appear three times in the Joseph materials in the context of famine (Gen 45:11, 47:12, 50:21). The famine context is significant in light of Deut 8:3, where Moses states that Yahweh "caused you famine."

30. See, e.g., Newman, *Praying by the Book*, 88–91. Gili Kugler has argued that the use of the root *nʾṣ* in Neh 9:18 also draws on Num 14:11 and 23 ("Present Affliction," 611). The reference to "wonders" in Neh 9:17 may also be drawn from the non-Deuteronomic spies account (cf. Num 14:11, 22, which use "signs" instead); note, however, that alongside their different nouns, these verses also use different verbs.

31. See Boda, *Praying the Tradition*, 78–79. Boda rightly observes that the possessive pronoun in v. 23 must refer to the Exodus generation, but he does not observe how Neh 9 combines conflicting pentateuchal views of generation change.

32. Gilbert has rightly observed that vv. 13 and 14 likely distinguish between the direct revelation of the Decalogue and the laws that Moses mediated to the Israelites ("Place de la loi," 311).

33. The reference to the manna in Neh 9:15 ("bread from heaven") is most straightforwardly related to Exod 16 and not to Num 11 or Deut 8. Exod 16:4 is the only pentateuchal instance of "bread from heaven." The lawgiving draws upon Exod 19–20, while the water reference is likely to Exod 17:1b–7. However, the actual language used in the water reference comes from the parallel (P) story in Num 20:2, 3b–4, 6–13, which uses the phrase "water from the rock" (v. 8). On the source division of Num 20, see Baden, "Narratives of Numbers 20–21." On the nonsequential narration of events in Neh 9 generally, see esp. Williamson, "Structure and Historiography," 122–23; Boda, *Praying the Tradition*, 77–80.

34. See, e.g., Williamson, "Structure and Historiography," 128. The prayer in Neh 9:6–37 is regularly dated to the postexilic/Persian period (Gilbert, "Place de la loi," 315; Williamson, "Structure and Historiography," 129–31; Newman, *Praying by the Book*, 57; Boda, *Praying the Tradition*, 189–95 [for an overview of scholarly proposals for the prayer's date and social location, see Boda, *Praying the Tradition*, 4–19]). Others have argued for a preexilic date for the prayer (e.g., Welch, Kugler), but such claims encounter a number of challenges, including the text's conflationary interaction with pentateuchal texts (as well as other biblical texts), a hallmark of late (especially postexilic) biblical compositions.

35. With regard to generation change specifically, the logic of the additions in Deut 1–2 was probably anticipated by—and is largely identical with—the interpretive logic evinced by Neh 9.

36. It is striking, then, that in its current position, the Levites offer the prayer in Neh 9 immediately after an extensive session of reading in "the scroll of the teaching of Yahweh, their god" (Neh 9:3). The scroll highlighted here is probably to be understood as pentateuchal (cf. esp. vv. 26, 29; Williamson, "Structure and Historiography," 129; Boda, *Praying the Tradition*, 186; for discussion of the term *tôrâ* as a general reference to the divine will, see Gilbert, "Place de la loi," 312–13).

37. See, e.g., Schiffman, "Deuteronomic Paraphrase"; Crawford, *Rewriting Scripture*, 93–102.

38. For a fuller discussion, see Stackert, "Cultic Status."

39. Milgrom references Num 18:2 but does not spell out its significance. Moreover, he suggests in a footnote that even in this context the Levitical service of 11Q19 60:14 could entail sacrificial officiation (Milgrom, "Studies in the Temple Scroll," 503). Johann Maier follows Milgrom in the view that the Levites are subservient to the priests here (*Temple Scroll*, 130), yet his translation on p. 52 does not reflect the alteration to Deut 18:7 in 60:14. One might prefer the *nota accusativi* before *h'wmdym* in the Temple Scroll's rendering, but the author here makes his revision with minimal intervention.

40. The discussion of this example draws from Stackert, "Before and After Scripture."

41. It has been suggested that the Temple Scroll's revoicing of Deuteronomic law, transforming it (mostly) into divine speech rather than Mosaic speech, was an attempt to combat the view that Deuteronomy was a commentary of second rank. Yet it is hardly clear that this perspective is implied by the Temple Scroll's legal voicing. Drawing as it does on a range of pentateuchal laws and in light of its narrative framework, the Temple Scroll's legislative voicing is just as easily understood as a harmonizing feature and an attempt to secure its own authority. It need not reveal anything concerning the assumed status of Deuteronomic law among those it opposes. What can be said without controversy is that the Temple Scroll presents Deuteronomic law as equivalent to other pentateuchal legislation. For discussion of the Temple Scroll's revoicing of Deuteronomic law and its potential implications, including for understanding the scroll as a new Torah or an extension of the Torah, see esp. Schiffman, "Theology"; Otto, "*Temple Scroll* and Pentateuch"; Kratz, "Law and Narrative," 118–19.

42. As others have recognized, it is likely that the scriptural *Vorlage* from which the Temple Scroll author worked aligned in significant ways with the LXX and not the MT. See Yadin, *Temple Scroll*, 2: 228–29; Schiffman, "Deuteronomic Paraphrase," 564–65; Crawford, *Rewriting Scripture*, 95–96.

43. Yadin, *Temple Scroll*, 1: 383–85, 2: 227–29. Several scholars have substantially followed Yadin's analysis; see, e.g., Schiffman, "Deuteronomic Paraphrase"; Crawford, *Rewriting Scripture*, 94–96; Paganini, *Rezeption des Deuteronomiums*, 44–51.

44. Bernstein and Koyfman, "Interpretation of Biblical Law," 84. As Bernstein and Koyfman note, in proper cases of *gezera shava*, the interpreted expression appears only twice in the Torah, as in the case of the "do not fear" command in Deut 1:17 and 18:22. Yadin also notes that these are the only two occurrences of *l' tgwr[w]* in the Pentateuch (*Temple Scroll*, 2: 229).

45. It is possible that the death penalty in the hypothetical case of prophetic inducement to apostasy in Deut 13:2–6 may also have helped smooth the way for this penalty's introduction in 11Q19 51:17, but this is not necessary.

46. See, e.g., Van Seters, "Etiology," 359; Brettler, *Creation of History*, 67–68.

47. For discussion of this example, see esp. Kratz, "'Place Which He Has Chosen'"; Weissenberg, "Centrality of the Temple."

48. The text here follows the reconstruction of *DJD*, which represents a combination of readings. For B 27–30, see 4Q394 3–7 ii:14–17 and 4Q397 3:1–3. For B 60–61, see 4Q394 8 iv:10–11 and 4Q396 1–2 ii:11, iii:1. See now also the new edition by Reinhard G. Kratz in Kratz, ed., *Interpreting and Living*, 32–53.

49. For discussion of approximate quotation, including this example, see Schorch, "Which Kind of Authority?," 3–4.

50. One recent argument for understanding Deut 1:5 as a characterization of D's laws as interpretive bases its claim especially in early reception history. See

Gertz, "Compositional Function," 40–41. Gertz argues that the ancient versions and in particular 1Q22 (1QWords of Moses) 2:8 confirm that the verb *b'r* was understood to mean "to expound/interpret" by early interpreters. Leaving aside whether these early Jewish interpretations should guide the understanding of Deut 1:5, it is important to contextualize the example in 1Q22. Doing so reveals several problems with Gertz's reading. (Gertz does not actually treat this text in detail.) While *lb'r* is clearly preserved in 1Q22 2:8, what comes immediately before it is partially broken, and the immediately following text (the beginning of the next line) is missing entirely. 1Q22 2:8 comes in the context of Moses's commissioning of the judges in the wilderness, as found in Deut 1:9–18; 1Q22 2:7 clearly reflects knowledge of Deut 1:12. Yet because of the brokenness of its surroundings, it is difficult to make sense of *lb'r* in 2:8. The relevant section in lines 8–9 reads (with *DJD* reconstruction):

[hbw lkm ḥkmym 'šr y]'św lb'r
[lkm wlbny]km ['t] kwl dbry ht[wrh] h'lh

As indicated here, the agent of the action denoted by *lb'r* is not preserved, and the speculative reconstruction proposed by *DJD* creates an idiosyncratic (even dubious) formulation (*y'św lb'r*). Moreover, even if this reconstruction is accepted, it is hardly clear that it refers to interpretation and not promulgation/communication. In view of these details, the claim that 1Q22 2:8 clarifies the meaning of *b'r* in Deut 1:5 cannot be sustained. For further discussion, and alternative reconstruction that responds in part to the issues raised here, see Feldman, "Moses' Farewell," 207–8.

51. See, e.g., *b. Pesaḥ.* 6b; *Mek. Besh.* 7; *Sipre Num.* 64; *Eccl. Rab.* 1:12. On the origin and various meanings and applications of this rabbinic dictum, see, e.g., Kasher, "Interpretation of Scripture," 558–60, 590–91. For the debates among the medieval Jewish commentators (e.g., Nahmanides and Abarbanel vs. Rashi and Ibn Ezra) concerning the issue of chronological presentation in the Torah, see Elman, "Moses ben Nahman," 423–27.

52. *B. 'Erub.* 13b; *b. Giṭ.* 6b. The example of this quotation from *'Erubin* is particularly instructive because it comes in the context of a dispute between the houses of Hillel and Shammai. Although both are validated, the perspective of the house of Hillel is accepted and defended as halakhah on the basis of its members' humility. This example shows the impossibility of reconciling opposing viewpoints and the eventual preference of one over the other. For discussion of the acceptance of Hillel over Shammai, see, e.g., Halivni, *Revelation Restored,* 87–89.

Chapter 5. Dating Deuteronomic Composition

1. Scholars have, of course, suggested other possible datings for D. For example, some have tried to correlate (at least an early form of) D with the reform of

Hezekiah described in 2 Kgs 18:3–4, 16, 22 and 2 Chr 29–31; 32:12 (e.g., Weinfeld, *Deuteronomic School*, 164; Weinfeld, *Deuteronomy 1–11*, 83–84; Rose, *5. Mose*,
23; Steymans, "Deuteronomy 28," 12). Others have argued for even earlier dates,
including dates based on D's posited northern origin (see, e.g., Alt, "Heimat
des Deuteronomiums"; Rofé, *Deuteronomy*, 7–9; for discussion and critique, see
Knoppers, "Northern Context"), D's supposed reflection of real socioeconomic
details (e.g., Richter, "Question of Provenance"), and similarities between D
and Hittite texts (see the discussion in Chapter 3).

2. De Wette's dissertation is regularly cited as the origin of the "de Wette hypothesis." Yet several scholars, including John W. Rogerson (*W. M. L. de Wette*,
40), Eran Viezel, ("Précédent juif de De Wette"), and Harvey, Jr., and Halpern
("'*Dissertatio Critica*,'" 60–61, 73), have noted that the "de Wette hypothesis" did
not actually originate with de Wette. Moreover, de Wette hardly emphasized
the Josianic book find at all in his dissertation, making only a passing reference
to it in footnote 5.

3. De Wette, *Beiträge*, 179; see also Harvey, Jr., and Halpern, "'*Dissertatio Critica*,'"
61–65.

4. Harvey, Jr., and Halpern, "'*Dissertatio Critica*,'" 84.

5. For further discussion, see Stackert, *Prophet Like Moses*, 2–19.

6. Wellhausen, *Prolegomena*, 76–78, 366–68.

7. Wellhausen, *Prolegomena*, 508–9; also cited in Weinfeld, *Place of the Law*, 4.

8. Wellhausen, "Israel," *Encyclopaedia Britannica* (1881); repr. in *Prolegomena*, 509–
10; also quoted by Weinfeld, *Place of the Law*, 5.

9. Wellhausen, *Composition*, 186–93; *Prolegomena*, 33, 280.

10. Harvey, Jr., and Halpern, "'*Dissertatio Critica*,'" 84.

11. Harvey, Jr., and Halpern, "'*Dissertatio Critica*,'" 84.

12. Commenting on Wellhausen's reordering of the source materials in de Wette's
analysis, Harvey, Jr., and Halpern note, "Wellhausen thought he had found
de Wette standing on his head, and so turned him upside down" ("'*Dissertatio
Critica*,'" 72). This is perhaps best exemplified in Wellhausen's reorientation of
de Wette's judgment regarding the similarity between Deuteronomic law and
later rabbinic thought and the latter's dissimilarity from other pentateuchal
legislation: "The doctrine of law and religion that emanates from our book
seems manifestly different and dissonant with that of the preceding books: indeed, that doctrine is of the sort that seems to approximate, in a certain fashion
later, rabbinical doctrine. What the preceding books contain as simple, natural and unsophisticated, our book presents as embellished, more refined, and
corrupted" (ibid., 79–80). Wellhausen retained de Wette's basic devolutionary
schema and his value judgment upon it, but he repopulated the points on the
timeline: from "the preceding books," JE remained early and "natural," but P
became the pinnacle of corruption.

13. "Ohne W. M. L. de Wette, kein Wellhausen" (Otto, "Deuteronomium als archimedischer Punkt," 322). Otto goes on to claim that the de Wette hypothesis

was such a fundamental part of the Graf-Wellhausen Documentary Hypothesis that damage to one necessarily implied damage to the other. Yet as I have discussed here, though Wellhausen thoroughly integrated de Wette's dating of D into his reconstruction of Israelite religion on the basis of the pentateuchal sources, de Wette's observations regarding the separation of D from the other pentateuchal works is quite independent of the dating that he posited for D. For Wellhausen, too, situating D in the late seventh century was hardly determinative for his source division; neither was this absolute dating of primary importance for his historical reconstruction. Much more important was his *sequencing* of the sources, with P following D.

14. For discussion of the varied relevance of the book find account for contemporary readers, see Henige, "Found But Not Lost."

15. A voluminous amount of scholarship critiques the de Wette hypothesis, its reliance upon 2 Kgs 22–23, and its conceptualization of D's role in the reform. For both softer and harder critiques, see, e.g., Weinfeld, "Cult Centralization"; Levin, "Joschija"; Niehr, "Reform des Joschija"; Henige, "Found But Not Lost"; Pakkala, "Date of the Oldest Edition," 390–91. For a recent reassertion of the basic contours of the de Wette hypothesis, see Na'aman, "'Discovered Book.'"

16. De Wette, *Beiträge*, 170–79. Notably, de Wette stopped short of asserting some of his stronger suspicions, stating that he did not want to transgress "the laws of history" ("die Gesetze der Geschichte," 179).

17. Uehlinger, "Was There a Cult Reform?," 279.

18. Uehlinger, "Was There a Cult Reform?," 292–95.

19. Uehlinger, "Was There a Cult Reform?," 299. For discussion of the recently unearthed temple at Moza from the Iron IIA period that may have also functioned later, see Kisilevitz, "Judahite Temple."

20. Spieckermann, *Juda unter Assur*, esp. 79–112. For critique of Spieckermann, see esp. Mordechai Cogan, "Judah under Assyrian Hegemony."

21. Uehlinger, "Was There a Cult Reform?," 300–305. See also Weinfeld, "Worship of Molech," 149–54); Weinfeld, *Deuteronomy 1–11*, 17, 74–76, 206.

22. Uehlinger, "Was There a Cult Reform?," 303, 306.

23. Otto, "Deuteronomium als archimedischer Punkt." For brief arguments along similar lines, see already Frankena, "Vassal-Treaties," 152–53. More recently, see Watanabe, "Esarhaddon's Succession Oath Documents Reconsidered," 164.

24. Otto, "Deuteronomium als archimedischer Punkt," 338.

25. Steymans, "Deuteronomy 28," 11–12; Steymans, "Deuteronomy 13," 102–3, 130–32. For the historicity of the Josianic book find and reform, Steymans relies especially on Pietsch, *Kultreform Josias*.

26. See, e.g., Perlitt, *Bundestheologie im Alten Testament*, 279–83; Weinfeld, *Deuteronomic School*, 122; Stackert, *Prophet Like Moses*, 31–32. As discussed above, Otto prefers a Josianic date, but he has acknowledged that D may have originated earlier in the seventh century: "If we are looking for an *Urdeuteronomium*, then it was this loyalty oath to YHWH as the literary core section of Deuteronomy.

It was written between 672 and 612 BCE and most probably during the reign of king Josiah" ("Political Theology," 65). Others have also offered a hybrid account that includes both Manassite and Josianic dates (e.g., Haran, *Temples and Temple Service*, 137–38).

27. Frankena, "Vassal-Treaties," 151. Holloway argues for the use of both Assyrian and local gods in loyalty oath ceremonies (*Aššur Is King!*, 175–76). For critique, see Berlejung, "Assyrians in the West," 35–36.

28. Knoppers, "Deuteronomic Law of the King"; Knoppers, "Rethinking the Relationship"; Levinson, "Reconceptualization."

29. Levinson, "Reconceptualization," 527. Many scholars, observing the inconsistency between D's restrictions on the monarchy and a royal commissioning of a work that includes them, have argued that the law of the king must be a late addition or a basis for dating the whole of D as late. See, e.g., Lohfink, "Distribution of the Functions of Power," 345–46; Pakkala, "Date of the Oldest Edition," 392–93.

30. Levinson, "Reconceptualization," 528.

31. Nicholson, "'Do Not Dare.'"

32. Wazana, "Law of the King," 170; see also Crouch, *Making of Israel*, 179–80. For questions in response to Wazana, see Markl, "Deuteronomy's Anti-King," 173. Others have connected D's law of the king to Assyria in other ways. For example, Nicholson argued that the prohibition against a foreign king in Deut 17:15 should be understood in relation to the long experience of Judah across the seventh century and reflects a retrospective on a century of rule by "the Great King" (i.e., the Assyrian emperors) in Judah ("'Do Not Dare,'" 59–61).

33. Following Weinfeld (*Deuteronomic School*, 168–69; cf. 281, 368), Wazana connects the reference to accumulating horses in Egypt with Hos 11:5 (Wazana, "Law of the King," 182–83). It is worth noting that SAA 19 159 (ND 2765) reports Judah's delivery of horses to Assyria during the reign of Sargon II. Cf. Morton Cogan, *Imperialism and Religion*, 118.

34. For an archaeological reconstruction of a substantial, noncentralized Judean leadership in the seventh century that would provide context for Wazana's suggestion, see Maier and Shai, "Reassessing." For evidence of scribal practice in the late Iron Age outside of state-sponsored centers, see Sanders, *Invention of Hebrew*, 131.

35. Of course, depending upon the details of the proposal, a correlation between D's allegory and its dating is possible for any of the options reviewed here, as the Wazana interpretation just reviewed attests.

36. Römer, *Deuteronomistic History*, 115–33.

37. Kratz, *Composition*, 132.

38. Pakkala, "Date of the Oldest Edition." For critique of Pakkala, see MacDonald, "Issues in the Dating of Deuteronomy." Pakkala offered further response to MacDonald in "Dating of Deuteronomy."

39. For an extended discussion of this issue, see Stackert, "Political Allegory."

40. Note that alongside the one attestation *nś' ḥēṭ'* in Ezekiel, there are nine occurrences of *nś' 'āwôn* (4:4, 5, 6; 14:10; 18:19 [with *bêt* preposition]; 18:20 [twice]; 44:10, 12). On the possible general linguistic and conceptual ties between the biblical expressions and their Mesopotamian parallels, see Wells, *Law of Testimony*, 73–78; Lam, *Patterns of Sin*, 55–58.

41. See Magdalene, Wunsch, and Wells, *Fault, Responsibility, and Administrative Law*, 31–58.

42. The Judean examples are not yet published. They will appear in Wunsch, *Judeans by the Waters of Babylon*. The relevant text numbers are BaAr 6 4 and BaAr 6 83. I am grateful to Dr. Wunsch for sharing these examples with me.

43. See now the publication of an initial subset of Judean documents from the David Sofer Collection in Pearce and Wunsch, *Documents*. These tablets date from the year 572 BCE to the year 477 and thus add significantly to what was previously known about Judeans in Babylonia from the documents of the Murašû archive, which date to the second half of the fifth century BCE (Pearce and Wunsch, *Documents*, 4–5). See also the helpful recent discussions in Pearce, "New Evidence"; Zadok, "Judeans in Babylonia."

44. Stackert, "Political Allegory," 218–20.

45. Lipschits, "Long Seventh Century." See also the recent survey by Kelle ("Judah in the Seventh Century"). As Lipschits and others have observed, the period between 701 BCE and 586 BCE attests no significant destruction in Judah. This means that there are few secure contexts for situating archaeological finds during this period.

46. See, e.g., Schloen, *House of the Father*, 141–47; Faust, "Interests of the Assyrian Empire"; Faust, "Southern Levant," 113–15; Faust, "Assyrian Century"; Bagg, "Palestine under Assyrian Rule," 131. Note, too, Faust's observation that the Levantine regions that were made provinces were not nearly as prosperous as those regions that maintained semiautonomy. This detail underscores that the Assyrians did not invest to develop local economies ("Southern Levant," 105–6).

47. See, e.g., Finkelstein and Na'aman, "Judahite Shephelah"; Faust, "Settlement and Demography," 172–73.

48. On the possibility of displacement of residents from the Shephelah to the areas surrounding Jerusalem and the development of the Jerusalem economy, see Gadot, "In the Valley of the King."

49. See Mayer, "Sennacherib's Campaign," 173–79 (note that Mayer includes transliterations and translations of the different versions of the campaign). As Mayer observes, it is likely that the southern Levantine rebellion was a response to the battlefield death of Sargon II in 705 BCE and ensuing political upheaval for Assyria. Its timeframe may have covered the entire period between 705 and 701 BCE. As several scholars have noted, transitions of power were moments of

political vulnerability and tumult in the Neo-Assyrian empire. See, e.g., Radner, "Revolts in the Assyrian Empire," 48.

50. On the importance of Ashdod as an Assyrian province that ensured Assyrian access to Egypt, see Lipschits, "Long Seventh Century," 19–20; Faust, "Southern Levant," 98–99. For discussion of Esarhaddon's campaign against Egypt, including the circuitous route he took to get there, see Spalinger, "Esarhaddon and Egypt"; Radner, "Esarhaddon's Expedition," 305–14. In less than a decade, however, Egypt again established its independence after a series of battles with Assurbanipal. See B. Schipper, "Egyptian Imperialism," 270–71.

51. See, e.g., Morton Cogan, *Imperialism and Religion*, 72; Bagg, "Palestine under Assyrian Rule," 125. Mayer concludes similarly: "From the Assyrian point of view, launching a full-scale offensive against the capital of Jerusalem would have been superfluous and even senseless" ("Sennacherib's Campaign," 184).

52. See, e.g., Mayer, "Sennacherib's Campaign," 179–81.

53. For discussion of Ekron's relationship to the Assyrian empire and Padi's rulership of the city-state, see esp. Na'aman, "Ekron under the Assyrian and Egyptian Empires."

54. See Stade, "Miscellen," 172–73, 180–82; Childs, *Isaiah and the Assyrian Crisis*, 69–103.

55. For comparable avian comparisons in the Amarna letters, see Mayer, "Sennacherib's Campaign," 179.

56. This does not mean, however, that Assyria paid no attention to Judah in the aftermath of Hezekiah's capitulation. Berlejung has argued that a *qēpu* official ("trusted official") from the Neo-Assyrian empire was likely installed in Judah to oversee it, even though Judah was not itself made a province ("Assyrians in the West," 23–24, 32; for discussion of the Assyrian *qēpu* official more generally, see Dubovský, "King's Direct Control"). Dubovský has also accumulated evidence that suggests Assyria established an intelligence network in the southern Levant in the late eighth and seventh centuries to aid its regional governance (*Hezekiah and the Assyrian Spies*, 189–221).

57. See Esarhaddon's Nineveh A and F/S prisms (RINAP 4 1 v:55; 4 5 viii:8') and Assurbanipal's Prism Inscription C (ii:27). In each case, Manasseh is portrayed as a dutiful client ruler who paid tribute to the empire. For discussion, see, e.g., Morton Cogan, *Imperialism and Religion*, 67–68; Gane, "Role of Assyria"; W. Morrow, "Have Attempts?," 139.

58. For an attempt to reconstruct an "archaeology of Manasseh," see Finkelstein, "Days of Manasseh." For critique, see Lipschits, "Long Seventh Century," 34.

59. For analysis of the biblical treatment of Manasseh, including comparison with the nonbiblical data, see, e.g., Stavrakopoulou, *King Manasseh*, esp. 15–72; Knauf, "Glorious Days"; Machinist, "Manasseh of Judah."

60. See, e.g., the discussion in Radner, "Revolts in the Assyrian Empire," 52–53.

61. See B. Schipper, "Egyptian Imperialism," 283; Lipschits, "Long Seventh Century," 27–28. Both Schipper (273–79) and Uehlinger ("Was There a Cult Re-

form?," 295) have highlighted the prominence of Egyptian material culture remains in the Levant from the second half of the seventh century.

62. Dion, "Deuteronomy 13," 204–5.

63. As several scholars have observed, the Sargonids of the seventh century significantly increased the usage of *adê* oaths in their diplomatic relations. See, e.g., Tadmor, "Treaty and Oath"; M. Fales, "After Ta'yinat," 135; Radner, "Neo-Assyrian Treaties as a Source," 310–12. For recent discussion of the impact of the Assyrian empire upon Deuteronomic texts, see Brett, *Locations of God*, 34–40.

64. This likely explains why there have been few attempts to situate EST in this broader context when evaluating its impact on D. Notable exceptions are Tadmor, "Treaty and Oath," and Lauinger, "Literary Connections." The evidence of the Tayinat EST exemplar suggests that it was a display tablet and, based on its find spot, that it was installed inside the Neo-Assyrian temple there (labeled by the excavators Building XVI) and perhaps also was brought out on special occasions for viewing. Yet what is unknown is when precisely the Building XVI temple, with its copy of EST installed within it, was destroyed. For discussion of Building XVI, see Harrison and Osborne, "Building XVI," and esp. Osborne et al., "Urban Built Environments," 277–93.

65. George, "Tablet of Destinies"; Parpola and Watanabe, *Neo-Assyrian Treaties and Loyalty Oaths*, xxxvi; Watanabe, "Esarhaddon's Succession Oath Documents Reconsidered," 162–63.

66. Lauinger, "Neo-Assyrian *adê*," 108–14. See now also Watanabe, "Adoration of Oath Documents." On the *akītu* festival more generally, see, among others, Toorn, "Babylonian New Year Festival"; Sommer, "Babylonian Akitu Festival." For emphasis upon the ritual use of treaty tablets, see already McCarthy, *Treaty and Covenant*, 157.

67. Parpola and Watanabe, *Neo-Assyrian Treaties and Loyalty Oaths*, 22.

68. On Zakutu generally, see Melville, *Naqia/Zakutu*. On the Zakutu treaty in particular, see pp. 79–90.

69. Parpola and Watanabe raise the possibility that the text's reference to Esarhaddon only as "lord" and not as "king" may mean that its oath was imposed before Esarhaddon's accession to the throne (*Neo-Assyrian Treaties and Loyalty Oaths*, xxviii). This conclusion is unlikely, however, in view of the fact that the *adê* texts regularly refer to the king as "lord" and as a rule do not use this title for the crown prince in his current status (for illuminating examples, see SAA 2 6: 188–91, 298–301; for a rare case in which Assurbanipal is called "lord" in EST, see line 506; note the alternative usage in lines 201–11). There are also instances in the *adê* texts where the king is referenced only as "lord" and not as "king" (e.g., SAA 2 6: 393–94).

70. Note that even though copies of EST directed to all of the different individuals and subgroups of the empire are not extant, the content of the *adê* text makes clear that all Assyrians and others subject to the Assyrian king were bound by its demands (e.g., SAA 2 6:62–82). Moreover, as Simo Parpola has

observed, *LSA* 1–3 appear to be letters concerning the enactment of the *adê*'s oath across the empire (*Letters from Assyrian Scholars*, 2: 3–6). For discussion of the mass production of *adê* tablets to serve this end, see Lauinger, "Neo-Assyrian Scribes."

71. Wiseman has suggested that "it was customary for a new king to call on the people to renew their oath of loyalty at the earliest public meeting after his accession" (*Vassal-Treaties*, 9).

72. Parpola, "Neo-Assyrian Treaties," 168–69. A. Kirk Grayson insists that the imposition of the Zakutu *adê*'s oath upon Šamaš-šumu-ukin occurred upon the latter's accession to the throne of Babylon, presumably because his accession could have emboldened him to challenge Assurbanipal ("Akkadian Treaties," 130, 132, 138). Yet it should be noted that the text makes no reference to Šamaš-šumu-ukin's new position or to the people of Babylonia as his subjects. Grayson dates the Zakutu *adê* to the year 668 BCE, but Parpola and Watanabe leave open the possibility that it dates to late 669 BCE and do not connect it directly with the accession of Šamaš-šumu-ukin (*Neo-Assyrian Treaties and Loyalty Oaths*, xxxi). Given the Zakutu *adê*'s reference to Assurbanipal as "king of Assyria," Radner's 672 BCE dating is unlikely ("Neo-Assyrian Treaties as a Source," 313). As noted, Assurbanipal only ascended to the throne in 669 BCE. Wiseman suggested two possible occasions for the Zakutu *adê*: the death of Esarhaddon or the revolt of Šamaš-šumu-ukin in 652 BCE (*Vassal-Treaties*, 9). For critique of the latter suggestion, see Parpola, "Neo-Assyrian Treaties," 168 n. 23. For detailed treatment of the relationship between Assurbanipal and Šamaš-šumu-ukin, see Zaia, "My Brother's Keeper."

73. For discussion of the familial relationships of Esarhaddon and Assurbanipal, see esp. Watanabe, "Aššurbanipal and His Brothers"; Radner, "Trials of Esarhaddon." Note, too, Melville's observation that there is no evidence that Assurbanipal actually encountered any rebellion at his accession or in the early years of his reign. It is possible, then, that Zakutu was simply carrying out plans set in place before Esarhaddon's death and not responding to any specific threat (*Naqia/Zakutu*, 89–90).

74. Tadmor, "Treaty and Oath," 150–51.

75. See, e.g., SAA 2 6:9–10.

76. For discussion of the succession *adê*s as distinctive among the preserved Assyrian *adê* texts, see esp. Radner, "Neo-Assyrian Treaties as a Source," 316–19.

77. It should be observed that Assurbanipal did himself issue other *adê*s; see SAA 2 9 and 10. Note, too, that Parpola and Watanabe characterize Šamaš-šumu-ukin's rebellion against Assurbanipal as a violation of the Zakutu *adê*, not EST (*Neo-Assyrian Treaties and Loyalty Oaths*, xxxi–xxxii).

78. Lauinger, "Some Preliminary Thoughts," 11–12. See also Radner's discussion of the divinized *adê* tablet and later development of "the King's Tablet" as one of

the cursing parties alongside the gods named in *adê* texts ("Neo-Assyrian Treaties as a Source," 320–25).

79. Lauinger, "Iqqur *īpuš*," 230–32.

80. Watanabe, "Adoration of Oath Documents," esp. 73–84.

81. Crouch similarly emphasizes the importance of the tablet's communication of power as an object, not as a text whose linguistic content was paramount (*Israel and the Assyrians*, 154–56).

82. On the seal impressions on the EST *adê* tablets, see, e.g., Watanabe, "Siegelung"; Watanabe, "Adoration of Oath Documents"; Lauinger, "Neo-Assyrian *adê*," esp. 108–10.

83. Lauinger, "Literary Connections," 94–97. Lauinger also substantiates his argument through an explanation of the shift from EST's use of perfect (t-infix) verbs to describe the writing and establishment of the *adê* to a durative form to describe its swearing: "Your father wrote (this) in the *adê*-agreement, he established (the *adê*-agreement), and he makes us swear (it)" (EST lines 357–58) (see Lauinger, "Literary Connections," 96).

84. Parpola and Watanabe, *Neo-Assyrian Treaties and Loyalty Oaths*, xlii.

85. Note that Lauinger makes this argument alongside a tentative proposal linking the reconstructed Assyrian *akītu* practice with the prescription in Deut 31:9–13 that the Levites read out Yahweh's laws every seven years among all the Israelites at Sukkot ("Literary Connections," 97–98). While the parallel between these practices is suggestive, it is quite general and thus difficult to judge as a potential instance of direct influence (which is how Lauinger prefers to understand it).

86. Steymans, "Neuassyrische Vertragsrhetorik," 96; Steymans, "Deuteronomy 28," 9–10.

87. Radner, "Assyrische tuppi adê," 372–73; Lauinger, "Neo-Assyrian *adê*," 113–14.

88. Harrison and Osborne, "Building XVI," 125–26; Osborne et al., "Urban Built Environments," 262–63.

89. Lauinger, "Neo-Assyrian *adê*," 113–14.

90. Tadmor also argues against the presence of an EST tablet in Jerusalem. However, in his view, this is because it is unlikely that Manasseh was forced to swear this oath, which he suggests was imposed only on newer subject polities ("Treaties and Oaths," 151).

91. On the Assyrian province of Samerina, see, e.g., Itach, "Kingdom of Israel," 67–73; Morton Cogan, *Imperialism and Religion*, 97–108; Faust, "Southern Levant," 102–3. On the Assyrian provinces in the southern Levant more generally, see esp. Zilberg, "Assyrian Provinces."

92. For a catalogue of Judean interactions with Assyria during the Neo-Assyrian westward expansion in the eighth to seventh centuries, see Wright, *Inventing God's Law*, 96–106. For documents related to Assyrian/Judean interactions, see Zilberg, "Assyrian Empire and Judah." For additional discussion of interactions

between center and periphery in the Neo-Assyrian empire more generally, including the practice of delivering tribute to the center, see Holloway, *Aššur Is King!*, 223–319; W. Morrow, "Tribute from Judah"; Berlejung, "Assyrians in the West," 22–30.

93. For arguments in favor of an EST tablet in Jerusalem, see Frankena, "Vassal-Treaties," 151; Berlejung, "Assyrians in the West," 23–24; Levinson and Stackert, "Between the Covenant Code," 132; Steymans, "Deuteronomy 28," 11. Radner endorses the presence of an *adê* in Jerusalem, but she is hesitant to designate which one ("Assyrische tuppi adê," 374–75). Quick acknowledges the possibility of an EST tablet in Jerusalem but as discussed in Chapter 3 suggests against the evidence that its Akkadian would have been inaccessible to Judean scribes (*Deuteronomy 28*, 63).

94. M. Fales, "After Tayinat," 151–52. See also Radner, "Neo-Assyrian Treaties as a Source," 314–16.

95. Steymans, "Deuteronomy 13," 113.

96. On the mass production of EST tablets, see esp. Lauinger, "Neo-Assyrian Scribes," passim; M. Fales, "After Tayinat," 148. This deposition scenario also permits a tantalizing suggestion for understanding the famous command in the Decalogue, "You shall have no other gods before my face" (Deut 5:7). The prepositional phrase "before my face" is most naturally understood as locative, and the designation of "gods" should probably be extended beyond the narrow category of divine beings to divinized objects (i.e., any entity participating in the category of the divine). Given these details and the fact that an EST tablet would certainly be considered "other"/foreign, it is possible that the deposition of a divinized object such as an EST tablet within a Yahwistic sanctuary is the kind of practice that the Decalogue line targets. For further discussion of possible connections between EST and the Decalogue prohibitions against the veneration of objects, see Koch, "Bundestheologie und autoritativer Text." On the possible Neo-Assyrian practice of creating divinized images of the king and installing them in temples, see Holloway, *Aššur Is King!*, 178–93.

97. Note that Wazana's argument for subversive intent in Deut 17:14–20 addresses precisely those issues that Crouch raises in her argument against subversive intent in D's claimed reuse of EST (see *Israel and the Assyrians*, 147–56). Rather than requiring widespread specialized knowledge of a cuneiform text, Wazana's argument requires D's audience to be familiar only with relatively common imperial ideology and practices. For Judean familiarity with such phenomena, see Berlejung, "Assyrians in the West," 31–32.

98. See, e.g., Morton Cogan, *Imperialism and Religion*, 88; Mordechai Cogan, "Judah under Assyrian Hegemony"; McKay, *Religion in Judah*, 67; Berlejung, "Assyrians in the West," 37–38. On emulation rather than compulsion as the primary mode of Judean interaction with Neo-Assyrian culture, see Bagg, "Palestine under Assyrian Rule," 128–29.

99. See esp. Spieckermann, *Juda unter Assur,* 333–38, 369–72. Given the requirement in EST that the oath-taker acknowledge Assur and that its tablet be set up and treated like a god, Quick's claim that "nowhere do the *adê* documents impose cultic measures" requires revision (*Deuteronomy 28,* 62). Berlejung's suggestion that "the content of these treaties is purely political and economic" ("Assyrians in the West," 37) should also be nuanced—at least from the perspective of Assyria's subjects. Note Radner's observations on EST, which she suggests are particularly relevant for the Judean context: "What is certain, however, is that at least from 672 BC onwards, the god Aššur was made manifest across the empire in the form of such sacred texts, transcending the confines of his temple in the city of Assur. Due to the extensive and deliberate dissemination of the succession treaty tablets, the idea that the god was present in these texts must have been widely familiar in the Assyrian influence sphere" ("Neo-Assyrian Treaties as a Source," 315).

100. This observation raises the possibility that D's arguments could be understood as anti-Assyrian at a remove, refracted through an anti-Assyrianism already in E. For an argument along these lines, see Wright, *Inventing God's Law,* 115–17, 344–52 (for the correspondence between Wright's Covenant Code Narrative and E, see 493 n. 49).

101. This is not to say that E knew nothing of monarchy or had no views on it. For discussion of antimonarchic perspectives in E, including in its laws, see Chavel, "Kingdom of Priests," esp. 197–201.

102. See the discussion above.

103. See, e.g., Dion, "Deuteronomy 13," 199; Otto, *Deuteronomium: Politische Theologie,* 69; W. S. Morrow, "Cuneiform Literacy," 211. More recently, Morrow has reversed his position ("Have Attempts?," 157–58).

104. Rose, *5. Mose,* 23; Bloch-Smith, "Assyrians Abet Israelite Cultic Reforms." See also the discussion of Knauf, who ties cult centralization in Deut 12 to the time of Manasseh and the archaeological evidence of the period ("Glorious Days," 184–88).

105. See Stade, "Miscellen," 173–80; Childs, *Isaiah and the Assyrian Crisis,* 118–24.

Bibliography

Addis, W. E. *The Documents of the Hexateuch.* 2 vols. London: David Nutt, 1892.

Albertz, Rainer. "A Possible *Terminus Ad Quem* for the Deuteronomistic Legislation—A Fresh Look at Deut 17:16." Pages 271–96 in *Homeland and Exile: Studies in Honour of Bustenay Oded.* Edited by Gershon Galil, Markham Geller, and Alan Millard. VTSup 130. Boston: Brill, 2009.

Allen, Spencer L. "Rearranging the Gods in Esarhaddon's Succession Treaty (SAA 2 6:414–465)." *WdO* 43 (2013): 1–24.

Alt, Albrecht. "Die Heimat des Deuteronomiums." Pages 250–75 in *Kleine Schriften zur Geschichte des Volkes Israel.* Edited by Albrecht Alt. 3 vols. Munich: Beck, 1953–1959.

Alter, Robert. *The Art of Biblical Narrative.* New York: Basic Books, 1981.

———. "How Convention Helps Us Read: The Case of the Bible's Annunciation Type-Scene." *Prooftexts* 3 (1983): 115–30.

———. *The Pleasures of Reading in an Ideological Age.* New York: Simon & Schuster, 1989.

Araújo, Reginaldo Gomez de. *Theologie der Wüste im Deuteronomium.* ÖBS 17. Frankfurt am Main: Peter Lang, 1999.

Arnold, Bill T. "Deuteronomy's Book and Hammurapi's Stela: The Referent of 'This *Sēpher*' in Deuteronomy 28:58." *VT* 71 (2021): 1–18.

———. "Number Switching in Deuteronomy 12–26 and the Quest for *Ur-deuteronomium.*" *ZABR* 23 (2017): 163–80.

———. "Reexamining the 'Fathers' in Deuteronomy's Framework." Pages 10–41 in *Torah and Tradition: Papers Read at the Sixteenth Joint Meeting of the Society for Old Testament Study and the Oudtestamentisch Werkgezelschap, Edinburgh, 2015.* Edited by Klaas Spronk and Hans M. Barstad. *OtSt* 70. Leiden: Brill, 2017.

Aster, Shawn Zelig. "The Image of Assyria in Isaiah 2:5–22: The Campaign Motif Reversed." *JAOS* 127 (2007): 249–78.

Avrahami, Yael. *The Senses of Scripture: Sensory Perception in the Hebrew Bible.* LHBOTS 545. New York: T&T Clark, 2012.

Baden, Joel S. *The Composition of the Pentateuch: Renewing the Documentary Hypothesis.* AYBRL. New Haven: Yale University Press, 2012.

———. "The Deuteronomic Evidence for the Documentary Theory." Pages 327–44 in *The Pentateuch: International Perspectives on Current Research*. Edited by Thomas B. Dozeman, Konrad Schmid, and Baruch J. Schwartz. FAT 78. Tübingen: Mohr Siebeck, 2011.

———. *J, E, and the Redaction of the Pentateuch*. FAT 68. Tübingen: Mohr Siebeck, 2009.

———. "Literary Allusions and Assumptions about Textual Familiarity." Pages 114–30 in *Subtle Citation, Allusion, and Translation in the Hebrew Bible*. Edited by Ziony Zevit. Sheffield: Equinox, 2017.

———. "The Narratives of Numbers 20–21." *CBQ* 76 (2014): 634–52.

———. "The Original Place of the Priestly Manna Story in Exodus 16." *ZAW* 122 (2010): 491–504.

———. "The Re-Emergence of Source Criticism: The Neo-Documentary Hypothesis." *Bible and Interpretation*. May 2012. https://bibleinterp.arizona.edu/articles/bad368008.

Bagg, Ariel M. "Palestine under Assyrian Rule: A New Look at the Assyrian Imperial Policy in the West." *JAOS* 133 (2013): 119–44.

Bar-On (Gesundheit), Shimon. "The Festival Calendars in Exod XXIII 14–19 and XXXIV 18–26." *VT* 48 (1998): 161–95.

Barr, James. *Comparative Philology and the Text of the Old Testament: With Additions and Corrections*. Winona Lake, IN: Eisenbrauns, 1987.

Barton, John. *Oracles of God: Perceptions of Ancient Prophecy in Israel after the Exile*. Rev. ed. Oxford: Oxford University Press, 2007.

———. "The Prophets and the Cult." Pages 111–22 in *Temple and Worship in Biblical Israel: Proceedings of the Oxford Old Testament Seminar*. Edited by John Day. LHBOTS 422. London: T&T Clark, 2005.

———. "Wellhausen's *Prolegomena to the History of Israel:* Influences and Effect." Pages 316–29 in *Text and Experience: Towards a Cultural Exegesis of the Bible*. Edited by Daniel Smith-Christopher. BibSem 35. Sheffield: Sheffield Academic Press, 1995.

Beentjes, Pancratius C. "Inverted Quotations in the Bible: A Neglected Stylistic Pattern." *Biblica* 63 (1982): 506–23.

Bell, Catherine. *Ritual Theory, Ritual Practice*. New York: Oxford University Press, 1992.

Ben-Dov, Jonathan. "Writing as Oracle and as Law: New Contexts for the Book-Find of King Josiah." *JBL* 127 (2008): 223–39.

Beneviste, Émile. *Problèmes de linguistique générale*. 2 vols. 2nd ed. Paris: Gallimard, 1986.

Ben Zvi, Ehud. "Revisiting 'Boiling in Fire' in 2 Chronicles 35:13 and Related Passover Questions: Text, Exegetical Needs and Concerns, and General Implications." Pages 238–50 in *Biblical Interpretation in Judaism and Christianity*. Edited by Peter J. Haas and Isaac Kalimi. LHBOTS 439. New York: T&T Clark, 2006.

Berlejung, Angelika. "The Assyrians in the West: Assyrianization, Colonialism, Indifference, or Development Policy?" Pages 21–60 in *Congress Volume Helsinki 2010*. Edited by Martti Nissinen. VTSup 148. Leiden: Brill, 2012.

Berman, Joshua. "CTH 133 and the Hittite Provenance of Deuteronomy 13." *JBL* 130 (2011): 25–44.

———. "Historicism and Its Limits: A Response to Bernard M. Levinson and Jeffrey Stackert." *JAJ* 4 (2013): 297–309.

———. "Histories Twice Told: Deuteronomy 1–3 and the Hittite Treaty Prologue Tradition." *JBL* 132 (2013): 229–50.

———. *Inconsistency in the Torah: Ancient Literary Convention and the Limits of Source Criticism.* New York: Oxford University Press, 2017.

Berner, Christoph. "Das Wasserwunder von Rephidim (Ex 17,1–7) als Schlüsseltext eines nachpriesterschriftlichen Mosebildes." *VT* 63 (2013): 193–209.

Bernstein, Moshe J., and Shlomo Koyfman. "The Interpretation of Biblical Law in the Dead Sea Scrolls." Pages 61–87 in *Biblical Interpretation at Qumran*. Edited by Matthias Henze. Studies in the Dead Sea Scrolls and Related Literature. Grand Rapids: Eerdmans, 2005.

Bertholet, Alfred. *Deuteronomium.* KHAT 5. Freiburg: J. C. B. Mohr, 1899.

Biberger, Bernd. *Unsere Väter und Wir: Unterteilung von Geschichtsdarstellungen in Generationen und das Verhältnis der Generationen im Alten Testament.* BBB 145. Berlin: Philo, 2003.

Blenkinsopp, Joseph. *The Pentateuch: An Introduction to the First Five Books of the Bible.* ABRL. New York: Doubleday, 1992.

Bloch, Yigal. "Aramaic Influence and Inner Diachronic Development in Hebrew Inscriptions of the Iron Age." Pages 83–112 in *Advances in Biblical Hebrew Linguistics: Data, Methods, and Analyses*. Edited by Adina Moshavi and Tania Notarius. LSAWS 12. Winona Lake, IN: Eisenbrauns, 2017.

Bloch-Smith, Elizabeth. "Assyrians Abet Israelite Cultic Reforms: Sennacherib and the Centralization of the Israelite Cult." Pages 35–44 in *Exploring the Longue Durée: Essays in Honor of Lawrence E. Stager*. Edited by J. David Schloen. Winona Lake, IN: Eisenbrauns, 2009.

Boda, Mark J. *Praying the Tradition: The Origin and Use of Tradition in Nehemiah 9.* BZAW 277. Berlin: de Gruyter, 1999.

Borger, Riekele. "Zu den Asarhaddon-Verträgen aus Nimrud." *ZA* 54 (1961): 173–96.

Botterweck, G. Johannes, Helmer Ringgren, and Heinz-Josef Fabry. *Theological Dictionary of the Old Testament.* 15 vols. Grand Rapids: Eerdmans, 1974–2006.

Boyd, Samuel L. "Exodus 21:35 and the Composition and Date of the Covenant Code." *WdO* 48 (2018): 9–23.

———. "The Flood and the Problem of Being an Omnivore." *JSOT* 43 (2019): 163–78.

———. *Language Contact, Colonial Administration, and the Construction of Identity in Ancient Israel: Constructing the Context for Contact.* HSM 66. Leiden: Brill, 2021.

Boyd, Samuel Lanham. "Contact and Context: Studies in Language Contact and Literary Strata in the Hebrew Bible." Ph.D. diss., University of Chicago, 2014.

Braulik, Georg. "The Sequence of the Laws in Deuteronomy 12–26 and in the Decalogue." Pages 313–35 in *A Song of Power and the Power of Song: Essays on the Book of Deuteronomy*. Edited by Duane L. Christensen. SBTS 3. Winona Lake, IN: Eisenbrauns, 1993.

Braulik, Georg, and Norbert Lohfink. "Deuteronomium 1,5 באר את־התורה הזאת: 'er verlieh dieser Tora Rechtskraft.'" Pages 34–51 in *Textarbeit: Studien zu Texten und ihrer Rezeption aus dem Alten Testament und der Umwelt Israels: Festschrift für Peter Weimar zur Vollendung seines 60. Lebensjahres mit Beiträgen von Freunden, Schülern und Kollegen*. Edited by Klaus Kiesow and Thomas Meurer. AOAT 294. Münster: Ugarit-Verlag, 2003.

Brekelmans, Christianus. "Wisdom Influence in Deuteronomy." Pages 28–38 in *La Sagesse de l'Ancien Testament*. Edited by Maurice Gilbert. BETL 51. Louvain: Louvain University Press, 1978.

Brett, Mark G. *Locations of God: Political Theology in the Hebrew Bible*. New York: Oxford University Press, 2019.

Brettler, Marc Zvi. *The Creation of History in Ancient Israel*. New York: Routledge, 1995.

Carasik, Michael. *Theologies of the Mind in Biblical Israel*. StBibLit 85. New York: Peter Lang, 2006.

Carr, David M. "Rethinking the Materiality of Biblical Texts: From Source, Tradition and Redaction to a Scroll Approach." *ZAW* 132 (2020): 594–621.

Chavel, Simcha (Simeon). "The Legal Literature of the Hebrew Bible." Pages 227–72 in vol. 1 of *The Literature of the Hebrew Bible: Introductions and Studies*. Edited by Zipora Talshir. 2 vols. Jerusalem: Yad Ben-Zvi Press, 2011 (in Hebrew).

Chavel, Simeon. "A Kingdom of Priests and Its Earthen Altars in Exodus 19–24." *VT* 65 (2015): 169–222.

———. "The Literary Development of Deuteronomy 12: Between Religious Ideal and Social Reality." Pages 303–26 in *The Pentateuch: International Perspectives on Current Research*. Edited by Thomas B. Dozeman, Konrad Schmid, and Baruch J. Schwartz. FAT 78. Tübingen: Mohr Siebeck, 2011.

———. *Oracular Law and Priestly Historiography in the Torah*. FAT/II 71. Tübingen: Mohr Siebeck, 2014.

Childs, Brevard S. *The Book of Exodus: A Critical, Theological Commentary*. OTL. Philadelphia: Westminster, 1974.

———. "Deuteronomic Formulae of the Exodus Traditions." Pages 29–39 in *Hebräische Wortforschung: Festschrift zum 80. Geburtstag von Walter Baumgartner*. Edited by Walter Baumgartner, Benedickt Hartmann, Ernst Jenni, Edward Yechezkel Kutscher, Victor Maag, Isaac Leo Seeligmann, and Rudolf Smend. VTSup 16. Leiden: Brill, 1967.

———. *Isaiah and the Assyrian Crisis*. SBT/II 3. London: SCM, 1967.

Cholewiński, Alfred. *Heiligkeitsgesetz und Deuteronomium: Eine vergleichende Studie.* AnBib 66. Rome: Biblical Institute Press, 1976.

Clements, R. E. "Deuteronomy and the Jerusalem Cult Tradition." *VT* 15 (1965): 300–312.

Cogan, Mordechai. "Judah under Assyrian Hegemony: A Reexamination of *Imperialism and Religion.*" *JBL* 112 (1993): 403–14.

Cogan, Morton (Mordechai). *Imperialism and Religion: Assyria, Judah and Israel in the Eighth and Seventh Centuries B.C.E.* Missoula, MT: Scholars Press, 1974.

Cohen, Harold R. (Chaim). *Biblical Hapax Legomena in the Light of Akkadian and Ugaritic.* SBLDS 37. Missoula, MT: Scholars Press, 1978.

Couroyer, Bernard. "La Tablette du Coeur." *RB* 90 (1983): 416–34.

Craigie, Peter C. *The Book of Deuteronomy.* NICOT. Grand Rapids: Eerdmans, 1976.

Crawford, Sidnie White. *Rewriting Scripture in Second Temple Times.* Grand Rapids: Eerdmans, 2008.

Crouch, C. L. *Israel and the Assyrians: Deuteronomy, the Succession Treaty of Esarhaddon, and the Nature of Subversion.* ANEM 8. Atlanta: SBL Press, 2014.

———. *The Making of Israel: Cultural Diversity in the Southern Levant and the Formation of Ethnic Identity in Deuteronomy.* VTSup 162. Leiden: Brill, 2014.

Crouch, C. L., and Jeremy M. Hutton. *Translating Empire: Tell Fekheriyeh, Deuteronomy, and the Akkadian Treaty Tradition.* FAT 135. Tübingen: Mohr Siebeck, 2019.

Daube, David. *Studies in Biblical Law.* Cambridge: Cambridge University Press, 1947.

Dillmann, August. *Die Bücher Numeri, Deuteronomium und Josua.* 2nd ed. KHAT. Leipzig: S. Hirzel, 1886.

Dion, Paul E. "Deuteronomy 13: The Suppression of Alien Religious Propaganda in Israel during the Late Monarchical Era." Pages 147–216 in *Law and Ideology in Monarchic Israel.* Edited by B. Halpern and D. W. Hobson. JSOTSup 124. Sheffield: JSOT Press, 1991.

Dobbs-Allsopp, F. W. *On Biblical Poetry.* New York: Oxford University Press, 2015.

Dogniez, Cécile. "The Greek Translation of the Pentateuch." Pages 111–32 in *The Oxford Handbook of the Pentateuch.* Edited by Joel S. Baden and Jeffrey Stackert. Oxford: Oxford University Press, 2021.

Driver, S. R. *A Critical and Exegetical Commentary on Deuteronomy.* 3rd ed. ICC. Edinburgh: T&T Clark, 1902.

Dubovský, Peter. *Hezekiah and the Assyrian Spies: Reconstruction of the Neo-Assyrian Intelligence Services and Its Significance for 2 Kings 18–19.* BibOr 49. Roma: Editrice Pontificio Istituto Biblico, 2006.

———. "King's Direct Control: Neo-Assyrian *Qēpu* Officials." Pages 449–60 in *Organization, Representation, and Symbols of Power in the Ancient Near East: Proceedings of the 54th Rencontre Assyriologique Internationale at Würzburg 20–25 July 2008.* Edited by Gernot Wilhelm. Winona Lake, IN: Eisenbrauns, 2012.

Dyk, P. J. van. "The Function of So-Called Etiological Elements in Narratives." *ZAW* 102 (1990): 19–33.

Ehrlich, Arnold B. *Randglossen zur hebräischen Bibel: Textkritisches, sprachliches und sachliches.* 7 vols. Leipzig: J. C. Hinrichs, 1908–1913.

Eidevall, Gören. *Amos: A New Translation with Introduction and Commentary.* AYB 24G. New Haven: Yale University Press, 2017.

———. "Prophetic Cult-Criticism in Support of Sacrificial Worship?: The Case of Jeremiah." Pages 151–67 in *Sacrifice, Cult, and Atonement in Ancient Judaism and Early Christianity: Constituents and Critique.* Edited by Henrietta L. Wiley and Christian A. Eberhart. Atlanta: SBL Press, 2017.

Elman, Yaakov. "Moses ben Nahman/Nahmanides (Ramban)." Pages 416–32 in *Hebrew Bible/Old Testament: The History of Its Interpretation.* Edited by Magne Sæbø. 3 vols. Göttingen: Vandenhoeck & Ruprecht, 1996.

Fabrikant-Burke, O. Y. "Tradition as Innovation: Ancient Harmonistic Theologising in the Temple Sermon (Jeremiah 7:1–8:3)." *JTS* 71 (2020): 458–85.

Fabry, Heinz-Josef. "לב; לבב." *TDOT* 7: 399–437.

Fales, F. Mario. "The Use and Function of Aramaic Tablets." Pages 89–124 in *Essays on Syria in the Iron Age.* Edited by Guy Bunnens. ANESSup 7. Louvain: Peeters, 2000.

Fales, Frederick Mario. "Aramaic Epigraphy from Assyria: New Data and Old Issues." Pages 5–16 in *New Perspectives on Aramaic Epigraphy in Mesopotamia, Qumran, Egypt and Idumea.* Edited by Aren M. Maeir, Angelika Berlejung, Esther Eshel, and Takayoshi M. Oshima. ORA 40. Tübingen: Mohr Siebeck, 2021.

———. "Multilingualism on Multiple Media in the Neo-Assyrian Period: A Review of the Evidence." *SAAB* 16 (2007): 95–122.

Fales, Mario. "After Ta'yinat: The New Status of Esarhaddon's *adê* for Assyrian Political History." *RA* 106 (2012): 133–58.

Faust, Avraham. "The Assyrian Century in the Southern Levant: An Overview of the Reality on the Ground." Pages 20–55 in *The Southern Levant under Assyrian Domination.* Edited by Shawn Zelig Aster and Avraham Faust. University Park, PA: Eisenbrauns, 2018.

———. "The Interests of the Assyrian Empire in the West: Olive Oil Production as a Test-Case." *JESHO* 54 (2011): 62–86.

———. "Settlement and Demography in Seventh-Century Judah and the Extent and Intensity of Sennacherib's Campaign." *PEQ* 140 (2008): 168–94.

———. "The Southern Levant under the Neo-Assyrian Empire: A Comparative Perspective." Pages 97–127 in *Imperial Peripheries in the Neo-Assyrian Period.* Edited by Craig W. Tyson and Virginia R. Hermann. Boulder: University Press of Colorado, 2018.

Feldman, Ariel. "Moses' Farewell Address according to 1QWords of Moses (1Q22)." *JSP* 23 (2013): 201–14.

Finkelstein, Israel. "The Archaeology of the Days of Manasseh." Pages 169–87 in *Scripture and Other Artifacts: Essays on the Bible and Archaeology in Honor of*

Philip J. King. Edited by Michael D. Coogan, J. Cheryl Exum, and Lawrence Stager. Louisville: Westminster John Knox, 1994.

Finkelstein, Israel, and Nadav Na'aman. "The Judahite Shephelah in the Late 8th and Early 7th Centuries BCE." *TA* 31 (2004): 60–79.

Finsterbusch, Karin. "'Ich habe meine Tora in ihre Mitte gegeben': Bemerkungen zu Jer 31,3." *BN* 49 (2005): 86–92.

Fishbane, Michael. *Biblical Interpretation in Ancient Israel.* Rev. ed. Oxford: Clarendon, 1988.

Fletcher, Angus. *Allegory: The Theory of a Symbolic Mode.* Rev. ed. Princeton: Princeton University Press, 2012.

Folmer, Margaretha. "Aramaic as *Lingua Franca.*" Pages 373–99 in *A Companion to Ancient Near Eastern Languages.* Edited by Rebecca Hasselbach-Andee. Hoboken, NJ: Wiley, 2020.

Fox, Michael V. "Frame-Narrative and Composition in the Book of Qohelet." *HUCA* 48 (1977): 83–106.

Frankena, Rintje. "The Vassal-Treaties of Esarhaddon and the Dating of Deuteronomy." *OtSt* 14 (1965): 122–54.

Friedman, Richard Elliott. "Three Major Redactors of the Torah." Pages 31–44 in *Birkat Shalom: Studies in the Bible, Ancient Near Eastern Literature, and Post-Biblical Judaism: Presented to Shalom M. Paul on the Occasion of His Seventieth Birthday.* Edited by Chaim Cohen, Victor Avigdor Hurowitz, Avi M. Hurvitz, Yochanan Muffs, Baruch J. Schwartz, and Jeffrey H. Tigay. Winona Lake, IN: Eisenbrauns, 2008.

Frye, Northrop. *The Anatomy of Criticism: Four Essays.* Princeton: Princeton University Press, 1957.

Fuad, Chelcent. "The Innovation of the Pentateuchal Tithe Laws." *VT,* forthcoming.

Gadot, Yuval. "In the Valley of the King: Jerusalem's Rural Hinterland in the 8th–4th Centuries BCE." *TA* 42 (2015): 3–26.

Gane, Roy. "The Role of Assyria in the Ancient Near East during the Reign of Manasseh." *AUSS* 35 (1997): 21–32.

Geller, Stephen A. "Some Pitfalls in the 'Literary Approach' to Biblical Narrative." *JQR* 74 (1984): 408–15.

Genette, Gérard. *Narrative Discourse: An Essay in Method.* Translated by Jane E. Lewin. Ithaca, NY: Cornell University Press, 1980.

———. *Paratexts: Thresholds of Interpretation.* Translated by Jane E. Lewin. Literature, Culture, Theory 20. New York: Cambridge University Press, 1997.

George, Andrew R. "Sennacherib and the Tablet of Destinies." *Iraq* 48 (1986): 133–46.

Germany, Stephen. *The Exodus-Conquest Narrative: The Composition of the Non-Priestly Narratives in Exodus–Joshua.* FAT 115. Tübingen: Mohr Siebeck, 2017.

Gertz, Jan Christian. "The Compositional Function and Literary-Historical Setting of Deuteronomy 1–3." Pages 27–47 in *Writing, Rewriting, and Overwriting in the Books of Deuteronomy and the Former Prophets: Essays in Honour of Cynthia*

Edenburg. Edited by Ido Koch, T. Römer, and O. Sergi. BETL 304. Leuven: Peeters, 2019.

Gilbert, Maurice. "La place de la loi dans la prière de Néhémie 9." Pages 307–16 in *De la Tôrah au Messie: études d'exégèse et d'herméneutique bibliques offerts à Henri Cazelles pour ses 25 années d'enseignement à l'Institut catholique de Paris (Octobre 1979)*. Edited by Maurice Carrez, Joseph Doré, and Pierre Grelot. Paris: Desclée; 1981.

Gilmer, Harry W. *The If-You Form in Israelite Law.* SBLDS 15. Missoula, MT: Scholars Press, 1975.

Graham, William A. "Scripture." Pages 8194–8205 in vol. 12 of *Encyclopedia of Religion.* 15 vols. 2nd ed. Farmington Hills, MI: Thomason Gale, 2005.

Grayson, A. Kirk. "Akkadian Treaties of the Seventh Century BC." *JCS* 39 (1987): 127–60.

"The Great Isaiah Scroll." Digital Dead Sea Scrolls. Israel Museum. http://dss .collections.imj.org.il/isaiah.

Greenberg, Moshe. "נסה in Exodus 20:20 and the Purpose of the Sinaitic Theophany." *JBL* 79 (1960): 273–76.

———. "The Redaction of the Plague Narrative in Exodus." Pages 243–52 in *Near Eastern Studies in Honor of William Foxwell Albright.* Edited by H. Goedicke. Baltimore: Johns Hopkins University Press, 1971.

Greenstein, Edward L. "Theory and Argument in Biblical Criticism." Pages 77–93 in *Essays on Biblical Method and Translation.* Atlanta: Scholars Press, 1989.

Gross, Walter, ed. *Jeremia und die "deuteronomistische Bewegung."* BBB 98. Weinheim: Athenäem, 1995.

Halivni, David Weiss. *Revelation Restored: Divine Writ and Critical Responses.* Boulder, CO: Westview, 1997.

Haran, Menahem. "The Běrît 'Covenant': Its Nature and Ceremonial Background." Pages 203–19 in *Tehillah le-Moshe: Biblical and Judaic Studies in Honor of Moshe Greenberg.* Edited by Mordechai Cogan, Barry L. Eichler, and Jeffrey H. Tigay. Winona Lake, IN: Eisenbrauns, 1997.

———. *The Biblical Collection: Its Consolidation to the End of the Second Temple Times and Changes of Form to the End of the Middle Ages.* 4 vols. Jerusalem: Magnes, 1996–2014 (in Hebrew).

———. "Book-Size and the Device of Catch-Lines in the Biblical Canon." *JJS* 36 (1985): 1–11.

———. "Book-Size and the Thematic Cycles in the Pentateuch." Pages 165–76 in *Die Hebräische Bibel und ihre zweifache Nachgeschichte: Festschrift für Rolf Rendtorff zum 65. Geburtstag.* Edited by Erhard Blum, Christian Macholz, and Ekkehard Stegemann. Neukirchen-Vluyn: Neukirchener, 1990.

———. "Book-Scrolls at the Beginning of the Second Temple Period: The Transition from Papyrus to Skins." *HUCA* 54 (1983): 111–22.

———. "More Concerning Book-Scrolls in Pre-Exilic Times." *JJS* 35 (1984): 84–85.

———. "The Size of Books in the Bible and the Division of the Pentateuch and the Prophets: Paleographical and Compositional Aspects in the Arrangement of the Biblical Collection." *Tarbiz* 53 (1984): 329–52 (in Hebrew).

———. *Temples and Temple Service: An Inquiry into Biblical Cult Phenomena and the Historical Setting of the Priestly School.* Oxford: Clarendon, 1978. Repr., Winona Lake, IN: Eisenbrauns, 1985.

Harrison, Timothy P., and James F. Osborne. "Building XVI and the Neo-Assyrian Sacred Precinct at Tell Tayinat." *JCS* 64 (2012): 125–43.

Harshav, Benjamin. *Explorations in Poetics.* Stanford, CA: Stanford University Press, 2007.

Harvey, Jr., Paul B., and Baruch Halpern. "W. M. L. de Wette's '*Dissertatio Critica . . .*': Context and Translation." *ZABR* 14 (2008): 47–85.

Heidel, Alexander. *The Gilgamesh Epic and Old Testament Parallels.* 2nd ed. Chicago: University of Chicago Press, 1949.

Hendel, Ronald. "What Is a Biblical Book?" Pages 283–302 in *From Author to Copyist: Essays on the Composition, Redaction, and Transmission of the Hebrew Bible in Honor of Zipi Talshir.* Edited by Cana Werman. Winona Lake, IN: Eisenbrauns, 2015.

Henige, David. "Found But Not Lost: A Skeptical Note on the Document Discovered in the Temple under Josiah." *JHS* 7 (2007): 1–17. https://www.jhsonline.org/index.php/jhs/article/view/5657.

Hobson, Russell. *Transforming Literature into Scripture: Texts as Cult Objects at Nineveh and Qumran.* London: Routledge, 2014.

Holladay, William L. "The Background of Jeremiah's Self-Understanding: Moses, Samuel, and Psalm 22." *JBL* 83 (1964): 153–64.

———. "Jeremiah and Moses: Further Observations." *JBL* 85 (1966): 17–27.

Holloway, Steven W. *Aššur Is King! Aššur Is King! Religion in the Exercise of Power in the Neo-Assyrian Empire.* CHANE 10. Leiden: Brill, 2002.

Holmstedt, Robert D. "Analyzing זו Grammar and Reading זו Texts of Ps 68:9 and Judg 5:5." *JHS* 14 (2014): 1–27. https://www.jhsonline.org/index.php/jhs/article/view/29339.

Hölscher, Gustav. "Komposition und Ursprung des Deuteronomiums." *ZAW* 40 (1922): 161–255.

Horowitz, Wayne, Takayoshi Oshima, and Seth L. Sanders. *Cuneiform in Canaan: The Next Generation.* University Park, PA: Eisenbrauns, 2018.

Horst, Friedrich. *Das Privilegrecht Yahves: Rechtsgeschichtliche Untersuchungen zum Deuteronomium.* Göttingen: Vandenhoeck & Ruprecht, 1930.

Hossfeld, Frank-Lothar. "Der Dekalog als Grundgesetz—eine Problemanzeige." Pages 46–59 in *Liebe und Gebot: Studien zum Deuteronomium.* Edited by Reinhard G. Kratz and Hermann Spieckermann. FRLANT 190. Göttingen: Vandenhoeck & Ruprecht, 2000.

Houtman, Cornelis. *Exodus.* 4 vols. HCOT. Leuven: Peeters, 1993–2002.

Itach, Gilad. "The Kingdom of Israel in the Eighth Century: From a Regional Power to Assyrian Provinces." Pages 57–77 in *Archaeology and History of Eighth-Century Judah*. Edited by Zev I. Farber and Jacob L. Wright. ANEM 23. Atlanta: SBL Press, 2018.

Japhet, Sara. *I & II Chronicles*. OTL. Louisville: Westminster/John Knox, 1993.

Jassen, Alex P. *Mediating the Divine: Prophecy and Revelation in the Dead Sea Scrolls and Second Temple Judaism*. STDJ 68. Leiden: Brill, 2007.

———. "The Pesharim and the Rise of Commentary in Early Jewish Biblical Interpretation." *DSD* 19 (2012): 363–98.

———. "Prophets and Prophecy in the Qumran Community." *AJSR* 32 (2008): 299–334.

Jindo, Job. "On the Biblical Notion of the 'Fear of God' as a Condition for Human Existence." *BibInt* 19 (2012): 433–53.

Kasher, Rimon. "The Interpretation of Scripture in Rabbinic Literature." Pages 547–94 in *Mikra: Text, Translation, Reading and Interpretation of the Hebrew Bible in Ancient Judaism and Early Christianity*. Edited by Martin Jan Mulder. Assen: Van Gorcum; Philadelphia: Fortress, 1988.

Kelle, Brad E. "Judah in the Seventh Century: From the Aftermath of Sennacherib's Invasion to the Beginning of Jehoiakim's Rebellion." Pages 350–82 in *Ancient Israel's History: An Introduction to Issues and Sources*. Edited by Bill T. Arnold and Richard S. Hess. Grand Rapids: Baker Academic, 2014.

Kisilevitz, Shua. "The Iron IIA Judahite Temple at Tel Moza." *TA* 42 (2015): 147–64.

Kislev, Itamar. "Joshua (and Caleb) in the Priestly Spies Story and Joshua's Initial Appearance in the Priestly Source: A Contribution to an Assessment of the Pentateuchal Priestly Material." *JBL* 136 (2017): 39–55.

Kline, Meredith G. *The Treaty of the Great King: The Covenant Structure of Deuteronomy: Studies and Commentary*. Grand Rapids: Eerdmans, 1963.

Knauf, Ernst Axel. "The Glorious Days of Manasseh." Pages 164–88 in *Good Kings and Bad Kings: The Kingdom of Judah in the Seventh Century BCE*. Edited by Lester L. Grabbe. LHBOTS 393. London: T&T Clark, 2005.

Knight, Douglas A., ed. *Julius Wellhausen and His* Prolegomena to the History of Israel. *Semeia* 25 (1982).

Knohl, Israel. *Sanctuary of Silence: The Priestly Torah and the Holiness School*. Translated by Jackie Feldman and Peretz Rodman. Minneapolis: Augsburg Fortress, 1995.

Knoppers, Gary N. "The Deuteronomist and the Deuteronomic Law of the King: A Reexamination of a Relationship." *ZAW* 108 (1996): 329–46.

———. "The Northern Context of the Law-Code in Deuteronomy." *HeBAI* 4 (2015): 162–83.

———. "Rethinking the Relationship between Deuteronomy and the Deuteronomistic History: The Case of Kings." *CBQ* 63 (2001): 393–415.

Koch, Christoph. "Bundestheologie und autoritativer Text im Deuteronomium: Das Tafelmotiv in Deuteronomium 5.9–10 vor dem Hintergrund altorientalischer Vertragspraxis." Pages 29–47 in *Covenant and Election in Exilic and Post-Exilic Judaism: Studies of the Sofja Kovalevskaja Research Group on Early Jewish Monotheism Vol. V.* Edited by Nathan MacDonald. FAT/II 79. Tübingen: Mohr Siebeck, 2015.

——. *Vertrag, Treueid und Bund: Studien zur Rezeption des altorientalischen Vertragsrechts im Deuteronomium und zur Ausbildung der Bundestheologie im Alten Testament.* BZAW 383. Berlin: de Gruyter, 2008.

Koller, Aaron. "Deuteronomy and Hittite Treaties." *Bible and Interpretation.* September 2014. https://bibleinterp.arizona.edu/articles/2014/09/kol388003.

König, Eduard. *Stilistik, Rhetorik, Poetik in Bezug auf die biblische Literatur.* Leipzig: T. Weicher, 1900.

Korošec, Viktor. *Hethitische Staatsverträge: Ein Beitrag zu ihrer juristischen Wertung.* Leipziger rechtswissenschaftliche Studien 60. Leipzig: T. Weicher, 1931.

Kort, Wesley A. *"Take, Read": Scripture, Textuality, and Cultural Practice.* University Park: Pennsylvania State University Press, 1996.

Kratz, Reinhard G. *The Composition of the Narrative Books of the Old Testament.* Translated by John Bowden. London: T&T Clark, 2005.

——. "Der Dekalog im Exodusbuch." *VT* 44 (1994): 205–38.

——. "The Headings of the Book of Deuteronomy." Pages 31–47 in *Deuteronomy in the Pentateuch, Hexateuch, and the Deuteronomistic History.* Edited by R. F. Person, Jr., and K. Schmid. FAT/II 56. Tübingen: Mohr Siebeck, 2012.

——, ed. *Interpreting and Living God's Law at Qumran: Miqṣat Ma'aśe Ha-Torah, Some Works of the Torah (4QMMT).* SAPERE 37. Tübingen: Mohr Siebeck, 2020.

——. "Law and Narrative in Deuteronomy and the Temple Scroll." Pages 109–22 in *The Reception of Biblical War Legislation in Narrative Contexts.* Edited by Christoph Berner and Harald Samuel. BZAW 460. Berlin: de Gruyter, 2015.

——. "The Pentateuch in Current Research: Consensus and Debate." Pages 31–61 in *The Pentateuch: International Perspectives on Current Research.* Edited by Thomas B. Dozeman, Konrad Schmid, and Baruch J. Schwartz. FAT 78. Tübingen: Mohr Siebeck, 2011.

——. "'The Place Which He Has Chosen': The Identification of the Cult Place of Deut. 12 and Lev. 17 in 4QMMT." Pages *57–*80 in *Meghillot: Studies in the Dead Sea Scrolls 5–6. A Festschrift for Devorah Dimant.* Edited by Moshe Bar-Asher and Emanuel Tov. Jerusalem: Bialik Institute; Haifa: Haifa University Press, 2007.

Kreuzer, Siegfried. "Die Exodustradition im Deuteronomium." Pages 81–106 in *Das Deuteronomium und seine Querbeziehungen.* Edited by Timo Veijola. SFEG 62. Helsinki: Finnische Exegetische Gesellschaft; Göttingen: Vandenhoeck & Ruprecht, 1996.

Krüger, Thomas. "Das 'Herz' in der alttestamentlichen Anthropologie." Pages 103–18 in *Anthropologische Aufbrüche: Alttestamentliche und interdisziplinäre Zugänge zur historischen Anthropologie.* Edited by Andreas Wagner. FRLANT 232. Göttingen: Vandenhoeck & Ruprecht, 2011.

Kuenen, Abraham. "Bijdragen to de critiek van Pentateuch en Jozua: III. De uitzending der verspieders." *Theologisch Tijdschrift* 11 (1877): 545–66.

———. *An Historico-Critical Inquiry into the Origin and Composition of the Hexateuch (Pentateuch and Book of Joshua).* Translated by Philip H. Wicksteed. London: Macmillan, 1886.

Kugel, James L. *Traditions of the Bible: A Guide to the Bible As It Was at the Start of the Common Era.* Cambridge, MA: Harvard University Press, 1998.

Kugler, Gili. "Moses Died and the People Moved On: A Hidden Narrative in Deuteronomy." *JSOT* 43 (2019): 191–204.

———. "Present Affliction Affects the Representation of the Past: An Alternative Dating of the Levitical Prayer in Nehemiah 9." *VT* 63 (2013): 605–26.

———. "The Threat of Annihilation of Israel in the Desert: An Independent Tradition within Two Stories." *CBQ* 78 (2016): 632–47.

———. *When God Wanted to Destroy the Chosen People: Biblical Traditions and Theology on the Move.* BZAW 515. Berlin: de Gruyter, 2019.

Kukkonen, Karin, and Sonja Klimek, eds. *Metalepsis in Popular Culture.* Narratologia 28. Berlin: de Gruyter, 2011.

Lam, Joseph. *Patterns of Sin in the Hebrew Bible: Metaphor, Culture, and the Making of a Religious Concept.* New York: Oxford University Press, 2016.

Lambert, David. "Fasting as a Penitential Rite: A Biblical Phenomenon?" *HTR* 96 (2003): 477–512.

Lauinger, Jacob. "*Iqqur īpuš* at Tel Tayinat." *JCS* 68 (2018): 229–48.

———. "Literary Connections and Social Contexts: Approaches to Deuteronomy in Light of the Assyrian *adê* Tradition." *HeBAI* 8 (2019): 87–100.

———. "The Neo-Assyrian *adê*: Treaty, Oath, or Something Else?" *ZABR* 19 (2013): 99–115.

———. "Neo-Assyrian Scribes, 'Esarhaddon's Succession Treaty,' and the Dynamics of Textual Mass Production." Pages 285–314 in *Texts and Contexts: The Circulation and Transmission of Cuneiform Texts in Social Space.* Edited by Paul Delnero and Jacob Lauinger. SANER 9. Boston: de Gruyter, 2015.

———. "Some Preliminary Thoughts on the Tablet Collection in Building XVI from Tell Tayinat." *JCSMS* 6 (2011): 5–14.

Lester, Mark. "Deuteronomy 28:58, CTH 53, and the Rhetoric of Self-Reference." *VT* 70 (2020): 645–66.

Levenson, Jon D. *The Hebrew Bible, the Old Testament, and Historical Criticism: Jews and Christians in Biblical Studies.* Louisville: Westminster/John Knox, 1993.

Levering, Miriam, ed. *Rethinking Scripture: Essays from a Comparative Perspective.* Albany: State University of New York Press, 1989.

Levin, Christoph. "Joschija im deuteronomistischen Geschichtswerk." *ZAW* 96 (1984): 351–71.

———. "On the Cohesion and Separation of Books within the Enneateuch." Pages 127–54 in *Pentateuch, Hexateuch, or Enneateuch?: Identifying Literary Works in Genesis through Kings*. Edited by Thomas B. Dozeman, Thomas Römer, and Konrad Schmid. SBLAIL 8. Atlanta: Society of Biblical Literature, 2011.

Levinson, Bernard M. "'But You Shall Surely Kill Him!': The Text-Critical and Neo-Assyrian Evidence for MT Deut 13:10." Pages 37–63 in *Bundesdokument und Gesetz: Studien zum Deuteronomium*. Edited by Georg Braulik. HBS 4. Freiburg: Herder, 1995.

———. *Deuteronomy and the Hermeneutics of Legal Innovation*. New York: Oxford University Press, 1997.

———. "Esarhaddon's Succession Treaty as the Source for the Canon Formula in Deuteronomy 13:1." *JAOS* 130 (2010): 337–47.

———. "The Neo-Assyrian Origins of the Canon Formula in Deuteronomy 13:1." Pages 25–45 in *Scriptural Exegesis: The Shapes of Culture and the Religious Imagination (Essays in Honour of Michael Fishbane)*. Edited by Deborah A. Green and Laura Lieber. Oxford: Oxford University Press, 2009.

———. "The Reconceptualization of Kingship in Deuteronomy and the Deuteronomistic History's Transformation of Torah." *VT* 51 (2001): 511–34.

———. "Recovering the Lost Original Meaning of ולא תכסה עליו (Deuteronomy 13:9)." *JBL* 115 (1996): 601–20.

———. "Revisiting the 'and' in Law and Covenant in the Hebrew Bible: What the Evidence from Tel Tayinat Suggests about the Relationship between Law and Religion in the Ancient Near East." *Maarav* 24 (2020): 27–43.

———. "Textual Criticism, Assyriology, and the History of Interpretation: Deuteronomy 13:7a as a Test Case in Method." *JBL* 120 (2001): 211–43.

Levinson, Bernard M., and Jeffrey Stackert. "Between the Covenant Code and Esarhaddon's Succession Treaty: Deuteronomy 13 and the Composition of Deuteronomy." *JAJ* 3 (2012): 123–40.

———. "The Limitations of 'Resonance': A Response to Joshua Berman on Historical and Comparative Method." *JAJ* 4 (2013): 310–33.

Lipschits, Oded. "The Long Seventh Century BCE: Archaeological and Historical Perspectives." Pages 7–41 in *The Last Century in the History of Judah: The Seventh Century BCE in Archaeological, Historical, and Biblical Perspectives*. Edited by Filip Čapek and Oded Lipschits. SBLAIL 37. Atlanta: SBL Press, 2019.

Lohfink, Norbert. "Die Bundesurkunde des Königs Josias—Eine Frage an die Deuteronomiumforschung." *Biblica* 44 (1963): 261–88, 461–98.

———. "Canonical Signals in the Additions in Deuteronomy 1.39." Pages 30–43 in *Seeing Signals, Reading Signs: The Art of Exegesis*. Edited by M. A. O'Brien and H. N. Wallace. JSOTSup 415. London: T&T Clark, 2004.

————. "Das Deuteronomium: Jahwegesetz oder Mosegesetz?: Die Subjektzuordnung bei Wörtern für 'Gesetz' im Dtn und in der dtr Literatur." *TP* 65 (1990): 387–91.

————. "Distribution of the Functions of Power: The Laws concerning Public Offices in Deuteronomy 16:18–18:22." Pages 336–52 in *A Song of Power and the Power of Song: Essays on the Book of Deuteronomy*. Edited by Duane L. Christensen. SBTS 3. Winona Lake, IN: Eisenbrauns, 1993.

————. *Die Väter Israels im Deuteronomium: Mit einer Stellungnahme von Thomas Römer.* OBO 111. Fribourg: Editions Universitaires; Göttingen: Vandenhoeck & Ruprecht, 1991.

————. "Zum deuteronomischen Zentralisationsformel." *Biblica* 65 (1984): 297–329.

Long, Burke O. *The Problem of Etiological Narrative in the Old Testament*. BZAW 108. Berlin: A. Töpelmann, 1968.

MacDonald, Nathan. "Anticipations of Horeb: Exodus 17 as Inner-Biblical Commentary." Pages 7–19 in *Studies on the Text and Versions of the Hebrew Bible in Honour of Robert Gordon*. Edited by Geoffrey Khan and Diana Lipton. Leiden: Brill, 2012.

————. "Issues in the Dating of Deuteronomy: A Response to Juha Pakkala." *ZAW* 122 (2010): 431–35.

————. *Not Bread Alone: The Uses of Food in the Old Testament*. Oxford: Oxford University Press, 2008.

Machiela, Daniel A. "The Qumran Pesharim as Biblical Commentaries: Historical Context and Lines of Development." *DSD* 19 (2012): 313–62.

Machinist, Peter. "Assyria and Its Image in the First Isaiah." *JAOS* 103 (1983): 719–37.

————. "Manasseh of Judah: A Case Study in Biblical Historiography." Pages 183–228 in *Stones, Tablets, and Scrolls: Periods of the Formation of the Bible*. Edited by Peter Dubovský and Federico Giuntoli. Archaeology and Bible 3. Tübingen: Mohr Siebeck, 2020.

Magdalene, F. Rachel, Cornelia Wunsch, and Bruce Wells. *Fault, Responsibility, and Administrative Law in Late Babylonian Texts*. Mesopotamian Civilizations 23. University Park, PA: Eisenbrauns, 2019.

Maier, Aren M., and Itzhaq Shai. "Reassessing the Character of the Judahite Kingdom: Archaeological Evidence for Non-Centralized, Kinship-Based Components." Pages 323–40 in *From Sha'ar Hagolan to Shaaraim: Essays in Honor of Prof. Yosef Garfinkel*. Edited by Saar Ganor, Igor Kreimerman, Katharina Streit, and Madeleine Mumcuoglu. Jerusalem: Israel Exploration Society, 2016.

Maier, Johann. *The Temple Scroll: An Introduction, Translation, and Commentary*. JSOTSup 34. Sheffield: Sheffield Academic, 2009.

Malul, Meir. *The Comparative Method in Ancient Near Eastern and Biblical Legal Studies*. AOAT 227. Kevelaer: Butzon & Bercker; Neukirchen-Vluyn: Neukirchener, 1990.

Markl, Dominik. "Deuteronomy's 'Anti-King': Historicized Etiology or Political Program?" Pages 165–86 in *Changing Faces of Kingship in Syria-Palestine 1500–500*

BCE. Edited by Agustinus Gianto and Peter Dubovský. AOAT 459. Münster: Ugarit-Verlag, 2018.

———. "Deuteronomy's Frameworks in Service of the Law (Deut 1–11; 26–34)." Pages 271–83 in *Deuteronomium—Tora für eine neue Generation*. Edited by Georg Fischer, Dominik Markl, and Simone Paganini. BZABR 17. Wiesbaden: Harrassowitz, 2011.

———. *Gottes Volk im Deuteronomium*. BZABR 18. Wiesbaden: Harrassowitz, 2012.

Marquis (Feldman), Liane M. "The Composition of Numbers 32: A New Proposal." *VT* 63 (2013): 408–32.

Maskow, Lars. *Tora in der Chronik: Studien zur Rezeption des Pentateuchs in den Chronikbüchern*. FRLANT 274. Göttingen: Vandenhoeck & Ruprecht, 2019.

Mastnjak, Nathan. *Deuteronomy and the Emergence of Textual Authority in Jeremiah*. FAT/II 87. Tübingen: Mohr Siebeck, 2016.

Mattison, Kevin. *Rewriting and Revision as Amendment in the Laws of Deuteronomy*. FAT/II 100. Tübingen: Mohr Siebeck, 2018.

Mayer, Walter. "Sennacherib's Campaign of 701 BCE: The Assyrian View." Pages 168–200 in *Like a Bird in a Cage: The Invasion of Sennacherib in 701 BCE*. Edited by Lester L. Grabbe. JSOTSup 363. London: Sheffield Academic, 2003.

Mayes, A. D. H. *Deuteronomy*. NCB. London: Marshall, Morgan & Scott, 1979.

McCarthy, Dennis J. *Treaty and Covenant: A Study in Form in the Ancient Oriental Documents and in the Old Testament*. 2nd ed. AnBib 21a. Rome: Biblical Institute Press, 1981.

McHale, Brian, and Eyal Segal. "Small World: The Tel Aviv School of Poetics and Semiotics." Pages 196–215 in *Theoretical Schools in the Twentieth-Century Humanities: Literary Theory, History, Philosophy*. Edited by Marina Grishakova and Silvi Salupere. New York: Routledge, 2015.

McKay, John W. "Man's Love for God in Deuteronomy and the Father/Teacher–Son/Pupil Relationship." *VT* 22 (1972): 426–35.

———. *Religion in Judah under the Assyrians 732–609 BCE*. SBT/II 26. London: SCM Press, 1973.

Melville, Sarah C. *The Role of Naqia/Zakutu in Sargonid Politics*. SAAS 9. Helsinki: Neo-Assyrian Text Corpus Project, 1999.

Mendenhall, George E. "Covenant Forms in Israelite Tradition." *BA* 17 (1954): 49–76.

———. "The Suzerainty Treaty Structure: Thirty Years Later." Pages 85–100 in *Religion and Law: Biblical-Judaic and Islamic Perspectives*. Edited by Edwin B. Firmage, Bernard G. Weiss, and John W. Welch. Winona Lake, IN: Eisenbrauns, 1990.

Menken, Maarten J. J., and Steve Moyise, eds. *Deuteronomy in the New Testament: The New Testament and the Scriptures of Israel*. LNTS 358. London: T&T Clark, 2007.

Milgrom, Jacob. "Concerning Jeremiah's Repudiation of Sacrifice." *ZAW* 89 (1977): 273–75.

————. *Leviticus 23–27: A New Translation with Introduction and Commentary*. AB 3B. New York: Doubleday, 2001.

————. "Studies in the Temple Scroll." *JBL* 97 (1978): 501–23.

Millard, Alan R. "Assyria, Aramaeans and Aramaic." Pages 203–14 in *Homeland and Exile: Biblical and Ancient Near Eastern Studies in Honour of Bustenay Oded*. Edited by Gershon Galil, Markham Geller, and Alan Millard. VTSup 130. Leiden: Brill, 2009.

Miller, Geoffrey P. "J as Constitutionalist: A Political Interpretation of Exodus 17:8–16 and Related Texts." *Chicago-Kent Law Review* 70 (1995): 1829–47.

Milstein, Sara J. "Making a Case: The Repurposing of 'Israelite Legal Fictions' as Post-Deuteronomic Law." Pages 161–81 in *Supplementation and the Study of the Hebrew Bible*. Edited by Saul M. Olyan and Jacob L. Wright. BJS 361. Providence: Brown Judaic Studies, 2018.

————. *Tracking the Master Scribe: Revision through Introduction in Biblical and Mesopotamian Literature*. New York: Oxford University Press, 2016.

Mintz, Alan. "On the Tel Aviv School of Poetics." *Prooftexts* 4 (1984): 215–35.

Moore, George Foote. *A Critical and Exegetical Commentary on Judges*. 2nd ed. ICC. Edinburgh: T&T Clark, 1918.

Moran, William. "The Ancient Near Eastern Background of the Love of God." *CBQ* 25 (1963): 77–87.

Morrow, William. "Have Attempts to Establish the Dependency of Deuteronomy on the Esarhaddon Succession Treaty (EST) Failed?" *HeBAI* 8 (2019): 133–58.

————. "Tribute from Judah and the Transmission of Assyrian Propaganda." Pages 183–92 in *"My Spirit at Rest in the North Country" (Zechariah 6.8): Collected Communications to the XXth Congress of the International Organization for the Study of the Old Testament, Helsinki 2010*. Edited by H. M. Niemann and M. Augustin. BEATAJ 57. Oxford: Peter Lang, 2011.

Morrow, William S. "Cuneiform Literacy and Deuteronomic Composition." *BO* 62 (2005): 204–13.

Mulder, Martin Jan, and Harry Sysling, eds. *Mikra: Text, Translation, Reading & Interpretation of the Hebrew Bible in Ancient Judaism & Early Christianity*. Peabody, MA: Hendrickson, 2004.

Myers, Jacob M. *Ezra-Nehemiah*. AB 14. Garden City, NY: Doubleday, 1956.

Na'aman, Nadav. "The 'Discovered Book' and the Legitimation of Josiah's Reform." *JBL* 130 (2011): 47–62.

————. "Ekron under the Assyrian and Egyptian Empires." *BASOR* 332 (2003): 81–91.

Najman, Hindy. *Seconding Sinai: The Development of Mosaic Discourse in Second Temple Judaism*. JSJSup 77. Leiden: Brill, 2003.

Nelson, Richard D. *Deuteronomy: A Commentary*. OTL. Louisville: Westminster John Knox, 2002.

————. *Joshua: A Commentary*. OTL. Louisville: Westminster John Knox, 1997.

Newman, Judith H. *Praying by the Book: The Scripturalization of Prayer in Second Temple Judaism.* SBLEJL 14. Atlanta: Scholars Press, 1999.

Nicholson, Ernest. "'Do Not Dare to Set a Foreigner Over You': The King in Deuteronomy and 'The Great King.'" *ZAW* 118 (2006): 46–61.

Niehr, Herbert. "Die Reform des Joschija: Methodische, historische und religionsgeschichtliche Aspekte." Pages 33–55 in *Jeremia und die "deuteronomistische Bewegung."* Edited by Walter Gross. BBB 98. Weinheim: Beltz Athenäum, 1995.

Nielsen, Eduard. *Deuteronomium.* HAT I/6. Tübingen: Mohr Siebeck, 1995.

Nihan, Christophe. *From Priestly Torah to Pentateuch: A Study in the Composition of the Book of Leviticus.* FAT/II 25. Tübingen: Mohr Siebeck, 2007.

———. "The Holiness Code between D and P: Some Comments on the Function and Significance of Leviticus 17–26 in the Composition of the Torah." Pages 81–122 in *Das Deuteronomium zwischen Pentateuch und Deuteronomistischem Geschichtswerk.* Edited by Eckart Otto and Reinhard Achenbach. FRLANT 206. Göttingen: Vandenhoeck & Ruprecht, 2004.

———. "The Priestly Laws of Numbers, the Holiness Legislation, and the Pentateuch." Pages 109–37 in *Torah and the Book of Numbers.* Edited by Christian Frevel, Thomas Pola, and Aaron Schart. FAT/II 62. Tübingen: Mohr Siebeck, 2013.

Nissinen, Martti. *References to Prophecy in Neo-Assyrian Sources.* SAAS 7. Helsinki: Neo-Assyrian Text Corpus Project, 1998.

Noth, Martin. *The Deuteronomistic History.* JSOTSup 15. Sheffield: JSOT Press, 1981.

Osborne, James F., Timothy P. Harrison, Stephen Batiuk, Lynn Welton, J. P. Dessel, Elif Denel, and Özge Demirci. "Urban Built Environments in Early 1st Millennium B.C.E. Syro-Anatolia: Results of the Tayinat Archaeological Project, 2004–2016." *BASOR* 382 (2019): 261–312.

Oswald, Wolfgang. "Defeating Amalek, Defending the Constitution: The Political Theory of Ex 17:8–16." Pages 61–72 in *The Reception of Biblical War Legislation in Narrative Contexts: Proceedings of the EABS Research Group "Law and Narrative."* Edited by Christoph Berner and Harald Samuel. BZAW 460. Berlin: de Gruyter, 2015.

Otto, Eckart. "Anti-Achaemenid Propaganda in Deuteronomy." Pages 547–56 in *Homeland and Exile: Studies in Honour of Bustenay Oded.* Edited by Gershon Galil, Markham Geller, and Alan Millard. VTSup 130. Boston: Brill, 2009.

———. *Deuteronomium 1–11.* HThKAT. 2 vols. Freiburg: Herder, 2012.

———. *Deuteronomium 12–34.* HThKAT. 2 vols. Freiburg: Herder, 2016–2017.

———. "Das Deuteronomium als archimedischer Punkt der Pentateuchkritik: Auf dem Wege zu einer Neubegründung der de Wette'schen Hypothese." Pages 321–40 in *Deuteronomy and Deuteronomic Literature: Festschrift C. H. W. Brekelmans.* Edited by M. Vervenne and J. Lust. Leuven: Peeters, 1997.

———. *Das Deuteronomium im Pentateuch und Hexateuch: Studien zur Literaturgeschichte von Pentateuch und Hexateuch im Lichte des Deuteronomiumrahmens.* FAT 30. Tübingen: Mohr Siebeck, 2000.

————. *Das Deuteronomium: Politische Theologie und Rechtsreform in Juda und Assyrien.* BZAW 284. Berlin: Walter de Gruyter, 1999.

————. "Das Heiligkeitsgesetz Leviticus 17–26 in der Pentateuchredaktion." Pages 65–80 in *Altes Testament, Forschung und Wirkung: Festschrift für Henning Graf Reventlow.* Edited by Peter Mommer and Winfred Thiel. Frankfurt am Main: P. Lang, 1994.

————. "The History of the Legal-Religious Hermeneutics of the Book of Deuteronomy from the Assyrian to the Hellenistic Period." Pages 211–50 in *Law and Religion in the Eastern Mediterranean: From Antiquity to Early Islam.* Edited by Anselm C. Hagedorn and Reinhard G. Kratz. Oxford: Oxford University Press, 2013.

————. "Innerbiblische Exegese im Heiligkeitsgesetz Levitikus 17–26." Pages 125–96 in *Levitikus als Buch.* Edited by H.-J. Fabry and H.-W. Jüngling. BBB 119. Berlin: Philo, 1999.

————. *Kontinuum und Proprium: Studien zur Sozial- und Rechtsgeschichte des Alten Orients und des Alten Testaments.* Wiesbaden: Harrassowitz, 1996.

————. "Mose, der erste Schriftgelehrte: Deuteronomium 1,5 in der Fabel des Pentateuch." Pages 273–84 in *L'Ecrit et l'Esprit: Etudes d'histoire du texte et de théologie biblique en hommage à Adrian Schenker.* Edited by D. Boehler, I. Himbaza, and P. Hugo. OBO 214. Fribourg: Academic Press; Göttingen: Vandenhoeck & Ruprecht, 2005.

————. "Political Theology in Judah and Assyria: The Beginning of the Hebrew Bible as Literature." *SEÅ* 65 (2000): 59–76.

————. "*Temple Scroll* and Pentateuch: A Priestly Debate about the Interpretation of the Torah." Pages 59–74 in *The Qumran Legal Texts between the Hebrew Bible and Its Interpretation.* Edited by Kristin De Troyer and Armin Lange. CBET 61. Leuven: Peeters, 2011.

————. "Die Ursprünge der Bundestheologie im Alten Testament und im Alten Orient." *ZABR* 4 (1998): 1–84.

————. "Von der Gerichtsordnung zum Verfassungsentwurf: Deuteronomische Gestaltung und deuteronomistische Interpretation im 'Ämtergesetz' Dtn 16,18–18,22." Pages 142–55 in *"Wer ist wie du, HERR, unter den Göttern?": Studien zur Theologie und Religionsgeschichte Israels für Otto Kaiser zum 70. Geburtstag.* Edited by Ingo Kottsieper, Jürgen van Oorschot, Diethard Römheld, and Harald Martin Wahl. Göttingen: Vandenhoeck & Ruprecht, 1994.

Paganini, Simone. *"Nicht darfst du zu diesen Wörtern etwas hinzufügen": Die Rezeption des Deuteronomiums in der Tempelrolle: Sprache, Autoren, Hermeneutik.* BZABR 11. Wiesbaden: Harrassowitz, 2009.

Paget, James Carleton, and Joachim Schaper, eds. *The New Cambridge History of the Bible. Vol. 1, From the Beginnings to 600.* Cambridge: Cambridge University Press, 2013.

Pakkala, Juha. "The Date of the Oldest Edition of Deuteronomy." *ZAW* 121 (2009): 388–401.

———. "The Dating of Deuteronomy: A Response to Nathan MacDonald." *ZAW* 123 (2011): 431–36.

———. *Intolerant Monolatry in the Deuteronomistic History.* Helsinki: Finnish Exegetical Society; Göttingen: Vandenhoeck & Ruprecht, 1999.

———. "Textual Developments within Paradigms and Paradigm Shifts." *HeBAI* 3 (2014): 327–42.

Parpola, Simo. *Letters from Assyrian Scholars to the Kings Esarhaddon and Assurbanipal.* 2 vols. AOAT 5. Kevelaer: Butzon & Bercker, 1970–1983.

———. "Neo-Assyrian Treaties from the Royal Archives of Nineveh." *JCS* 39 (1987): 161–89.

Parpola, Simo, and Kazuko Watanabe. *Neo-Assyrian Treaties and Loyalty Oaths.* SAA 2. Helsinki: Helsinki University Press, 1988.

Pearce, Laurie E. "New Evidence for Judeans in Babylonia." Pages 399–411 in *Judah and the Judeans in the Persian Period.* Edited by Oded Lipschits and Manfred Oeming. Winona Lake, IN: Eisenbrauns, 2006.

Pearce, Laurie E., and Cornelia Wunsch. *Documents of Judean Exiles and West Semites in Babylonia in the Collection of David Sofer.* CUSAS 28. Bethesda, MD: CDL Press, 2014.

Perlitt, Lothar. *Bundestheologie im Alten Testament.* WMANT 36. Neukirchen-Vluyn: Neukirchener Verlag, 1969.

———. "Wovon der Mensch lebt (Dtn 8, 3b)." Pages 74–96 in *Deuteronomium-Studien.* FAT 8. Tübingen: Mohr Siebeck, 1994.

Pietsch, Michael. *Die Kultreform Josias: Studien zur Religionsgeschichte Israels in der späten Königszeit.* FAT 86. Tübingen: Mohr Siebeck, 2013.

Polk, Nicholas O. "Deuteronomy and Treaty Texts: A Critical Reexamination of Deuteronomy 13, 17, 27, and 28." Ph.D. diss., University of Chicago, 2020.

Polzin, Robert. *Moses and the Deuteronomist: A Literary Study of the Deuteronomistic History, Part I: Deuteronomy, Joshua, Judges.* New York: Seabury, 1980.

Preuss, H. D. *Deuteronomium.* EdF 164. Darmstadt: Wissenschaftliche Buchgesellschaft, 1982.

Quick, Laura. *Deuteronomy 28 and the Aramaic Curse Tradition.* Oxford: Oxford University Press, 2018.

Quilligan, Maureen. *The Language of Allegory: Defining the Genre.* Ithaca, NY: Cornell University Press, 1979.

Rad, Gerhard von. *The Problem of the Hexateuch and Other Essays.* Translated by E. W. Trueman Dicken. Edinburgh: Oliver & Boyd, 1966.

Radner, Karen. "Assyrische *ṭuppi adê* als Vorbild für Deuteronomium 28,20–44?" Pages 351–78 in *Die deuteronomistischen Geschichtswerke: Redaktions- und religionsgeschichtliche Perspektiven zur "Deuteronomismus"—Diskussion im Tora und Vorderen Propheten.* Edited by Jan Christian Gertz, Doris Prechel, Konrad Schmid, Markus Witte, and Johannes F. Diehl. BZAW 365. Berlin: de Gruyter, 2006.

———. "Esarhaddon's Expedition from Palestine to Egypt in 671 BCE: A Trek through Negev and Sinai." Pages 305–14 in *Fundstellen: Gesammelte Schriften zur*

Archäologie und Geschichte Altvorderasiens ad honorem Hartmut Kühne. Edited by Dominik Bonatz, Rainer M. Czichon, and F. Janoscha Kreppner. Wiesbaden: Harrassowitz, 2008.

———. "Neo-Assyrian Treaties as a Source for the Historian: Bonds of Friendship, the Vigilant Subject and the Vengeful King's Treaty." Pages 309–28 in *Writing Neo-Assyrian History: Sources, Problems, and Approaches.* Edited by G. B. Lanfranchi, R. Mattila, and R. Rollinger. SAAS 29. Helsinki: Neo-Assyrian Text Corpus Project, 2019.

———. "Revolts in the Assyrian Empire: Succession Wars, Revolts against a False King and Independence Movements." Pages 41–54 in *Revolt and Resistance in the Ancient Classical World and the Near East: In the Crucible of Empire.* Edited by John J. Collins and J. G. Manning. CHANE 85. Leiden: Brill, 2016.

———. "The Trials of Esarhaddon: The Conspiracy of 670 BC." *Isimu: Revista sobre Oriente Próximo y Egipto en la antigüedad* 6 (2003): 165–84.

Ramos, Melissa. "A Northwest Semitic Curse Formula: The Sefire Treaty and Deuteronomy 28." *ZAW* 128 (2016): 205–20.

Ratzon, Eshbal, and Nachum Dershowitz. "The Length of a Scroll: Quantitative Evaluation of Material Reconstructions." *PLOS One* 15.10 (2020): 1–26.

Richter, Sandra Lynn. "The Question of Provenance and the Economics of Deuteronomy." *JSOT* 42 (2017): 23–50.

Rofé, Alexander. *Deuteronomy: Issues and Interpretation.* OTS. Edinburgh: T&T Clark, 2002.

———. "The Strata of the Law about the Centralization of Worship in Deuteronomy and the History of the Deuteronomic Movement." Pages 221–26 in *Congress Volume: Uppsala 1971.* Edited by P. A. H. de Boer. VTSup 22. Leiden: Brill, 1972.

Rogerson, John W. *W. M. L. de Wette, Founder of Modern Biblical Criticism: An Intellectual Biography.* JSOTSup 126. Sheffield: JSOT Press, 1992.

Rollston, Christopher A. "Inscriptional Evidence for the Writing of the Earliest Texts of the Bible—Intellectual Infrastructure in Tenth- and Ninth-Century Israel, Judah, and the Southern Levant." Pages 15–45 in *The Formation of the Pentateuch: Bridging the Academic Cultures of Europe, Israel, and North America.* Edited by Jan C. Gertz, Bernard M. Levinson, Dalit Rom-Shiloni, and Konrad Schmid. FAT 111. Tübingen: Mohr Siebeck, 2016.

———. *Writing and Literacy in the World of Ancient Israel: Epigraphic Evidence from the Iron Age.* ABS. Atlanta: Society of Biblical Literature, 2010.

Römer, Thomas. *Israels Väter: Untersuchungen zur Väterthematik im Deuteronomium und in der deuteronomistischen Tradition.* OBO 99. Fribourg: Editions Universitaires; Göttingen: Vandenhoeck & Ruprecht, 1990.

———. *The So-Called Deuteronomistic History: A Sociological, Historical and Literary Introduction.* London: T&T Clark, 2005.

Römer, Thomas C., and Marc Z. Brettler. "Deuteronomy 34 and the Case for a Persian Hexateuch." *JBL* 119 (2000): 401–19.

Rose, Martin. *5. Mose Teilband 1: 5. Mose 12–25: Einführung und Gesetze.* ZBK AT 5.1. Zürich: Theologisher Verlag Zürich, 1994.

Rosenberg, Joel. *King and Kin: Political Allegory in the Hebrew Bible.* ISBL. Bloomington: Indiana University Press, 1986.

Rüterswörden, Udo. "Dtn 13 in der neueren Deuteronomiumforschung." Pages 185–203 in *Congress Volume Basel 2001.* Edited by André Lemaire. VTSup 92. Leiden: Brill, 2002.

Sæbø, Magne, ed. *Hebrew Bible, Old Testament: The History of Its Interpretation. Vol. 1, From the Beginnings to the Middle Ages (until 1300).* Göttingen: Vandenhoeck & Ruprecht, 1996.

Sanders, Seth L. *From Adapa to Enoch: Scribal Culture and Religious Vision in Judea and Babylon.* TSAJ 167. Tübingen: Mohr Siebeck, 2017.

————. *The Invention of Hebrew.* Traditions. Urbana: University of Illinois Press, 2009.

————. "What If There Aren't Any Empirical Models for Pentateuch Criticism?" Pages 281–304 in *Contextualizing Israel's Sacred Writings: Ancient Literacy, Orality, and Literary Production.* Edited by Brian B. Schmidt. AIL 22. Atlanta: SBL Press, 2015.

Sandmel, Samuel. "Parallelomania." *JBL* 81 (1962): 1–13.

Schaper, Joachim. "The 'Publication' of Legal Texts in Ancient Judah." Pages 225–36 in *The Pentateuch as Torah: New Models for Understanding Its Promulgation and Acceptance.* Edited by Bernard M. Levinson and Gary N. Knoppers. Winona Lake, IN: Eisenbrauns, 2007.

Schearing, Linda S., and Steven L. McKenzie, eds. *Those Elusive Deuteronomists: The Phenomenon of Pan-Deuteronomism.* JSOTSup 268. Sheffield: Sheffield Academic Press, 1999.

Schiffman, Lawrence H. "The Deuteronomic Paraphrase of the *Temple Scroll.*" *RevQ* 15 (1992): 543–67.

————. "The Theology of the *Temple Scroll.*" *JQR* 85 (1994): 109–23.

Schipper, Bernd U. "Egyptian Imperialism after the New Kingdom: The 26th Dynasty and the Southern Levant." Pages 268–90 in *Egypt, Canaan and Israel: History, Imperialism, Ideology and Literature.* Edited by S. Bar, D. Kahn, and J. J. Shirley. CHANE 52. Leiden: Brill, 2011.

Schipper, Jeremy. *Ruth: A New Translation with Introduction and Commentary.* AYB 7D. New Haven: Yale University Press, 2016.

Schloen, J. David. *The House of the Father as Fact and Symbol: Patrimonialism in Ugarit and the Ancient Near East.* Winona Lake, IN: Eisenbrauns, 2001.

Schmid, Konrad. "Buchtechnische und sachliche Prolegomena zur Enneateuchfrage." Pages 1–14 in *Auf dem Weg zur Endgestalt von Genesis bis II Regum.* Edited by M. Beck and U. Schorn. BZAW 370. Berlin: de Gruyter, 2006.

————. *Genesis and the Moses Story: Israel's Dual Origins in the Hebrew Bible.* Translated by James D. Nogalski. Siphrut 3. Winona Lake, IN: Eisenbrauns, 2010.

Schmitz, Thomas A. *Modern Literary Theory and Ancient Texts: An Introduction.* Malden, MA: Blackwell, 2007.

Schniedewind, William M. *How the Bible Became a Book: The Textualization of Ancient Israel.* Cambridge: Cambridge University Press, 2004.

———. "Scripturalization in Ancient Judah." Pages 305–21 in *Contextualizing Israel's Sacred Writings: Ancient Literacy, Orality, and Literary Production.* Edited by Brian B. Schmidt. AIL 22. Atlanta: SBL Press, 2015.

———. *A Social History of Hebrew: Its Origins through the Rabbinic Period.* AYBRL. New Haven: Yale University Press, 2013.

Schorch, Stefan. "The Samaritan Version of Deuteronomy and the Origin of Deuteronomy." Pages 23–37 in *Samaria, Samarians, Samaritans: Studies on Bible, History and Linguistics.* Edited by József Zsengellér. Studia Samaritana 6. Berlin: de Gruyter, 2011.

———. "Which Kind of Authority?: The Authority of the Torah during the Hellenistic and the Roman Periods." Pages 1–15 in *Scriptural Authority in Early Judaism and Ancient Christianity.* Edited by Isaac Kalimi, Tobias Nicklas, and Geza G. Xeravitz. DCLS 16. Berlin: de Gruyter, 2013.

Schwartz, Baruch J. "Joseph's Descent into Egypt: The Composition of Genesis 37 from Its Sources." *Beit Mikra* 55 (2010): 1–30 (in Hebrew).

———. "How the Compiler of the Pentateuch Worked: The Composition of Genesis 37." Pages 263–78 in *The Book of Genesis: Composition, Reception, and Interpretation.* Edited by Craig A. Evans, Joel N. Lohr, and David L. Petersen. VTSup 152. Leiden: Brill, 2012.

———. "The Torah: Its Five Books and Four Documents." Pages 161–225 in vol. 1 of *The Literature of the Hebrew Bible: Introductions and Studies.* Edited by Zipora Talshir. 2 vols. Jerusalem: Yad Ben-Zvi Press, 2011 (in Hebrew).

Seidel, Moshe. "Parallels between Isaiah and Psalms." *Sinai* 38 (1955–1956): 149–72, 229–40, 272–80, 335–55 (in Hebrew).

Sharp, Carolyn J. *Prophecy and Ideology in Jeremiah: Struggles for Authority in the Deutero-Jeremianic Prose.* OTS. London: T&T Clark, 2003.

Shaver, Judson R. *Torah and the Chronicler's History Work: An Inquiry into the Chronicler's References to Laws, Festivals and Cultic Institutions in Relation to Pentateuchal Legislation.* BJS 196. Atlanta: Scholars Press, 1989.

Ska, Jean-Louis. "La structure du Pentateuque dans sa forme canonique." *ZAW* 113 (2001): 331–52.

Smend, Rudolf. "Julius Wellhausen and His *Prolegomena to the History of Israel.*" *Semeia* 25 (1982): 1–20.

———. "Wellhausen in Greifswald." *ZTK* 78 (1981): 141–76.

Smith, Barbara Herrnstein. *On the Margins of Discourse: The Relation of Literature and Language.* Chicago: University of Chicago Press, 1978.

Smith, Wilfred Cantwell. *What Is Scripture?: A Comparative Approach.* Minneapolis: Fortress, 1993.

Sommer, Benjamin D. "The Babylonian Akitu Festival: Rectifying the King or Renewing the Cosmos?" *JANES* 27 (2000): 81–95.

———. *The Bodies of God and the World of Ancient Israel.* Cambridge: Cambridge University Press, 2009.

Sonnet, Jean-Pierre. *The Book within the Book: Writing in Deuteronomy.* BibInt 14. Leiden: Brill, 1997.

———. "The Fifth Book of the Pentateuch: Deuteronomy in Its Narrative Dynamic." *JAJ* 3 (2012): 197–234.

———. "If-Plots in Deuteronomy." *VT* 63 (2013): 453–70.

Spalinger, Anthony J. "Esarhaddon and Egypt: An Analysis of the First Invasion of Egypt." *Orientalia* (1974): 295–326.

Speiser, Ephraim A. *Genesis: Introduction, Translation, and Notes.* AB 1. Garden City, NY: Doubleday, 1964.

Spieckermann, Hermann. *Juda unter Assur in der Sargonidenzeit.* FRLANT 129. Göttingen: Vandenhoeck & Ruprecht, 1982.

Stackert, Jeffrey. "Before and After Scripture: Narrative Chronology in the Revision of Torah Texts." *JAJ* 4 (2013): 168–85.

———. "The Cultic Status of the Levites in the Temple Scroll: Between History and Hermeneutics." Pages 197–212 in *Levites and Priests in Biblical History and Tradition.* Edited by Mark A. Leuchter and Jeremy M. Hutton. AIL 9. Atlanta: Society of Biblical Literature, 2011.

———. "Holiness Code and Writings." Pages 389–96 in vol. 1 of *The Oxford Encyclopedia of the Bible and Law.* Edited by Brent A. Strawn. 2 vols. New York: Oxford University Press, 2015.

———. "The Holiness Legislation and Its Pentateuchal Sources: Revision, Supplementation, and Replacement." Pages 173–90 in *The Strata of the Priestly Writings: Contemporary Debate and Future Directions.* Edited by Sarah Shectman and Joel S. Baden. ATANT 95. Zurich: Theologischer Verlag Zürich, 2009.

———. "How the Priestly Sabbaths Work: Innovation in Pentateuchal Priestly Ritual." Pages 79–111 in *Ritual Innovation in the Hebrew Bible and Ancient Judaism.* Edited by Nathan MacDonald. BZAW 468. Berlin: Walter de Gruyter, 2016.

———. "Pentateuchal Coherence and the Science of Reading." Pages 253–68 in *The Formation of the Pentateuch: Bridging the Academic Cultures of Europe, Israel, and North America.* Edited by Jan C. Gertz, Bernard M. Levinson, Dalit Rom-Shiloni, and Konrad Schmid. FAT 111. Tübingen: Mohr Siebeck, 2016.

———. "Political Allegory in the Priestly Source: The Destruction of Jerusalem, the Exile and Their Alternatives." Pages 211–26 in *The Fall of Jerusalem and the Rise of the Torah.* Edited by Peter Dubovský, Dominik Markl, and Jean-Pierre Sonnet. Tübingen: Mohr Siebeck, 2016.

———. *A Prophet Like Moses: Prophecy, Law, and Israelite Religion.* New York: Oxford University Press, 2014.

———. "The Relationship of the Pentateuchal Codes." Pages 297–314 in *The Oxford Handbook of the Pentateuch*. Edited by Joel S. Baden and Jeffrey Stackert. Oxford: Oxford University Press, 2021.

———. *Rewriting the Torah: Literary Revision in Deuteronomy and the Holiness Legislation*. FAT 52. Tübingen: Mohr Siebeck, 2007.

———. "Why Does Deuteronomy Legislate Cities of Refuge?: Asylum in the Covenant Collection (Exodus 21:12–14) and Deuteronomy (19:1–13)." *JBL* 125 (2006): 23–49.

———. "The Wilderness Period without Generation Change: The Deuteronomic Portrait of Israel's Forty-Year Journey." *VT* 70 (2020): 696–721.

Stade, Bernhard. "Miscellen: Anmerkungen zu 2 Kö. 15–21." *ZAW* 6 (1886): 156–89.

Stavrakopoulou, Francesca. *King Manasseh and Child Sacrifice: Biblical Distortions of Historical Realities*. BZAW 338. Berlin: de Gruyter, 2004.

Sternberg, Meir. "If-Plots: Narrativity and the Law Code." Pages 29–107 in *Theorizing Narrativity*. Edited by John Pier and José Ángel García Landa. Narratologia 12. Berlin: de Gruyter, 2008.

———. *The Poetics of Biblical Narrative: Ideological Literature and the Drama of Reading*. ISBL. Bloomington: Indiana University Press, 1985.

Steuernagel, Carl. *Übersetzung und Erklärung der Bücher Deuteronomium und Josua und allgemeine Einleitung in den Hexateuch*. HKAT I, 3. Göttingen: Vandenhoeck & Ruprecht, 1900.

Steymans, Hans Ulrich. "Eine assyrische Vorlage für Deuteronomium 28, 20–44." Pages 119–41 in *Bundesdokument und Gesetz: Studien zum Deuteronomium*. Edited by Georg Braulik. HBS 4. Freiburg: Herder, 1995.

———. *Deuteronomium 28 und die adê zur Thronfolgeregelung Asarhaddons: Segen und Fluch im Alten Orient und in Israel*. OBO 145. Freiburg: Universitätsverlag, 1995.

———. "Deuteronomy 13 in Comparison with Hittite, Aramaic and Assyrian Treaties." *HeBAI* 8 (2019): 101–32.

———. "Deuteronomy 28 and Tell Tayinat." *Verbum et Ecclesia* 34.2 (2013): 1–13.

———. "Die neuassyrische Vertragsrhetorik der 'Vassal Treaties of Esarhaddon' und das Deuteronomium." Pages 89–152 in *Das Deuteronomium*. Edited by Georg Braulik. ÖBS 23. Frankfurt: Peter Lang, 2003.

Strawn, Brent A. "Moses at Moab, Lincoln at Gettysburg?: On the Genre of Deuteronomy, Again." *ZABR* 24 (2018): 153–210.

———. "Slaves and Rebels: Inscription, Identity, and Time in the Rhetoric of Deuteronomy." Pages 161–91 in *Sepher Torath Mosheh: Studies in the Composition and Interpretation of Deuteronomy*. Edited by Daniel I. Block and Richard L. Schultz. Peabody, MA: Hendrickson, 2017.

Tadmor, Hayim. "The Aramaization of Assyria: Aspects of Western Impact." Pages 449–70 in *Mesopotamien und seine Nachbarn*. Edited by J.-J. Nissen, J. Renger, and H. Kühne. Berlin: Reimer, 1982.

———. "Treaty and Oath in the Ancient Near East: A Historian's Approach." Pages 127–52 in *Humanizing America's Iconic Book: Society of Biblical Literature Centennial Addresses 1980*. Edited by Gene M. Tucker and Douglas A. Knight. Chico: Scholars Press, 1982.

Talmon, Shemaryahu. "The 'Desert Motif' in the Bible and in Qumran Literature." Pages 216–54 in *Literary Studies in the Hebrew Bible: Form and Content; Collected Studies*. Jerusalem: Magnes; Leiden: Brill, 1993.

Tanner, Hans Andreas. *Amalek: Der Feind Israels und der Feind Jahwes; Eine Studie zu den Amalektexten im Alten Testament*. Zürich: Theologischer Verlag Zürich, 2005.

Tanselle, G. Thomas. *A Rationale of Textual Criticism*. Philadelphia: University of Pennsylvania Press, 1989.

Taschner, Johannes. "Die Bedeutung des Generationswechsels für den Geschichtsrückblick in Dtn 1–3." *WD* 26 (2001): 61–72.

Thiel, Winfried. *Die deuteronomistische Redaktion von Jeremia 1–25*. WMANT 41. Neukirchen-Vluyn: Neukirchener Verlag, 1973.

———. *Die deuteronomistische Redaktion von Jeremia 26–45*. WMANT 52. Neukirchen-Vluyn: Neukirchener Verlag, 1981.

Thomason, Sarah. "Determining Language Contact Effects in Ancient Contact Situations." Pages 1–15 in *Lenguas en contacto: El testimonio escrito*. Edited by Pedro Bádenas de la Peña, Sofía Torallas Tovar, Eugenio R. Luján, and María Ángeles Gallego. Manuales y anejos de "Emerita" 46. Madrid: Cosejo Superior de Investigaciones Científicas, 2004.

Tigay, Jeffrey H. *Deuteronomy*. JPS Torah Commentary. Philadelphia: Jewish Publication Society, 1996.

———. "The Presence of God and the Coherence of Exodus 20:22–26." Pages 195–211 in *Sefer Moshe: The Moshe Weinfeld Jubilee Volume*. Edited by Chaim Cohen, Avi Hurvitz, and Shalom M. Paul. Winona Lake, IN: Eisenbrauns, 2004.

Toorn, Karel van der. "The Babylonian New Year Festival: New Insights from the Cuneiform Texts and Their Bearing on Old Testament Study." Pages 331–44 in *Congress Volume Leuven 1989*. Edited by J. A. Emerton. VTSup 43. Leiden: Brill, 1991.

Tov, Emanuel. "The Copying of a Biblical Scroll." Pages 107–27 in *Hebrew Bible, Greek Bible, and Qumran*. TSAJ 121. Tübingen: Mohr Siebeck, 2008.

———. *Textual Criticism of the Hebrew Bible*. 3rd ed., rev. and exp. Minneapolis: Fortress, 2012.

———. "Textual Harmonizations in the Ancient Texts of Deuteronomy." Pages 15–28 in *Mishneh Todah: Studies in Deuteronomy and Its Cultural Environment in Honor of Jeffrey H. Tigay*. Edited by Nili Sachar Fox, David A. Glatt-Gilad, and Michael J. Williams. Winona Lake, IN: Eisenbrauns, 2009.

Uehlinger, Christoph. "Was There a Cult Reform under King Josiah?: The Case for a Well-Grounded Minimum." Pages 279–316 in *Good Kings and Bad Kings:*

The Kingdom of Judah in the Seventh Century BCE. Edited by Lester L. Grabbe. LHBOTS 393. London: T&T Clark, 2005.

Van Seters, John. "Confessional Reformulation in the Exilic Period." *VT* 22 (1972): 448–59.

———. "Etiology in the Moses Tradition: The Case of Exodus 18." *HAR* 9 (1985): 355–61.

Veijola, Timo. *Das 5. Buch Mose. Deuteronomium. Kapitel 1,1–16,17*. ATD 8,1. Göttingen: Vandenhoeck & Ruprecht, 2004.

———. "'Der Mensch lebt nicht vom Brot allein': Zur literarischen Schichtung und theologischen Aussage von Deuteronomium 8." Pages 143–58 in *Bundesdokument und Gesetz: Studien zum Deuteronomium*. Edited by Georg Braulik. HBS 4. Freiburg: Herder, 1995.

———. *Moses Erben: Studien zum Dekalog, zum Deuteronomismus und zum Schriftgelehrtentum*. BWANT 149. Stuttgart: Kohlhammer, 2000.

Viezel, Eran. "Un précédent juif de De Wette: Un commentaire attribué à Rachi sur le livre des Chroniques Autour du livre trouvé au Temple par le prêtre Hilkiyyahou." *REJ* 170 (2011): 521–32.

Walton, Kendall L. *Mimesis as Make Believe: On the Foundations of the Representational Arts*. Cambridge, MA: Harvard University Press, 1990.

Watanabe, Kazuko. *Die adê-Vereidigung anlässlich der Thronfolgeregelung Asarhaddons*. BBaghM 3. Berlin: Gebr. Mann, 1987.

———. "Adoration of Oath Documents in Assyrian Religion and Its Development." *Orient* 55 (2020): 71–86.

———. "Aššurbanipal and His Brothers Considered from the References in the Esarhaddon Succession Oath Documents." *Orient* (2019, Supplement 1): 237–57.

———. "Esarhaddon's Succession Oath Documents Reconsidered in Light of the Tayinat Version." *Orient* 49 (2014): 145–70.

———. "Die Siegelung der 'Vasallenverträge Asarhaddons' durch den Gott Aššur." *BaghM* 16 (1985): 377–92.

———. "A Study of Assyrian Cultural Policy as Expressed in Esarhaddon's Succession Oath Documents." Pages 473–92 in vol. 2 of *"Now It Happened in Those Days": Studies in Biblical, Assyrian, and Other Ancient Near Eastern Historiography Presented to Mordechai Cogan on His 75th Birthday*. Edited by Amitai Baruchi-Unna, Tova L. Forti, Shmuel Ahituv, Israel Eph'al, and Jeffrey H. Tigay. 2 vols. Winona Lake, IN: Eisenbrauns, 2017.

Watts, James W. *Understanding the Pentateuch as a Scripture*. Hoboken, NJ: Wiley-Blackwell, 2017.

———. "Using Ezra's Time as a Methodological Pivot for Understanding the Rhetoric and Functions of the Pentateuch." Pages 489–506 in *The Pentateuch: International Perspectives on Current Research*. Edited by Thomas B. Dozeman, Konrad Schmid, and Baruch J. Schwartz. FAT 78. Tübingen: Mohr Siebeck, 2011.

Wazana, Nili. "The Law of the King (Deuteronomy 17:14–20) in Light of Empire and Destruction." Pages 169–94 in *The Fall of Jerusalem and the Rise of the Torah*. Edited by Peter Dubovský, Dominik Markl, and Jean-Pierre Sonnet. FAT 107. Tübingen: Mohr Siebeck, 2016.

Weinfeld, Moshe. "Cult Centralization in Israel in the Light of a Neo-Babylonian Analogy." *JNES* 23 (1964): 202–12.

———. *Deuteronomy 1–11: A New Translation with Introduction and Commentary*. AB 5. New York: Doubleday, 1991.

———. *Deuteronomy and the Deuteronomic School*. Oxford: Clarendon, 1972. Repr., Winona Lake, IN: Eisenbrauns, 1992.

———. "Jeremiah and the Spiritual Metamorphosis of Israel." *ZAW* 88 (1976): 17–56.

———. *The Place of the Law in the Religion of Ancient Israel*. VTSup 100. Leiden: Brill, 2004.

———. "Traces of Assyrian Treaty Formulae in Deuteronomy." *Biblica* 46 (1965): 417–27.

———. "The Worship of Molech and the Queen of Heaven and Its Background." *UF* 4 (1972): 133–54.

Weissenberg, Hanne von. "The Centrality of the Temple in 4QMMT." Pages 293–305 in *The Dead Sea Scrolls: Texts and Context*. Edited by Charlotte Hempel. STDJ 90. Leiden: Brill, 2010.

Weitzman, Steven. "Sensory Reform in Deuteronomy." Pages 123–39 in *Religion and the Self in Antiquity*. Edited by David Brakke, Michael L. Satlow, and Steven Weitzman. Bloomington: Indiana University Press, 2005.

Welch, Adam C. "The Source of Nehemiah IX." *ZAW* 47 (1929): 130–37.

Wellhausen, Julius. *Die Composition des Hexateuch und der historischen Bücher des Alten Testaments*. Berlin: G. Reimer, 1885. Repr., Berlin: Walter de Gruyter, 1963.

———. "Israel." Pages 396–432 in *Encyclopaedia Britannica*, vol. 13. 9th ed. Edited by W. Robertson Smith. Edinburgh: Adam & Charles Black, 1881. Repr. in *Prolegomena to the History of Ancient Israel*. Translated by Allan Menzies and J. Sutherland Black, with preface by W. Roberson Smith. Edinburgh: Adam & Charles Black, 1885.

———. *Prolegomena to the History of Ancient Israel*. New York: Meridian, 1957. Reprint of *Prolegomena to the History of Israel*. Translated by Allan Menzies and J. Sutherland Black, with preface by W. Roberson Smith. Edinburgh: Adam & Charles Black, 1885. Translation of *Prolegomena zur Geschichte Israels*. Berlin: G. Reimer, 1883. Revision of *Geschichte Israels. In zwei Bänden. Erster Band*. Berlin: G. Reimer, 1878.

Wells, Bruce. "Is It Law or Religion?: Legal Motivations in Deuteronomic and Neo-Babylonian Texts." Pages 287–309 in *Law and Religion in the Eastern Mediterranean: From Antiquity to Early Islam*. Edited by Anselm C. Hagedorn and Reinhard G. Kratz. Oxford: Oxford University Press, 2013.

————. *The Law of Testimony in the Pentateuchal Codes.* BZABR 4. Wiesbaden: Harrassowitz, 2004.

————. "What Is Biblical Law?: A Look at Pentateuchal Rules and Near Eastern Practice." *CBQ* 70 (2008): 223–43.

Westbrook, Raymond. "Biblical and Cuneiform Law Codes." *RB* 92 (1985): 247–64.

Wette, Wilhelm Martin Leberecht de. *Beiträge zur Einleitung in das Alte Testament.* 2 vols. Halle: Schimmelpfennig, 1806–1807.

————. "Dissertatio Critica qua a prioribus Deuteronomium Pentateuchi libris diversum alius cuiusdam recentioris auctoris opus esse monstratur." Pages 149–68 in *Opuscula Theologica.* 2nd ed. Berlin: G. Reimer, 1830.

Wevers, John William. *Notes on the Greek Text of Deuteronomy.* SCS 39. Atlanta: Scholars Press, 1995.

White, Hayden. *Metahistory: The Historical Imagination in Nineteenth-Century Europe.* Baltimore: Johns Hopkins University Press, 1973.

————. "The Value of Narrativity in the Representation of Reality." *Critical Inquiry* 7 (1980): 5–27.

Williamson, H. G. M. "Structure and Historiography in Nehemiah 9." Pages 117–31 in *Proceedings of the Ninth World Congress of Jewish Studies. Jerusalem. August 4–12, 1985. Panel Sessions: Bible Studies and the Ancient Near East.* Edited by M. Goshen Gottstein. Jerusalem: Magnes, 1988.

Wimbush, Vincent L., ed. *Theorizing Scriptures: New Critical Orientations to a Cultural Phenomenon.* Signifying (on) Scriptures. New Brunswick, NJ: Rutgers University Press, 2008.

Wiseman, Donald J. *The Vassal-Treaties of Esarhaddon.* London: British School of Archaeology in Iraq, 1958.

Wolf, Werner. "Illusion (Aesthetic)." Pages 270–87 in *Handbook of Narratology.* Edited by Peter Hühn, Jan Christoph Meister, John Pier, and Wolf Schmid. 2 vols. 2nd ed. Berlin: de Gruyter, 2014.

Wolff, Hans Walter. *Joel and Amos: A Commentary on the Books of the Prophets Joel and Amos.* Translated by Waldemar Janzen. S. Dean McBride, Jr., and Charles A. Muenchow. Edited by S. Dean McBride, Jr. Hermeneia. Philadelphia: Fortress, 1977.

Wright, David P. *Inventing God's Law: How the Covenant Code of the Bible Used and Revised the Laws of Hammurabi.* New York: Oxford University Press, 2009.

Wunsch, Cornelia. *Judeans by the Waters of Babylon: New Historical Evidence in Cuneiform Sources from Rural Babylonia in the Schoyen Collection.* BaAr 6. Dresden: ISLET, forthcoming.

Yadin, Yigael. *The Temple Scroll.* 3 vols. Jerusalem: Israel Exploration Society, Institute of Archaeology of the Hebrew University of Jerusalem, Shrine of the Book, 1983.

Zadok, Ran. "Judeans in Babylonia—Updating the Dossier." Pages 109–29 in *Encounters by the Rivers of Babylon: Scholarly Conversations between Jews, Iranians and Babylonians in Antiquity.* Edited by Uri Gabbay and Shai Secunda. TSAJ 160. Tübingen: Mohr Siebeck, 2014.

Zahn, Molly M. *Rethinking Rewritten Scripture: Composition and Exegesis in the 4QReworked Pentateuch Manuscripts.* STDJ 95. Leiden: Brill, 2011.

Zaia, Shana. "My Brother's Keeper: Assurbanipal versus Šamaš-šuma-ukīn." *JANEH* 6 (2019): 19–52.

Zilberg, Peter. "The Assyrian Empire and Judah: Royal Assyrian Archives and Other Historical Documents." Pages 383–405 in *From Sha'ar Hagolan to Shaaraim: Essays in Honor of Prof. Yosef Garfinkel.* Edited by Saar Ganor, Igor Kreimerman, Katharina Streit, and Madeleine Mumcuoglu. Jerusalem: Israel Exploration Society, 2016.

———. "The Assyrian Provinces of the Southern Levant: Sources, Administration, and Control." Pages 56–88 in *The Southern Levant under Assyrian Domination.* Edited by Shawn Zelig Aster and Avraham Faust. University Park, PA: Eisenbrauns, 2018.

Index of Ancient Sources

Index of Names and Subjects